CAMBRIDGE STUDIES IN LINGUISTICS

General Editors: W.SIDNEY ALLEN, B.COMRIE, C.J.FILLMORE
E.J.A.HENDERSON, F.W.HOUSEHOLDER, R.LASS, J.LYONS
R.B.LE PAGE, P.H.MATTHEWS, F.R.PALMER, R.POSNER, J.L.M.TRIM

Explanations in the study of
child language development

In this series

*Issued in hard covers and as a paperback

EXPLANATIONS IN THE STUDY OF CHILD LANGUAGE DEVELOPMENT

MARTIN ATKINSON

Lecturer in Linguistics
University of Essex

CAMBRIDGE UNIVERSITY PRESS
CAMBRIDGE
LONDON   NEW YORK   NEW ROCHELLE
MELBOURNE   SYDNEY

Published by the Press Syndicate of the University of Cambridge
The Pitt Building, Trumpington Street, Cambridge CB2 1RP
32 East 57th Street, New York, NY 10022, USA
296 Beaconsfield Parade, Middle Park, Melbourne 3206, Australia

First published 1982

Printed in Great Britain at The Pitman Press, Bath

Library of Congress catalogue card number: 81–10015

British Library Cataloguing in Publication Data
Atkinson, Martin
Explanations in the study of child language
development. – (Cambridge studies in linguistics,
ISSN 0068–676X; 35)
1. Children – Learning
I. Title
401'.9   LB1139.L3

ISBN 0 521 24302 5 hard covers
ISBN 0 521 28593 3 paperback

Contents

Preface

This book is an extensive revision of my doctoral dissertation, submitted to the University of Edinburgh in 1978. While the major arguments of the book are identical to those of the dissertation, there have been many changes in emphasis and, in the concluding chapter, an attempt to relate my work to that in learnability theory.

The dissertation grew out of a deep dissatisfaction with the state of theorising in language acquisition research. Many proposals, while superficially attractive, failed to stand up to critical analysis. This situation was uncomfortable, however, because I felt the lack of a coherent framework for analysis and was conscious of indulging in piecemeal sniping at theoretical ideas, often not succeeding in isolating that aspect of a suggestion which made it unsatisfactory. The result of my reflections on this state of affairs is a set of conditions, which I develop and attempt to justify in Chapter 1. The remainder of the book, with the exception of the concluding chapter, is an attempt to apply these conditions to theoretical proposals in the language acquisition literature. Inevitably, given the starting point, the tone of much of the discussion is negative; the theories we are confronted with are often bad theories. Furthermore, weakness infects theorising in this area from a number of directions and I believe that my conditions go some way towards identifying these directions, although I would not for a moment suggest that they approach completeness.

In writing a book of this sort, I have been conscious of the need to offer alternatives to the proposals I consider. On the whole, I have not done this, for the simple reason that I have no such alternatives; the study of language acqusition is extraordinarily difficult, and, perhaps, one should yield to the temptation of applauding what has been achieved and let matters rest there. But, if one believes, as I do, that very little has been achieved, despite a great deal of intellectual endeavour, such a strategy is not easily available. The one exception to this inability to present alternatives is contained in 7.4, where what is admittedly a very modest proposal does significantly better in terms of my analytic framework than its competitors.

A large number of people deserve acknowledgement for their help in leading me to formulate whatever is sensible in the pages that follow. Students and colleagues at the University of Edinburgh and at the University of Essex have patiently suffered one or other formulation of my ideas and have made many valuable comments and criticisms. I was fortunate enough to be employed for several years on a research project which brought together that rare blend of intellectual stimulation and human warmth. This was supplied by the late Renira Huxley, Patrick Griffiths and Alison Elliot. These last two read parts of an earlier version of the book and made many valuable and insightful comments. The whole dissertation on which the book is based was read by Doug Arnold, Ron Asher, Phil Johnson-Laird and Steve Pulman, each of whom contributed significantly to the subsequent revision. Of course, I am entirely responsible for what appears here. My greatest debt is owed to John Lyons who, as teacher, supervisor, colleague and editor, has been a constant source of encouragement and inspiration.

Mary Liddy did a large proportion of the typing, managing to remain competent and good-humoured. My thanks also to the staff at Cambridge University Press.

Colchester, March 1981   Martin Atkinson

1 Criteria for adequacy

In 1941 Roman Jakobson presented his theory of the child's phonological development in his *Kindersprache, Aphasie und allgemeine Lautgesetze*. Eventually translated as Jakobson (1968), this work was largely responsible for a resurgence in the study of the acquisition of phonology in the last decade. Many of the empirical claims made by Jakobson have been refuted by this study and the quality of data on which more satisfactory proposals can be based has risen sharply (see Ferguson 1977 for some recent discussion of this). Nevertheless, his theory remains attractive because of its comprehensiveness, its simplicity and its attempt to come to terms explicitly with developmental issues. In these respects it can be compared with work on the syntactic development of the child which culminated in the publication of Roger Brown's *A First Language* (1973). In this book Brown delivers a cautious and honest analysis of a number of different though related approaches to early child syntax; principally, proposals are compared in terms of their empirical consequences and are usually found to be wanting in certain respects. Overall, however, it is probably fair to say the more favoured analyses discussed by Brown come off rather better when confronted with acquisition data than do Jakobson's phonological suggestions. Despite this, I would claim that the theories which Brown presents and summarises so meticulously compare unfavourably with Jakobson's along a number of non-empirical parameters, and it is one of the major tasks of this book to substantiate this claim. At the outset it should be made clear that I shall not be involved in an attempt to relegate empirical adequacy from its position of supreme arbiter in theory evaluation; but there undoubtedly are other criteria which are used in judging theories in all areas of scientific investigation and, arguably, these criteria should be taken more seriously in domains where empirical adequacy is rarely, if ever, approached. The study of first language acquisition seems to me to be such a domain.

In what follows, then, I am concerned with theories in several areas of language development and, more particularly, with the explanatory status of such theories in some domain of this general area of study. To my knowledge there has been little systematic discussion of most of the issues raised here in the literature on language development, although some relevant concepts are available in the general field of child development.[1] Reasons why it is desirable to initiate this enquiry are not difficult to find. At a general level, it is useful for any discipline to be reflective and examine critically its own methods and standards. In the natural sciences theoretical insight and metatheoretical discussion have often gone hand in hand and we should always be aware of a proliferation of uncritical and uncriticised (from the standpoint of general principles) theories. More directly relevant is the fact that the field of child language development appears to be in great need of such a reflective treatment. A good deal of the theorising with which I am acquainted lacks rigour and direction, and is apparently divorced from any overall view of human development. One inevitable consequence of this is inconclusiveness in argumentation.

This lacuna of reflective criticism should not occasion much surprise as far as work on language is concerned, as it is commonly agreed that it is only in the last few decades that the tools for beginning to formulate theories at all adequately in this area have themselves been fashioned. I refer here particularly to the technical apparatus of descriptive linguistics. Without this apparatus discussions of language development were conducted in an often stimulating but theoretically impoverished framework. One can point to a concern with very general issues such as the ontogenesis of the functions of language (Bühler 1934), the emotional-intellectual issue (Leopold 1949), and the role of reinforcement and imitation in first language learning (Watson 1928, Mowrer 1960), but, with some exceptions, this work was conducted within some dominant psychological paradigm by investigators who were largely ignorant of the tools of descriptive linguistics.[2] During the second half of this century, however, and particularly during the last fifteen years, we have seen an enormous growth in the number of studies of different aspects of child language and a greater reliance on the concepts and techniques of descriptive linguistics as well as a rapprochement between linguists and psychologists leading to the development of theoretical statements which, in many cases, are clearly formulated and, one would expect, capable of evaluation. It seems to me that the time is ripe to submit some of these proposals to an analysis within a metatheoretical framework.

1.1 Fixing the domain of enquiry

Before I begin to discuss the nature of theories in language development there are some obvious preliminaries which must be mentioned. The task confronting a language acquisition theorist is to first specify that area of language structure or function with which he is to be concerned (more generally, we could consider the specification of any domain of an organism's structure or activity but in what follows I shall restrict myself to more particular formulations in terms of language and the human organism). To mention a few possibilities, this domain might be any of the following: the ability to produce syntactically structured utterances; the ability to comprehend such utterances; the ability to produce the forms of words; the ability to perform speech-acts; the knowledge underlying the ability to perform speech-acts; the ability to refer to concrete objects; the ability to comprehend the relational terms *more* and *less*. There is no attempt to be exhaustive here, and, in mentioning these domains, I do not wish to suggest that all of them would constitute equally fruitful areas of research. Some of them have been studied fairly intensively recently, but they are cited here merely to exemplify the notion 'domain of language development'. Nor do I wish to suggest at this stage that they all constitute clearly delimited and independent areas of research. Indeed, it may be non-sensical, as certain philosophers have urged (Stich 1971, Cooper 1975), to entertain 'knowledge underlying abilities', but child language theorists have manipulated such concepts and have constructed theories in such domains. A study of the activity of theorising can remain neutral on these questions.

1.2 Collecting the data

With his domain of interest fixed the theorist will attempt to collect relevant data. As he is involved in a *developmental* study he will do this at a number of points $t_1, \ldots, t_n$, these being construed either cross-sectionally or longitudinally. In practice he may focus on just one such point, thereby restricting his developmental considerations to comparisons between the child at this point and the adult. The t_i ($1 \leqslant i \leqslant n$) will, of course, normally denote time-intervals rather than points. The data which are considered relevant to a study can depend on a number of factors. Obviously the domain of enquiry is one of these – if, for example, we are concerned with some aspect of syntactic development, we may often be entitled to ignore phonetic details in a corpus of collected utterances. Also important, however, is a set of decisions which the theorist will take and which will be intimately linked to his views on the nature of psychological explanation. Is it necessary that data be collected in a restricted experimental context or can we also admit observational data? In an observational study are we justified in pursuing an interventionist methodology to increase the likelihood of interesting data? Should we allow an observer's interpretation of what a child meant by a particular utterance to count as legitimate data? Should we attempt to develop techniques to consult the child and to investigate his linguistic intuitions? Should we allow utterances which appear to be imitative of an earlier adult utterance the same status as spontaneous utterances? Such questions are important and may lead to different answers in different domains of enquiry. However, nothing in this book depends on providing such answers.

1.3 Developmental theories

According to the position I shall adopt in this book, developmental theories have two components. The first of these is a sequence of theories, each one corresponding to one of the time points at which data are collected and accounting for these data. Thus, if we collect data at $t_1, \ldots, t_n$ which are relevant to some domain D, we shall be obliged to construct theories $T_1, \ldots, T_n$ where T_i accounts for the data collected at t_i ($1 \leqslant i \leqslant n$). For example, we can imagine that D has been fixed as the knowledge which underlies the child's ability to produce and understand syntactically structured strings and that the data assumed relevant to D are the structured strings which are, in fact, produced by the child. Then the theorist might produce a sequence of grammars $G_1, \ldots, G_n$ in accordance with some general principles such that G_i accounts for the child's structured utterances at t_i ($1 \leqslant i \leqslant n$). There is nothing controversial in this characterisation and it accords well with general practice in developmental psychology. In particular, apart from an emphasis on theory construction as opposed to factual description, it is in total agreement with Simon's (1962) claim that 'We select certain instants in the course of . . . dynamic change, take "snapshots" of the system at those instants, and use these snapshots as descriptions of the system at a particular stage of development' (p. 130). Diagrammatically, what we have so far is:

$$\boxed{T_1} \rightarrow \boxed{T_2} \rightarrow \ldots \ldots \rightarrow \boxed{T_n}$$

$$t_1 \qquad\quad t_2 \qquad \ldots\ldots \qquad t_n$$

From now on I shall refer to such a sequence of theories by the ordered n-tuple $(T_1, \ldots, T_n)$.

The second component of a developmental theory is a *mechanism* for development. Given a sequence of theories $(T_1, \ldots, T_n)$ we want the theory to tell us why and how T_i gives way to T_{i+1} ($1 \leqslant i \leqslant n-1$). To illustrate, assume again that a theorist presents a sequence of grammars $(G_1, \ldots, G_n)$ to account for the knowledge underlying the child's ability to produce and comprehend syntactically structured strings at $t_1, \ldots, t_n$. One might consider the possibility that G_i is replaced by G_{i+1} ($1 \leqslant i \leqslant n-1$) wholly (or partially) on the basis of presentation of negative data, i.e. data which G_i cannot account for, in the child's linguistic environment. Alternatively, correction of the child's own utterances might be seen as a necessary condition for such a transition to take place and more flexibility could be introduced by considering variable criteria whereby more or fewer negative data (or correction) are necessary before the transition is implemented. None of this is intended to be convincing at this stage but illustrates the sorts of consideration which might be involved in specifying a mechanism. In general, then, a developmental theory will consist of an ordered $n+1$-tuple $(T_1, \ldots, T_n, M)$ where the T_i ($1 \leqslant i \leqslant n$) are as above and M is a mechanism responsible for the transition from T_i to T_{i+1} ($1 \leqslant i \leqslant n - 1$). For the remainder of this chapter I shall be concerned with what is involved in the claim that such a theory is explanatory.

1.4 A non-developmental condition

The discussion in the previous section begged an important question: what does it mean for a theory constructed for a particular time point to account for the relevant data at that time? It is clear that a necessary condition on an explanatory *developmental* theory is that it provide explanatory statements for any stage of the child's development in the domain of enquiry.[3] The problem as to what constitutes an explanatory statement for a stage in development does not seem to be distinct from the problem of explanation in psychology, and there are, of course, a number of positions taken by philosophers and psychologists on this issue.

Traditionally, psychological explanations have involved the formulation of laws relating mental states and observable behaviour (Fodor 1968, Paivio 1975), but, more recently, attempts have been made to eschew reference to behaviour and to focus attention on the axiomatisation of a range of possibilities (Pylyshyn 1973, Sloman 1978). Linguists are familiar with this latter strategy from the work of Chomsky (1965, 1976 and many other places) where the axiomatisation of the set of well-formed sentences in a language is referred to as a theory of linguistic competence. It is contrasted with a theory of linguistic performance in Chomsky's writings, which is directly concerned with the prediction and explanation of linguistic behaviour. Pylyshyn, approaching the issue from the perspective of artificial intelligence, distinguishes the 'epistemological problem' from the 'heuristic problem' and argues that psychology and computer modelling of psychological processes have suffered from a failure to draw this distinction. As a result the epistemological problem has been largely ignored by these disciplines.

It is not my purpose here to review the many positions which can be adopted within these broadly defined schools of thought. Suffice it to say that the traditional position has a number of *a priori* advantages which must be taken into account. First, it can be accommodated quite naturally to the deductive-nomological paradigm of explanation (see Hempel and Oppenheim 1948 and, for a discussion of this paradigm in a linguistic context, Lass 1980). According to this view of explanation, a phenomenon can be seen as explained if it is described by a statement which is a logical consequence of a conjunction of sentences describing antecedent conditions and laws. Alternatively, a phenomenon is predicted if the existence of antecedent conditions and laws leads us to expect the phenomenon on logical grounds. Because the 'axiomatisation of possibilities' position does not concern occurring phenomena it is clearly not assimilable to this paradigm in any direct way. Second, as is well known, the problem of providing a methodology for investigating the more recent position is a difficult one. To my knowledge, the most extensively researched competence theory is that developed within transformational generative grammar and it is riddled with serious methodological problems (see, for example, Derwing 1973, Botha 1973 and papers in Cohen 1974). When we take into account the fact that more direct experimental investigations of this competence theory have had inconclusive results (see Fodor, Bever and Garrett 1974 for an extensive summary), the magnitude of the problem becomes apparent. Finally, it is worth noting that the most extensive discussion of the notion of explanation in psychology takes place within the traditional account with perhaps the best-known example being Fodor (1968). There Fodor argues that an explanatory theory in psychology must meet three conditions:

(1) The components of the theory are functionally specified, i.e. in terms of what they do rather than in terms of their material realisation in some working model, e.g. the brain.

(2) The processes admitted by the theory correspond to processes in the organism.

(3) The theory predicts behaviour in the sense of specifying a set of input–output correspondences.[4]

(For a similar approach from the standpoint of artificial intelligence, see Boden 1977.) Whether or not we go along with Fodor's proposals is, to some extent, beside the point in the present context. It is sufficient to note that the question of the explanatory status of psychological theories has been raised and we might, therefore, expect purveyors of such theories to be sensitive to the relevant issues. What is more important is that the vast majority of theoretical models that I shall investigate in this book have to be construed as competence theories if they are to be intelligible. It is, therefore, unfortunate that this mode of psychological theorising has not, as yet, received the critical attention which it undoubtedly deserves. In the belief that such critical attention will be forthcoming I feel justified in formulating a first necessary condition on explanatory theories in language development:

> CONDITION I
> Given a theory T (= $(T_1, \ldots, T_n, M)$) in the domain of language development D, T is an explanatory theory in D only if T_i is an explanatory theory in D at t_i ($1 \leq i \leq n$), where the predicate 'is an explanatory theory in D at t_i' relies for its explication on adopting some view on the general problem of explanation in psychology.

I shall not pay much further attention to this condition for reasons already alluded to. It seems to me to be uncontroversial and to raise no special issues for developmental studies. To the extent that we are satisfied with our non-developmental psychological theories, as far as this condition is concerned, we shall also be satisfied with our developmental psychological theories.[5]

1.5 A developmental condition

We must now turn our attention to the fact that we are principally concerned with developmental theories. As well as imposing conditions on each of the static theories $T_1, \ldots, T_n$ which form part of T, we can also look to impose general constraints on the sequence of theories *qua* sequence such that the sequence provides us with a satisfactory theory of development in D. There is one immediate candidate for such a constraint and that is that each of the T_i ($1 \leq i \leq n$) should be constructed in accordance with some general notion of 'theory in D'. Thus, if we are investigating the child's developing lexical knowledge, we will bring to the task a set of assumptions concerning the lexicon, e.g. that it is a list of triples of phonological, syntactic and semantic features. Similarly, if we are concerned with the development of the ability to perform speech-acts, we will assume an inventory of speech-acts (perhaps admitting of internal structure in specified ways) and we shall be looking for the acquisition of *those* speech-acts and looking for phenomena which are explicable in terms of *that* internal structure. Of course, this is to say nothing more than that research should be theory-guided[6] but it has additional significance in a developmental context. It is only if theories in a sequence are constructed according to some general guide-lines that such theories are going to be *comparable* in any reasonably straightforward sense.

For simplicity let us consider a two-stage developmental theory $T = (T_1, T_2)$.[7] If this is presented as a developmental theory in some domain D we are committed to the view that T_1 explains the relevant data in D at t_1 and T_2 explains the relevant data in D at t_2; additionally, T_1 *changes* into T_2, T_2 *develops out of* T_1. These latter notions, we want to make sense of, and it is self-evident that, if T_1 and T_2 are constructed in accordance with completely different principles or in accordance with no principles at all, then our task is going to be more difficult.

Consider, then, the situation in which T_1 and T_2 are constructed according to the same general theory. It will follow from this that they have 'items' in common where by 'items' I wish to refer to all the constructs and construct-types which can occur in theories.[8] For example, we could consider again the case where the domain of investigation has been fixed as the knowledge underlying the ability to produce and comprehend syntactically structured strings and assume that we are presented with a theory $T = (G_1, G_2)$ where G_1 and G_2 are constructed in accordance with some general theory of linguistic structure. It will follow that G_1 and G_2 have items in common at some level of generality. G_1 and G_2 may, for example, employ the same set of syntactic categories or, perhaps, one employs a subset of the set of syntactic categories employed by the other. The sets of rules occurring in G_1 and G_2 may be identical, in a subset-superset relation, or have a non-empty intersection. The intersections of both sets of syntactic categories and of syntactic rules may be empty but G_1 and G_2 may employ rules of the same *type* and draw their syntactic categories from some antecedently defined set. In each of these cases I would wish to say that G_1 and G_2 are comparable in the required sense. In practice what this means is that we shall be able to contrast G_1 and G_2 along certain dimensions which we regard as significant in a developmental context.

We can now examine, in a general way, some of the consequences of discovering a $T = (T_1, T_2)$ such that T_1 and T_2 are not comparable in the required sense. The question as to whether this situation obtains in the language development literature is one to which I shall return on a number of occasions in the chapters which follow. To make the discussion slightly more concrete we can imagine that D has been fixed as above and that T_1 and T_2 are grammars, G_1 and G_2. Assume now that G_1 is constructed in accordance with the principles of systemic grammar as presented in, say, Halliday (1973) and that G_2 is constructed in accordance with the standard theory transformational grammar of Chomsky (1965).[9] We are immediately struck by the oddness of such a theory, and even if G_1 and G_2 were particularly successful in accounting for the relevant data at t_1 and t_2, we would be very unlikely to accept T as a cogent developmental theory. It would be unclear what it could mean for G_1 to develop into G_2 and we would be led to suspect the appropriateness of one or both of these theories. We might search for reasons to abandon G_1 or G_2 and look around for a theory to replace the abandoned one which is constructed in accordance with the principles of the retained theory. However, this is not the only possible response to the dilemma and an alternative is to accept that there is a more or less radical discontinuity in the child's development in D which is correlated with the switch from a theory of one kind to a theory of a totally different kind. We would be allowing the child to develop along a particular path for a certain period, suddenly abandoning it and adopting a quite different approach to the problem of learning his language.

I shall assume from now on that the acceptance of discontinuities of this sort in development is to be viewed with suspicion. I shall further insist that discontinuities need to be argued for, if we are not to see them as critical in the negative evaluation of a theory. Such argument may take a number of forms including, for example, the identification of similar formally relatable discontinuities in other domains of development leading to the suggestion that language and several other cognitive functions are merely reflecting a general developmental discontinuity. All I wish to claim at the moment is that some such argument is necessary.

Before formulating a condition based on the above discussion, it is useful to point out certain similarities and differences between the issues discussed in this section and Chomsky's numerous discussions of the motivation for, formulation of and application of an evaluation measure as part of a general linguistic theory. Chomsky usually presupposes and sometimes makes explicit the view that theories can only be meaningfully evaluated against each other (compared) if they are constructed on the basis of the same general assumptions.[10] There is one very important difference between this idea and what I have been discussing and that concerns the fact that when two theories (grammars) are presented to the evaluation measure one condition on them is that they both comprehend the same set of data: they are both observationally adequate. Using Chomsky's terminology, the evaluation measure, if successful, will select (prefer) the theory which is not only observationally adequate but also descriptively adequate. But *any* theory presented to the evaluation measure is assumed to be observationally adequate and hence all such theories are on an equal footing with respect to a set of data, in this case the set of well-formed sentences in the language under investigation. In the situation I have discussed above, however, the set of relevant data in D does not remain constant from t_1 to t_2 and this remains true if we are concerned with a competence theory as opposed to a performance theory.

To illustrate, if we fix D as the ability to perform speech-acts and we collect utterances of the child at t_1 and t_2 for analysis, then the two sets of utterances are not going to be identical. Furthermore, they will probably not even be identical if we consider them as sets of structural types rather than as sets of utterance tokens, such non-identity being exactly what we expect to find in studying development. In addition, there is no occasion for a comparison process to *select* or *prefer* T_1 to T_2 in these circumstances as they are theories for distinct sets of data. All of this is very obvious and we can safely conclude that, although Chomsky's evaluation measure is dealing in the same sorts of terms as the comparison process discussed here as far as reference to a general theory is concerned, the two concepts can in no sense be identified.

The first developmental condition can now be formulated as follows:

CONDITION II

Given a theory T (= (T₁, . . ., Tₙ, M)) in the domain of language development D, T is (standardly) an explanatory theory in D only if T_i is constructed in accordance with a particular general theory ($1 \leqslant i \leqslant n$). This ensures that the T_i ($1 \leqslant i \leqslant n$) are comparable in the required sense. If the T_i ($1 \leqslant i \leqslant n$) are not so constructed, then additional argument may restore the explanatory status of T.

Note immediately that there are two ways in which theories can fail to satisfy Condition II. It may be the case that no appropriate general theory exists and that theories are presented for each stage *ad hoc*. Alternatively, we may find situations where a general theory does exist but where particular stage theories violate its principles. Both of these situations are common in the acquisition literature.

1.6 The analysis of developmental sequences

Flavell (1972) is a systematic treatment of developmental sequences and, although he does not present his conclusions in terms of sequences of theories, many of the ideas he puts forward are relevant in the present context. He is concerned with 'the task of specifying just which sorts of sequences are theoretically interesting and which not; of finding parsimonious and theoretically revealing ways of classifying the interesting ones; of suggesting likely causal-developmental explanations for them; of asking whether there might also be aspects of cognitive growth for which a straightforward sequential, first-this-then-that sort of model would not be entirely adequate' (p. 281). In this section I shall be primarily concerned with examining Flavell's treatment of the first two of these tasks.

Flavell has a general idea of what constitutes an 'interesting' sequence. It is clear from his discussion that such a sequence must be concerned with theories in the same domain or in domains which are related in certain ways (see below), and the suggestion in the previous section that theories in such sequences must be constructed with reference to a general theory is consistent with his view that an interesting sequence 'would be one where we can at least imagine some sort of fairly direct, meaningful and substantive (i.e. other than merely temporal–sequential) relationship between the constituent items' (p. 285).

Interesting sequences are seen as belonging to one of five categories. If a sequence is an instance of *Addition*, it may be represented as:

$$(X_1, \{X_1, X_2\})$$

where X_2 enters the system at t_2 and X_1, already present at t_1, persists at t_2. In this formulation, X_1 and X_2 are *distinct* items.[11] A linguistic example is provided by the child's acquisition of verbal suffixes in English with the present progressive *-ing* being acquired before the regular past tense marker *-ed* which in turn is acquired before the present third person singular marker *-s*. Obviously, in this case, each of the acquisitions persists into the later stages.

In contrast, in cases of *Substitution*, an item appearing at t_1 is replaced by a distinct item at t_2, a situation we may represent as:

$$(X_1, X_2)$$

In this case, the acquisition of morphologically irregular past tense forms (e.g. *went*) and their subsequent replacement by overregularised forms (e.g. *goed*) is cited as illustration from the field of language development. Here, of course, the overregularised form is itself eventually replaced by the return of the appropriate strong form.[12]

Modification in a sequence involves an item present at t_1 changing into an item present at t_2. It differs from Addition and Substitution because these notions involve the introduction of *new* items between t_1 and t_2 and, in this sense, involve discontinuities when compared with Modification. Two subcategories of Modification are seen by Flavell as particularly important. According to *Differentiation* an item becomes more specific at t_2 than it was at t_1, i.e. we have something we could schematise as:

$$\left(X_1, \begin{bmatrix} X_1 \\ X_2 \end{bmatrix}\right)[13]$$

where X_2 represents a modification of X_1 resulting in the item

$$\begin{bmatrix} X_1 \\ X_2 \end{bmatrix}.$$

A simple linguistic example is provided by lexical development. Many concrete nominals enter the child's system with a range of reference which is too wide from the adult perspective. This range is subsequently narrowed as a second nominal from the same semantic field enters the system (see Clark 1973 and Chapter 3 for detailed discussion). *Generalisa-*

tion is opposed to Differentiation and is best viewed in terms of the removal of constraints on an item's functioning, i.e. we have:

$$\left(\begin{bmatrix} X_1 \\ X_2 \end{bmatrix}, X_1 \right)$$

We can, perhaps, conceive of an example from syntactic development (Flavell provides no linguistic examples in his paper) where at t_1 the child is assumed to operate with a set of syntactic rules (X_1) under a constraint on sentence length (X_2) and at t_2 this constraint disappears from the system (cf. p. 14 below and Chapter 5 for further discussion of this sort of sequence).

Flavell's category of *Inclusion* is best described in his own terms: 'It reflects the fact that developmental novelty is often had, neither by substantially modifying old items nor by adding or substituting new ones, but by linking existing items together to form new and larger cognitive units' (p. 310). From this it is clear that Flavell envisages a situation where items present at t_1 can enter into new relationships with each other at t_2 (perhaps maintaining their individual status), a development we might represent as:

$$(\{X_1, X_2\}, \{X_1, X_2, R(X_1, X_2)\})$$

where $R(X_1, X_2)$ represents the new item resulting from the integration of X_1 and X_2. An appropriate illustration of this notion is provided by Bellugi's (1971) claim concerning the child's inability at t_1 to apply a full sequence of transformational rules in the derivation of certain sentence types while providing evidence for controlling each of the rules individually, an inability the child overcomes by t_2.

The category of *Mediation*, the last one recognised by Flavell's taxonomy, is rather more amorphous than the preceding four. Roughly, (X_1, X_2) is analysable in terms of Mediation if X_1, in some sense, facilitates the acquisition of X_2. Mediation differs from Inclusion in that X_1 need not form a part of the more sophisticated developmental item and, given this level of generality, it is hardly surprising that superficially unrelated items may admit of analysis in terms of Mediation. In particular, Mediation may relate items in different domains of enquiry and this is especially significant when we attempt to relate developments in some linguistic domain with general cognitive developments (see 1.10 and Chapter 8 for more extensive discussion).[14]

An important generalisation emerges from the above if we exclude

Mediation as involving reference to fundamentally different sequences. This is that Addition, Modification (instanced by Differentiation) and Inclusion each involves the complication of the system under study via the introduction of new items: for Addition this simply involves another item alongside the original; for Modification (Differentiation) the new item further specifies an existing item; and for Inclusion the new item consists of a new relationship between existing items. Exceptions to the generalisation are provided by Substitution and by Modification (instanced by Generalisation) but for the latter it seems important to note that it typically involves the relaxation of constraints rather than the development of positively specified abilities. We might, therefore, anticipate that we shall find this phenomenon in a fairly restricted and well-defined context: one in which we are constructing theories of constraints. This leaves Substitution as the single exception to the claim that 'interesting' developmental sequences will have later members *additively more complex* than earlier members in the sense that they include all items from earlier members of the sequence plus some additional ones. Thus, at a certain level of generality, we only have two types of 'interesting' developmental sequence.

The notion of increasing complexity has played an important role in analyses of development and to say that two theories in a sequence are related additively in the way outlined above is a particularly clear interpretation of the notion. Thus, we find in Taylor (1971) in a discussion of alternatives to a Piagetian account of cognitive development: 'The major antagonist to a genetic psychology is thus an incremental view of learning, in which all development is seen as the addition (or sometimes subtraction) of homogeneous units such as Hull's sHr's (or "habits") linking stimuli and response' (p. 394), and, again, in Nagel (1957): 'The connotation of development thus involves two essential components. The notion of a system possessing a definite structure and a definite set of pre-existing capacities; and the notion of a sequential set of changes in the system, yielding relatively permanent but novel *increments* not only in its structure but in its modes of operation as well' (p. 17 – my emphasis – RMA). With a more biological tone, we find Harris (1957b, p. 3) saying: 'Discussions of development commonly include as essential the ideas of (1) organism conceived as living system; (2) time; (3) movement over time toward complexity of organization; (4) "hierarchization" or the comprehension of parts or part-systems into larger units or "wholes"; and (5) an end state of organization which is maintained with some stability or self-regulation.' Hamburger (1957, p. 49) puts the matter quite clearly when he states 'the term [development], in the most general sense, denotes a more or less continuous *process* which usually involves *progressive changes* from a more simple to a more complex structure or organizational pattern'.

Turning to discussion of this sort of issue in language development, there is one notable occasion where unease is expressed at a proposal which blatantly violates the principle now under consideration. This is Brown's (1973) criticism of Bloom's (1970) use of reduction transformations in child grammars on the grounds that the reduction transformation was something children would have to 'unlearn' with the consequence that later grammars, in this very local sense, would be less complicated than earlier ones (see Chapter 5 for extensive discussion). Fodor, Bever and Garrett refer to the position Brown criticises as 'mildly paradoxical' (1974, p. 487n) and so, although no logical incoherence attaches to the notion of the child and the theories which characterise his abilities becoming simpler as he gets older, there is something of a tradition which is uneasy with such a suggestion.

More positively, we might note here, in a preliminary fashion, a number of studies of different aspects of language development which appear to subscribe to additive complexity at some level of description. So, Brown and Hanlon (1970), an attempt to interpret the derivational theory of complexity (Fodor, Bever and Garrett 1974) in a developmental context, sees one aspect of learning syntax as the gradual accretion of transformational rules. In different domains E. Clark's (1973, 1974) attempts to construe the development of word-meanings in terms of the successive acquisition of semantic features and Halliday's (1975) hypotheses on the development of the child's 'functional meanings' can be seen as subscribing to formally similar claims, and, as will become apparent, these studies by no means exhaust the phenomena which have been examined in these terms.

The conclusion of all this is that for sequences which admit of analysis in terms of additive complexity we can formulate a further developmental condition:

CONDITION IIIa
Given a theory T (= $(T_1, \ldots, T_n, M)$) in the domain of language development D, if T admits of analysis in terms of additive complexity, then T is an explanatory theory in D only if T_{i+1} is additively more complex than T_i ($1 \leqslant i \leqslant n - 1$).

Corresponding to this we have a condition for theories which are theories of constraints and which are negatively interpreted:

CONDITION IIIb

Given a theory T $(= (T_1, \ldots, T_n, M))$ in the domain of language development D where D is a domain of constraints, if T admits of analysis in terms of additive complexity, then T is an explanatory theory in D only if T_{i+1} is less complex than T_i ($1 \leqslant i \leqslant n - 1$).[15]

For theories involving Substitution it is apparent that neither of these conditions is applicable.

Before leaving this discussion it is important to emphasise that the concept of complexity (and its converse, simplicity) involved in these conditions cannot be identified with the identically named notions which have been extensively studied by philosophers of science and transformational linguists. Briefly, the problem of simplicity in the philosophy of science has been construed in the following terms: if we have some domain of enquiry and two or more theories equally supported with respect to observations in this domain, then we should prefer the simplest of the set of theories where 'simplest' is understood in terms of judgements of elegance, generality of laws or rules, number of primitive terms, number of construct-types, etc. Transformational linguists have attempted to incorporate such ideas into the statement of an evaluation measure (see Halle 1961 for some early discussion), and, in a refreshing and insightful treatment of this area, Sober (1975) has argued, among other things, that the linguist's concern, particularly in the field of generative phonology, can be identified with that of the general philosopher of science. However, an observation already made in the previous section shows that the notion of simplicity which is important in this book cannot be identified with the traditional concept. This observation is simply that the traditional concept becomes applicable only when two or more theories comprehend the *same* set of data; but in a developmental study the data accounted for by two theories which we are interested in comparing are distinct.[16]

1.7 The need for further criteria

Imagine now that we are offered a theory in some domain of language development and, for simplicity, assume that it includes just two 'static' theories T_1 and T_2. Assume, furthermore, that the theory satisfies the conditions formulated so far, including IIIa – what this means is that T_2 utilises all the items appearing in T_1 plus some additional ones and we might represent this as:

$$(X_1, X_1 \oplus X_2)$$

where X_1 and X_2 refer to sets of items and '$\oplus$' is an operation which is neutral between Addition, Modification (Differentiation) and Inclusion from the previous section. The question we must now ask is whether the theorist can provide reasons for this sequence as against the alternative:

$$(X_2, X_1 \oplus X_2)$$

i.e. why do the items enter the developmental sequence in the order in which they do? Obviously, as things stand, the developmental theory corresponding to this second sequence is not a serious rival for the original model; by assumption the original sequence satisfies Condition I (T_1 is an adequate explanation for the relevant data in D at t_1) and there is no reason to believe that a theory using only the items from X_2 will satisfy this condition. Nevertheless, the point is clearly made that our original sequence, while, perhaps, providing an adequate *description* of the child's development in D, does not approach *explanation* of that development.

Exactly the same point can be made for theories which satisfy Condition IIIb when we now ask for reasons for the disappearance of items in a particular order. The case of theories which are related by Substitution, while slightly different in formulation, leads to a very similar question. Here an item is replaced and, if we assume a set of items which remains constant from t_1 to t_2, we have the representation:

$$(Y \oplus X_1, Y \oplus X_2)$$

and we can ask why we find this rather than the alternative:

$$(Y \oplus X_2, Y \oplus X_1)$$

i.e. why does X_1 enter the sequence before X_2?

The questions which are being asked here can be compared to the request for explanatory adequacy in the theory of transformational grammar, although the similarity should not be pushed too hard (see Chomsky 1964, 1965 and many other places, for extensive discussion). In both cases certain criteria for adequacy are established; in the case of transformational grammar, grammars must be observationally adequate and, in the case under discussion, theories must meet the sorts of conditions described above. In both cases, the problem arises when it is realised that the criteria do not enable us to formulate unique solutions – the theorist is faced with a surfeit of theories which satisfy his criteria. In both cases we require some additional machinery to determine the correct theory; in transformational grammar the correct theory is the descriptively adequate one and in language development the correct theory is the one which corresponds to the course of development as revealed by the relevant data (cf. Brainerd *et al.* 1978, 1979 for lengthy discussion of the descriptive and explanatory status of stages in Piagetian theory).

Although, to a large extent, theorists in child language development have not been concerned with these issues, there are a number of proposals in the literature which bear, more or less explicitly, on the question of explanation. These proposals fall into a small number of distinct types and it is the purpose of the next three sections to briefly review these.

1.8 Language-internal explanations

One strategy which can be contemplated on the path towards explanation is that of attempting to relate a set of developmental phenomena to some other area of language study. Broadly speaking, there are two such areas which have attracted attention: the comparison of linguistic systems and the postulation of linguistic universals, and the study of diachronic issues.

As far as the first of these is concerned, it is appropriate to restrict ourselves to sequences of theories which are related additively,[17] i.e. in the simplest case we have a sequence:

$$(X_1, X_1 \oplus X_2)$$

We can now imagine a linguistic theory making the claim that *all* the world's languages possess X_1 but only some of them possess X_2 (i.e. the claim that X_1 is an absolute universal – for the distinction between absolute, statistical and implicational universals, see Greenberg 1966), and we then have an instance of the general claim that the child learns first exactly what is common to all languages. Examples of this sort of suggestion can be found in McNeill's early views (1966) on the ontogenetic primacy of standard theory deep structures and grammatical relations, in Lyons' (1975) proposal that, with respect to certain deictic features, there is a universal core to the grammars of the world's languages and that it is this core which the child learns first, and in Jakobson's (1968) claim that there is a small set of universal phonological contrasts which correspond to the first contrasts learned by the child.

Obviously, it would be possible to formulate similar, if less interesting, claims on the basis of statistical universals, but more worthwhile, perhaps, are attempts to use implicational universals in developmental theories. Implicational universals have the form: if a language has X_2 then it has X_1, and, if we see the child's developing language system as constrained by a statement of this form, the development I am schematising as:

$$(X_1, X_1 \oplus X_2)$$

is permitted but the alternative:

$$(X_2, X_1 \oplus X_2)$$

is ruled out, as here we have the system manifesting X_2 without X_1 at t_1. Examples of the use of this sort of argumentation in the literature are provided again by Jakobson (1968) and also by Heider's (1971) investigation of Berlin and Kay's (1969) proposed implicational ordering of colour terms.

What should we make of the view that relating the emergence of linguistic items in a developmental theory to the distribution of those items in the world's languages constitutes an explanation of the developmental order? Investigators pursuing this sort of analysis have often felt the need for deeper principles to explain the *two* sets of related phenomena and this is surely correct; conceivably the facts from child language might be useful in explaining the distributional facts but there is little plausibility to an argument in the opposite direction. At the same time, it is important to recognise the importance of the step which has been taken when we discover identical principles operating in two different theories in this way. Such a discovery makes it more likely that the theories do constitute a first step towards explanation.

I shall say less here about the second method of enquiry which is internal to the study of language. Undoubtedly, there are important principles governing the course of language acquisition and language change (in both a historical and sociolinguistic context) as argued recently by Slobin (1977). However, insofar as explanation proceeds in one direction or the other, the traditional assumption has been that insight will be gained into language change via the study of language acquisition rather than vice versa (for a summary of traditional views on this matter and more recent analysis, see Baron 1977).

Returning to the question of the evaluation of theories, in this book I shall treat a successful attempt to relate developmental phenomena to other linguistic phenomena as a positive feature of a proposal. However, for the reasons briefly discussed in this section, I do not see such enterprises as bearing *directly* on the explanatory status of a developmental theory. Accordingly, I shall not formulate a condition based on this discussion.

1.9 Teleological explanations

In his discussion of developmental sequences Flavell (1972) mentions three kinds of explanation for such sequences. One of these, he calls 'item-structure explanation', and it is this that I am gracing with the attribute 'teleological' here. Flavell sees such explanations as being particularly compelling.[18]

What appears to be involved can easily be illustrated using a linguistic example. Imagine that we are investigating the child's developing syntactic competence and have produced a series of grammars which we claim to represent this competence. Assume further that there is a grammar in the sequence where the child is first credited with transformational rules; up to this point the child's grammars have consisted entirely of phrase-structure rules. If this grammar is G_k we can focus on the sub-sequence:

$$(G_{k-1}, G_k)$$

and ask why the item X_1 (the rule-type of phrase-structure rules) appears before the item X_2 (the rule-type of transformational rules), i.e. why we find:

$$(X_1, X_1 \oplus X_2)$$

rather than

$$(X_2, X_1 \oplus X_2)$$

It is immediately apparent that the theory we are using provides an answer: there is no sense in which the child could acquire transformational rules before phrase-structure rules because the former assume the latter in their functioning. To the extent that we are confident that the child is to acquire a grammar of this kind we have a fine explanation for why he approaches his goal in the manner he does.

A second example could be provided by considering a pair of rules which are intrinsically ordered. In this situation the rule which is ordered first creates the conditions for the second rule to apply and the second rule *cannot* apply unless the first one has already done so. Obviously, there is no sense in which the child could acquire the second of these rules before the first, and, again, we would have a theory-internal explanation for the order of emergence of certain items.

Note that if we are in a position to offer this sort of explanation, the order of acquisition of the items concerned becomes a non-empirical issue. Given our current way of conceptualising the items and our current views on theories in D, there is no possibility of the items being acquired in the reverse order. Of course, if we change our ideas on these matters, we may also change the empirical status of a particular sequence, although it is more likely that we should now be concerned with different items.

The teleological status of such explanations should be apparent from the examples I have given. We assume a well-defined end point in some developmental course and, *because of certain properties of that end point*, we are in a position to understand why items appear in the order in which they do. There does not appear to be anything particularly problematic about this way of doing things and the appropriateness of the proposed explanation will simply be a function of the appropriateness of the theory defining the end point. If we believe that children do acquire transformational grammars of a certain sort, sets of semantic features, inventories of speech-acts, etc., it is likely that some developmental statements will follow on logical, theory-internal grounds.[19]

A teleological explanation is only one type of explanation we might hope to find. The existence of such an explanation cannot, therefore, be imposed as a necessary condition on explanatory theories and the formulation of such a condition must await the discussion of the next section.

1.10 Reductive explanations

A position which has enjoyed a good deal of popularity in the last decade holds that aspects of language development can be explained by reference to the development of a general level of cognitive functioning (see, for example, Cromer 1974, 1976b; Sinclair 1971, 1975). The details of this position are quite complex and I wish to reserve an extensive discussion of them for Chapter 8. However, some preliminary remarks are in order here.

Imagine, then, that we have a two-term sequence of theories in some domain of language development D and that the two theories in the sequence are related additively, i.e. we have the schematic situation:

$$(X_1, X_1 \oplus X_2)$$

The sort of argument I am interested in here will attempt to identify, in a theory of general cognitive development, items corresponding to X_1 and X_2 and to relate the order of development of these cognitive items to that of X_1 and X_2. Similarly, if the two theories in the initial sequence are related by Substitution, i.e. we have:

$$(X_1, X_2)$$

the theorist will search his theory of general cognitive development for items corresponding to X_1 and X_2 looking at the developmental relations between them.[20]

It is immediately apparent that, if we view this task as that of relating *theories* of language development to *theories* of general cognitive development, it bears some resemblance to the problem of reductionism. Fodor (1978) has recently spelled out what is central in this issue. Briefly, each theoretical term in the reduced theory (in this case the theory of language development) must be paired with a theoretical term in the reducing theory (in this case the theory of general cognitive development), and the syntax of the reduced theory must be preserved in the reducing theory. While these notions are not directly applicable to much of what I shall consider in this book the following example appears to be in the spirit of Fodor's proposal. Suppose, again, that syntactic development has been studied in terms of transformational grammars and that the theorist presents a sequence of such grammars. The grammars will employ, among other things, a set of syntactic categories and it seems reasonable to ask that a reducing cognitive theory should employ theoretical terms corresponding to these. In addition, the categories will be manipulated in the grammars by certain formal operations and we might expect that just these operations will appear (along with others) in the reducing theory. Thus, if the grammars contain transformational rules, we ought to be able to identify formal operations which are structure-dependent in the required way in the theory of general cognitive development.

It is also clear that there will have to be sequential relations between corresponding items if the theory of cognitive development is to be explanatory in D. In particular, items must appear in general cognition *before* they appear in language. To obtain the reverse would be to move in the direction of explaining general cognitive development in terms of language development.

Summarising, there are three necessary conditions that we must impose on reductive explanations:

(1) Theoretical terms in the reduced theory must be systematically related to theoretical terms in the reducing theory.

(2) Formal operations in the reduced theory must be identifiable in the reducing theory.

(3) The relevant terms and operations must appear in the sequence of theories of general cognitive development before they appear in the sequence of theories in D.

Whether this set of conditions can be extended will be discussed in Chapter 8, but, as it stands, it will serve as a framework for some initial analysis.

Note now that the reducing theory in the above programme need not be a theory of general cognitive development. Alternatives which have received some discussion are theories of perceptual development and theories of social development. Usually, these latter have not been presented in a form which lends itself to this sort of analysis, but see Shields (1978) and the discussion in Chapter 9. A different sort of option is presented by the suggestion that we should look to theories of biological or neurological development. This can be seen as representing a maturational stance (see Flavell's 1972 concept of 'organism-structure explanation' and Brainerd's discussion of 'maturational variables [which] would presumably be neurological and hormonal events', 1978, p. 176), and also as moving in the direction of classical reductionism. Whether this move is likely to succeed is extremely doubtful, given the arguments in Fodor (1976).

Enough has been said to make clear the general outlines of a reductive explanation.[21] It remains, in this section, to briefly mention the third type of explanation countenanced in Flavell (1972), and to formulate a general condition.

The idea of an environmental explanation for a discovered order of development is, perhaps, the most straightforward we have considered. The theories which characterise the child's linguistic abilities are constructed on the basis of data which the child has available, and, if, given the sequence:

$$(X_1, X_1 \oplus X_2)$$

or the sequence

$$(X_1, X_2)$$

we can show that X_2 is simply not available to the child until after t_1, then we have an explanation for the ordering. Of course, if this explanation is correct, we would predict that altering the child's linguistic environment would lead to the alternative ordering. Despite its initial attractiveness, there is much that is obscure in this idea. Particularly, the problem of what data are available to the child and in what form requires a good deal of analysis (see papers in Snow and Ferguson 1977 for many interesting ideas). I shall return to discussion of this in Chapter 10.

In what follows, I shall assume that teleological, reductive and environmental explanations exhaust the category and that the theorist is obliged to try to formulate theories which conform to one of the three explanation-types. Accordingly, I now present a fourth condition on explanatory developmental theories:

CONDITION IV
Given a theory T $(= (T_1, \ldots, T_n, M))$ in the domain of language development D, T is an explanatory theory in D only if the sequence of theories $(T_1, \ldots, T_n)$ admits of a teleological, a reductive or an environmental explanation.[22]

1.11 The learning mechanism

The study of the mechanisms whereby the child's linguistic systems change has been neglected during the upsurge of interest in child language research during the last twenty years. Traditional psychological speculation on these issues saw mechanisms as being essentially data-driven, involving some version of associationism or behaviourism. More recently, from within linguistics, has come the suggestion that the child should be viewed as an active hypothesis-tester, his hypotheses being constrained by certain innately given principles. In this paradigm data merely support or refute a hypothesis and are not directly responsible for the formulation of such hypotheses.

Condition II above can be seen as a move in the direction of the hypothesis-testing alternative with its insistence that developmental theories should recognise the principles of some general theory in the domain in question. That condition is, however, neutral with regard to whether the general principles of theory construction are consistent with empiricist views on philosophy of mind or whether they require a richer rationalist stance (see Wexler and Culicover 1980). In addition, the nature of the learning mechanisms which interact with available data and with current hypotheses is not approached in this condition. Wexler and his associates have probably made the most interesting contributions to this topic in recent years (see, e.g., Hamburger and Wexler 1975, Culicover and Wexler 1977), but as Marshall (1979) points out any progress in this area has required remarkably rich assumptions, not only about the child's constraints on theory formation but also about the data available to the hypotheses-forming device. Because of the complexity of these issues, I shall present a summary of the main assumptions and conclusions of work in this field in Chapter 10 and there attempt to clarify any significance it might have for the major themes of this book. For now, having noted the importance of learning mechanisms, I merely state, in the form of a fifth condition, that an adequate theory must contain one.

CONDITION V

Given a theory T $(= (T_1, \ldots, T_n, M))$ in the domain of language development D, T is an explanatory theory in D only if M is specified in such a way as to explain the transition from T_i to T_{i+1} on the basis of data available at t_{i+1} $(1 \leqslant i \leqslant n - 1)$.

This concludes the presentation of the set of conditions I wish to consider in this book. Most of what follows is concerned with evaluating existing proposals within the framework the conditions provide. Often this will involve a good deal of interpretation and I may, on occasions, be accused of not giving the theorist the benefit of the doubt. I contend that it is a valuable exercise to discover where the doubt resides. Before commencing this general survey, however, I would like to begin to justify the claims with which I opened this chapter. This justification consists of an examination of Jakobson's theory of phonological development.

1.12 Summary of conditions

For ease of reference, I here bring together the full set of conditions introduced in this chapter:

CONDITION I

Given a theory T $(= (T_1, \ldots, T_n, M))$ in the domain of language development D, T is an explanatory theory in D only if T_i is an explanatory theory in D at t_i ($1 \leqslant i \leqslant n$), where the predicate 'is an explanatory theory in D at t_i' relies for its explication on adopting some view on the general problem of explanation in psychology.

CONDITION II

Given a theory T ($= (T_1, \ldots, T_n, M)$) in the domain of language development D, T is (standardly) an explanatory theory in D only if T_i is constructed in accordance with a particular general theory ($1 \leqslant i \leqslant n$). This ensures that the T_i ($1 \leqslant i \leqslant n$) are comparable in the required sense. If the T_i ($1 \leqslant i \leqslant n$) are not so constructed, then additional argument may restore the explanatory status of T.

CONDITION IIIa

Given a theory T ($= (T_1, \ldots, T_n, M)$) in the domain of language development D, if T admits of analysis in terms of additive complexity, then T is an explanatory theory in D only if T_{i+1} is additively more complex than T_i ($1 \leqslant i \leqslant n - 1$).

CONDITION IIIb

Given a theory T ($= (T_1, \ldots, T_n, M)$) in the domain of language development D where D is a domain of constraints, if T admits of analysis in terms of additive complexity, then T is an explanatory theory in D only if T_{i+1} is less complex than T_i ($1 \leqslant i \leqslant n - 1$).

CONDITION IV

Given a theory T ($= (T_1, \ldots, T_n, M)$) in the domain of language development D, T is an explanatory theory in D only if the sequence of theories ($T_1, \ldots, T_n$) admits of a teleological, a reductive or an environmental explanation.

CONDITION V

Given a theory T ($= (T_1, \ldots, T_n, M)$) in the domain of language development D, T is an explanatory theory in D only if M is specified in such a way as to explain the transition from T_i to T_{i+1} on the basis of data available at t_{i+1} ($1 \leqslant i \leqslant n - 1$).

2 *Jakobson's theory of phonological development*

Jakobson (1968) contains a large number of difficulties of interpretation. Perhaps most important among these is the fact that the author does not present a systematic set of phonological features in that work. For this we must look to later publications, e.g. Jakobson, Fant and Halle (1952) and Jakobson and Halle (1956). Additionally, despite the fact that Jakobson insists that phonological development should be viewed in terms of the acquisition of oppositions, he himself often talks of the acquisition of classes of consonants. This gets him into certain difficulties as we shall see. The fact that the theory lacks empirical support has already been mentioned in Chapter 1, and Kiparsky and Menn (1977) argue convincingly that it would be hard to imagine a corpus of data collected from a small child being sufficiently rich to refute the theory. Put alongside these facts the additional observations that Jakobson pays hardly any attention to the positions in which sounds appear and that he provides no explicit discussion of what it means to acquire a particular contrast, and it is apparent that his claims face many problems. Nevertheless, the theory has inspired a large number of studies which have assumed his framework (e.g. Velten 1943, Shvachkin 1948, Garnica 1971, 1973) and has provided the starting point for many less sympathetic treatments. More importantly, however, it retains many interesting features as a developmental theory, and this is sufficient reason to give it the role of exemplifying the concepts I have advanced in Chapter 1.[1]

2.1 What the theory says

Phonological development, according to Jakobson, consists, in part, of the acquisition of a set of distinctive oppositions. These oppositions are selected from a small set of oppositions which account for all possible phonological oppositions in the world's languages. In Jakobson, Fant and Halle (1952) and Jakobson and Halle (1956) a total of thirteen segmental oppositions is proposed and it is evident that in his earlier work Jakobson was moving in the direction of this list. The thirteen oppositions are: vocalic/non-vocalic; consonantal/non-consonantal; nasalised/non-nasalised; compact/non-compact; diffuse/non-diffuse;[2] abrupt/continuant; strident/ non-strident; checked/unchecked; voice/voiceless; tense/lax; grave/acute; flat/non-flat; sharp/non-sharp.

The first opposition to be acquired is that between a consonant and a vowel, this contrast providing the foundation for the syllable. It is important to be clear that it is the opposition which is acquired and not any particular sounds. So, although Jakobson suggests that the first vowel sound is usually a wide vowel (/a/) and the first consonant is usually a voiceless bilabial stop (/p/), nothing follows against his position if these suggestions are not always confirmed. With the first syntagmatic relations established, Jakobson takes up the development of paradigmatic opposi- tions within the consonantal system. This proceeds by the child distin- guishing nasal and oral stops followed by the acquisition of a contrast between labials and dentals. At this point the child may have a four-term consonantal system, e.g. /p/, /t/, /m/, /n/.

Jakobson next turns his attention to vowels, proposing that the next development takes place in the vowel system as the child begins to contrast wide and narrow vowels (/a/ and /i/). This is followed, most commonly, by a distinction, within the category of narrow vowels, between palatal and velar vowels (/i/ and /u/); an alternative, and less common development, is provided by the recognition of a third vowel height resulting in a linear vowel system (/i/, /e/, /a/).

Up to this point all children are claimed to go through exactly the same stages no matter what language they are learning. This is not so, however, for subsequent development. Nevertheless, generalisations can still be made and they have the form of implicational statements linking classes of sounds. Thus, Jakobson claims that the acquisition of fricatives is later than the acquisition of stops,[3] while recognising that not all children will acquire fricatives. In a similar vein is the claim that the development of front consonants precedes the development of back consonants, that the development of afficates follows the development of homorganic fricatives and that 'an opposition of two vowels of the same degree of aperture is not acquired by the child as long as a corresponding vocalic opposition of a narrower degree of aperture is lacking' (p. 56). There are many more examples of such implicational statements in Jakobson's monograph but there is little point in reproducing them here. Enough has been said for the reader to discern the outline of the proposals: that there is a phonological 'core' which all children learn in the same order and that subsequent development is describable by a series of implications.

2.2 Interpreting the theory

The reader will have noted that there are inconsistencies in the above brief exposition of Jakobson's views. Despite being urged to see development in terms of acquisition of oppositions or features, we are presented with a number of generalisations concerning traditional classes of consonants (e.g. labials). Our first task, then, is to try to produce a consistent interpretation of Jakobson's theory.

The first contrast is that between a consonant and a vowel and, of course, these are traditional labels for categories of sounds. Within Jakobson's system of distinctive features, these two categories are specified in terms of consonantal/non-consonantal and vocalic/non-vocalic. Thus the feature matrix corresponding to the traditional category of consonants would be:

$$\begin{bmatrix} + \text{cons} \\ - \text{voc} \end{bmatrix}$$

while that for the category of vowels would be:

$$\begin{bmatrix} - \text{cons} \\ + \text{voc} \end{bmatrix}$$

The point of this system is to enable the definition of the *four* major classes of sounds (consonants, vowels, liquids and glides) but it is not clear from Jakobson's remarks that he would wish to credit the child with the ability to make these distinctions at the beginnings of development. It is more appropriate to the spirit of his suggestion to credit the child with a single opposition, say consonantal/non-consonantal which distinguishes consonants, liquids and glides from true vowels[4] and I shall adopt this practice for the remainder of this chapter.

The first consonantal opposition is that between a nasal and an oral consonant and this gives rise to no problems, being mediated directly by the feature nasal/non-nasal. Labial consonants contrast with dental consonants by virtue of the former being grave while the latter are acute. It seems straightforward, therefore, to suggest that the acquisition of this contrast underlies the differentiation of labials and dentals. This completes the consonantal development which all children undergo and it is apparent that we can represent part of the child's phonological development as a sequence of three theories where each theory consists simply of a set of features. At the time corresponding to each theory the child is assumed to control those features contained in the theory. We can represent the situation as in Figure 2.1.

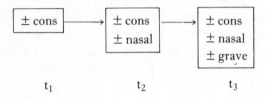

Figure 2.1

There are some immediate problems with this sequence. One is that acquired features appear to be highly restricted in their function. To illustrate, once the feature ± nasal has appeared at t_2 we might expect that a child learning a language with nasal vowels would be in a position to implement a contrast between oral and nasal vowels. This does not happen and, in fact, Jakobson goes to some lengths to point out the relatively late acquisition of nasal vowels and to explain it (see 2.3 below). Second, the feature ± grave introduced at t_3 distinguishes dental consonants from labials *and velars*. Yet, according to Jakobson, it is only labials which are contrasted with dentals at this stage and velars do not appear. Again, as we shall see, Jakobson approaches this problem.

Turning now to vowels, narrow vowels are differentiated from wide vowels in terms of diffuseness and compactness (see n.2). If we ignore the possibility of the linear vowel system, we can assume that the child acquires the feature ± diffuse with his wide vowel being − diffuse and his narrow vowel, + diffuse. The subsequent distinction between palatal and velar narrow vowels then refers to the feature ± grave already introduced into the consonantal system. Analogous to Figure 2.1, then, we have Figure 2.2, exhibiting the development of features relevant to vowel systems.[5]

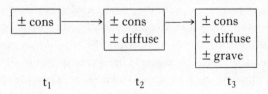

Figure 2.2

What of the implicational statements? How are we to interpret, for example, the claim that the acquisition of stops proceeds in advance of the acquisition of fricatives? In order to simplify the discussion, let us assume that the claim is restricted to one point of articulation. So, we might be considering the suggestion that /t/ and /d/ are acquired before /s/ and /z/. The feature which distinguishes stops from fricatives in Jakobson's system is ± continuant, and we might be tempted to say that there is some point in the child's development where his system contains − continuant (corresponding to stops) and that this point precedes the point where + continuant (corresponding to fricatives) enters the system. But this is impossible to reconcile with the features' role as *distinctive*, as we are now admitting a developing language system where − continuant does not serve to distinguish segments from other segments (those which are + continuant) but simply serves to define a class of sounds. Similar remarks can be made in connection with the other implicational statements mentioned above and it is obvious that there is a serious problem in interpreting Jakobson's theory in this regard. Because there remain interesting aspects of the implicational statements from the point of view of this book, despite the difficulties of interpreting them in Jakobson's own terms, I shall come back to them in the next section. One should not underestimate the seriousness of the above remarks, however, and it is worth pointing out that we shall come across similar problems when we look at the area of lexical development in Chapters 3 and 4.

2.3 Evaluating the theory

I shall consider each of the conditions formulated in Chapter 1 in turn.

It is difficult to see exactly how Condition I might be applied to the theory. Obviously, as it stands, it does not make predictions about behaviour for particular stages of development and it cannot be accommodated to any traditional psychological paradigm.[6] On the other hand, if we attempt to treat it as a competence theory we must face the difficulties associated with that notion (see Chapter 1), while noting that it is at best incomplete in this regard, as it deals only with the paradigmatic oppositions and says nothing about syntagmatic phonological constraints. In addition, the vagueness in Jakobson's methodology becomes crucial here. Most of the data he cites come from the child's spontaneous productions, but, arguably, a better indicator of phonological competence is the child's perceptions (see for example, Smith 1973, Stampe 1969). Again, the lack of a criterion for the acquisition of an opposition becomes crucial in this context, and, even if we allow that production data lead to interesting hypotheses about competence, we may still be confounded by the utilisation of a contrast in one position (e.g. initially) and its failure to appear elsewhere (e.g. medially).

It seems that we are forced to the conclusion that the theory does not satisfy Condition I, and this is a conclusion we shall meet repeatedly in this book.

Condition II requires the existence of a general theory which is instanced at the sampled stages of development. In Jakobson's case, this is provided by the set of thirteen segmental oppositions listed in 2.1. Any language system will be characterised, in part, by its selection from this total set and clearly this is true for the systems sketched above in Figures 2.1 and 2.2. Condition II is satisfied.

Similarly, Condition IIIa is satisfied in a reasonably straightforward way. What distinguishes later theories in the sequence from earlier theories is the addition of items (either features or, if we ignore the difficulties discussed in the previous section, values of features). So, looking at the sequence in Figure 2.1, we can schematise this as:

$$(X_1, X_1 \oplus X_2, X_1 \oplus X_2 \oplus X_3)$$

where X_1 is $\pm$ cons, X_2 is $\pm$ nasal and X_3 is $\pm$ grave. Similarly, if we consider the claim that stops are acquired before fricatives, this leads us to a sequence:

$$(X_1, X_1 \oplus X_2)$$

where X_1 is $-$ continuant and X_2 is $+$ continuant.[7]

Before moving on to Condition IV, it is important to mention Jakobson's systematic attempt to produce internal explanations for the order of development he postulates (cf. 1.8). Thus, he attempts to relate to the phonological development of the child, not only distributional facts from the world's languages, but also data from the breakdown of linguistic systems in patients who have suffered injury to the brain. He makes three general points:

(a) Those aspects of consonantal and vocalic development which are characteristic of all children define the minimal consonantal and vocalic systems in the world's languages. Taking Figure 2.1, this amounts to a claim that all languages distinguish consonants and vowels, nasal and oral consonants and (assuming the feature $\pm$ grave is restricted as it is in development) labial and dental consonants. For Figure 2.2, and continuing to ignore the possibility of linear vowel systems, all languages distinguish two vowel heights and, within the category of high vowels distinguish two in terms of back and front. If we consider any other phonological opposition, not only will it fall outside the universal sequence of development in children, but we shall also be able to find languages which do not make use of that opposition. Note that the actual order of acquisition of contrasts within this universal 'core' cannot be related to distributional facts because the relevant oppositions are assumed to appear in *all* languages. As far as language dissolution is concerned, the picture which is presented is the converse of that for acquisition. Contrasts from the universal 'core' will be the last to be lost as the phonological system breaks down.

(b) Outside the universal 'core' the order of acquisition of phonological units is related to a set of implicational universals which Jakobson refers to as Laws of Irreversible Solidarity. The claim that stops are acquired before fricatives is related to the claim that, in the languages of the world, we can find instances which lack fricatives while containing stops but no instances for which the opposite is true. Accordingly, we have an implicational universal of the form:

> If a language has fricatives then it has stops

and Jakobson formulates similar statements corresponding to several other of his developmental claims.[8] When language is breaking down oppositions disappear in the opposite order of appearance in acquisition.

(c) Sounds which are relatively rare in the world's languages are acquired late; this, of course, follows from (b). Thus, nasal vowels are relatively late to appear in the acquisition of French and Polish and have a limited distribution in the world's languages. Correspondingly, relatively rare sounds are lost early in language dissolution or by speakers who get no practice in speaking their native language.

These three points add up to an impressive array of evidence. Data from three distinct areas of enquiry point in the same direction and, while, as argued in Chapter 1, we cannot see this as counting as explanation, we can feel confident that the generalisations are not spurious and are likely to lead to interesting explanations. Jakobson is sensitive to this issue and, in the last part of his monograph, tries to confront it.

The best way for us to approach the problem is to consider satisfaction of Condition IV. The reader will recall that this condition recognises three types of explanation – teleological, reductive and environmental – and, for each of the developmental stages which Jakobson recognises, we can ask which, if any, of these categories is available to him.

As a preliminary, we can dispense with environmental explanations. There is no suggestion that the child learns the oppositions in a fixed order because they are presented to him in that order, nor is it likely that there are appropriate statistical imbalances between the oppositions in the child's linguistic environment. It would also appear not particularly fruitful to search for teleological explanations. The features in Jakobson's systems are largely independent of each other and, because of this, we are not going to find the acquisition of one opposition requiring the prior acquisition of another.[9] This leaves reductive explanations, and it is in this category that Jakobson's speculations most properly belong.

There is a good deal of obscurity in Jakobson's attempt to explain his proposed order of development. One source of this obscurity is his willingness to mix perceptual and motor categories when looking for antecedents for his oppositions. Another is a reliance on a principle of maximisation of contrast which is never clearly formulated, but which Jakobson appears to treat as governing a great deal of category learning. Nevertheless, the concern with explanation is a real one and deserves some attention. Recall then, Figure 2.1 with its three stages. Condition IV directs us to ask, in connection with the transition between t_1 and t_2, why it proceeds in this fashion rather than as in Figure 2.3. Jakobson's answer,

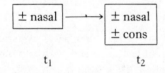

Figure 2.3

not presented in quite these terms, is that perceptually and articulatorily the categories corresponding to the ± cons distinction are more salient than those corresponding to the ± nasal distinction. As far as articulation is concerned, 'these two fundamental classes of speech sounds are contrasted with each other as closure and opening. The optimal opening is achieved in the wide *a*-vowel, while among the stop consonants it is the labial sounds which obstruct the entire oral cavity' (Jakobson 1968, p. 69), and, from the acoustic perspective, 'the labial stop presents a momentary frequency band, whereas in the vowel /a/ there is no strict limitation of time, and the energy is concentrated in a relatively narrow region of maximum aural sensitivity' (Jakobson and Halle 1956 p. 51). Thus the contrast between consonant and vowel is maximal and the best example of the consonantal category will be /p/ while the best example of the vowel category will be /a/. In this sense, Jakobson is in a position to make predictions not only about the acquisition of oppositions but also about the most likely phonetic realisations of these oppositions. Comparing the ± cons feature with ± nasal, we can note that the latter corresponds to an articulatory distinction where the oral cavity remains unchanged and to an acoustic distinction which involves the superimposition of nasal resonance onto an already existing pattern. It does appear to make sense to suggest that the categories, consonant and vowel, are perceptually and articulatorily more available than the categories, nasal and non-nasal.

Moving on now to the next transition in Figure 2.1, can we explain the appearance of ± nasal before ± grave? Furthermore, when ± grave appears, it is restricted to the consonantal system and it is phonetically realised by a labial rather than a velar. Can these additional facts be explained? As for the first of these questions, Jakobson considers the general configurations of the oral and nasal cavities. The distinction between an oral and nasal consonant can be viewed as a distinction between a single obstructed cavity and a single obstructed cavity together with an open subsidiary cavity. Thus, we have a major articulatory distinction between one and two cavities. Of course, the same is true for the distinction between oral and nasal vowels, but we know that this distinction is acquired relatively late. Jakobson is alive to this problem, however, and says 'a nasal vowel, which opposes a double open cavity to the simple open cavity of the oral vowel and thereby simply increases the vowel quality, is a much more complicated and much less opposing entity' (Jakobson 1968 p. 71). So, it is not simply the opposition of one cavity versus two but also the fact that for oral and nasal consonants the two cavities involved have different states that is important in maximising the contrast.[10] In comparison, the feature ± grave merely carries a distinction in the oral cavity. In acoustic terms too, the nasal consonant differs from its non-nasal counterpart in possessing a limited formant structure. For grave and acute consonants, however, all that differentiates them is their effect on the existing formant structures in adjacent vowels.

Why is ± grave first restricted to the consonantal system? Jakobson's answer to this refers to his views that there are two psychophysical dimensions along which consonants and vowels are characterised. Following Stumpf, he calls these 'chromatism' and 'lightness/darkness', the former corresponding to the compact/non-compact and diffuse/non-diffuse features and the latter corresponding to grave/acute. He then says: 'Chromatism is the specific phenomenal feature of vowels . . . consonants are sounds "without pronounced chromatism", and since the opposition of light and dark . . . increases as the chromatism decreases, it naturally forms the primary, and occasionally the only, axis of the consonantal system' (1968 pp. 75–6). So, grave/acute is the 'natural' classificatory dimension for consonants. To use an analogy, we can imagine two sets of objects, the members of one set differing obviously from each other with respect to colour and more subtly with respect to shape while the reverse is true for the second set, and being asked to sort the members of the sets into categories. It is highly likely that we would use colour as the critical attribute for the first set and shape for the second set. Whatever one may think of the obscurities in this account, it is undoubtedly asking the right questions. Note, further, that it attempts to explain why the compact/diffuse distinction, when it is first implemented, is restricted to the vowel system (Figure 2.2) as this is the 'natural' classificatory dimension for vowels, and to begin to classify consonants in these terms is to begin to look at their 'vowel-like' and less contrastive properties.

Finally, the question as to why + grave is first realised phonetically as /p/ receives a straightforward answer in articulatory terms. Grave consonants have the articulatory property of being produced with a larger and more compartmentalised resonating cavity than corresponding acute consonants. Given this, /p/ is a 'better' representative of the category of grave consonants than is /k/ (cf. the explanation above for why /p/ is the optimal consonant).

The analysis presented above only attempts to approach a small proportion of the total position Jakobson offers. It could be extended to take account of further aspects along similar lines. My aim, however, has not been to provide an exhaustive analysis, but rather to show the extent of Jakobson's concern. Because of this concern, I feel justified in concluding that Jakobson makes a serious attempt to provide reductive explanations for much of the development he envisages. To the extent that he is successful, his theory satisfies Condition IV.

Unfortunately, there is no discussion in Jakobson's work of any sort of mechanism for phonological development. We are left completely in the dark as to what sort of data lead the child to modify his set of features. Condition V is not satisfied.

This chapter has had two major functions. First, it has shown what is involved in one particular case in applying the abstract framework of Chapter 1. Second, it has shown that the theory under discussion, Jakobson's theory of phonological development, satisifies three of the five conditions from that framework, Conditions II, III and IV. It failed to satisfy Conditions I and V but, as we shall see, it is quite representative of theories in one or other domain of language development in that respect. More worthy of emphasis is its level of success. This level of success, added to the claims Jakobson makes about the relationships between different areas of language study, makes his theory one of the most attractive of those available from the perspective I am presenting in this book. I shall now turn to proposals which are often less satisfying.

3 Early lexical development

In this chapter, I am concerned with theories of the child's first words and, in particular, with views on the meanings of these early lexical items and the ways in which these meanings change as the lexicon grows. There are at least three reasonably coherent positions on these issues which have emerged during the last few years: the semantic feature hypothesis (SFH) associated principally with the work of E. Clark (1973, 1974), the functional core hypothesis (FCH) advanced by Nelson (1973a, 1973b, 1974, 1979), and the prototype hypothesis (PH), orginally put forward in restricted lexical domains by, e.g., Heider (1971), but more recently given some general currency by Bowerman (1978). I shall evaluate these in turn. As we shall see in the next chapter, the SFH and the PH have also been studied in connection with the later development of pairs of relational terms; this work will not be discussed here.

3.1 The semantic feature hypothesis

E. Clark's work represents one of the most systematic investigations of early lexical reference. The main ideas are contained in two papers (1973, 1974) and have been modified, to take account of some empirical inadequacies, in Clark (1975). I shall concentrate here on the unmodified theory, the justification for this being that I am not principally concerned with empirical adequacy in theory evaluation. Additionally, the unmodified theory is somewhat clearer in its claims than the later version. Criticisms of Clark's position, from different standpoints, can be found in Nelson (1974), Griffiths (1976) and Barrett (1978). Unless these criticisms seem particularly pertinent from the perspective I am developing, I shall not take them into account in what follows.

The pedigree of Clark's model is somewhat difficult to determine. In its notational devices it clearly owes a lot to the componential semanticists of anthropological linguistics (e.g. Lounsbury 1956), to the linguistic semantics of Katz and his associates (e.g. Katz 1972), and, from a slightly different perspective, to the ideas of Bierwisch (1970). However, it lacks the methodological constraints of the former in that, whereas the anthropological linguist can ask his native informant about the semantic relations between words and about the denotation classes of words, this strategy is not generally available to the child-language theorist. From the point of view of linguistic semantics, Clark's proposals lack philosophical motivation; there is no concern on her part for an explication of such notions as synonymy, ambiguity, paraphrase, analyticity, etc.[1] On the basis of considerations such as these, it seems fair to assert that Clark borrows little of substance from these approaches beyond the notational devices and, futhermore, we might note that there is no clear statement as to whether the theory only countenances binary features or admits n-valued features.[2]

The most central phenomenon tackled by the theory is that referred to as *overextension* where a small child uses a word which is recognised as a token of a word-form which exists in the adult language and does so in a non-standard fashion, i.e. uses it to refer to some object or event for which an adult would not judge it appropriate. Table 3.1 presents some examples collated by Clark in her 1973 paper.[3]

A good deal of evidence is now available from modern studies (e.g. Grieve and Hoogenraad 1977, Bowerman 1978) to attest to the generality of overextensions (for a cautionary note in this regard, see Griffiths 1976) and it is clear that Clark is using this aspect of the child's 'naming' behaviour to formulate hypotheses about the structure of the lexicon. The domain of enquiry D is this lexicon and the data regarded as relevant to D are children's uses of concrete nominals in a referential fashion.[4]

I now turn to what I regard as the central theses of the theory. There are at least six such theses:

(1)   The meaning of a word is to be understood as specifiable in terms of a set of features.[5]

(2)   The set of features which comprise the meaning of a word in the adult language may not be identical with the set of features comprising the meaning of the word for the child at the stage under investigation.[6]

(3)   The mismatch referred to in (2) is to be explained in terms of the child *sampling* from a certain set of features when he first encounters an application of the word.[7]

(4)   The subset sampled by the child is a subset of a set of *perceptual* (as

Table 3.1. *Some examples of overextension in child speech (adapted from E. Clark 1973, pp. 79–82)*

Language being learned	Child's form	First referent	Subsequent overextensions
English	bird	sparrows	cows, dogs, cats, any animal moving
Georgian	buti	ball	toy, radish, stone spheres at park entrance
Serbian	bebe	reflection of self in mirror	photograph of self, all photographs, all books with pictures, all books
English	kotibaiz	bars of cot	large toy abacus, toast rack with parallel bars, pictures of building with columns
French	bebe	baby	other babies, all small statues, figures in small pictures and prints
Russian	dany	sound of bell	clock, telephone, door bells
French	cola	chocolate	sugar, tarts, grapes, figs, peaches
Russian	va	white plush dog	muffler, cat, father's fur coat

opposed to conceptual or functional) features, which is somehow contingent on the perceptual properties of objects the word is typically used to refer to when the child first assimilates it into his lexicon.

(5) Development in this domain consists of the child simultaneously learning new words and features to distinguish them from words already learned, resulting in richer feature specifications for the words which have already been learned, with a gradual approximation to the adult meaning.[8]

(6) Features of meaning are acquired in an order from most general to least general.

There are many questions which one might wish to raise in connection with these theses, some of which are discussed below, but, for now, all I wish to do is cast the theory into terms which render the framework of Chapter 1 applicable. I submit that this procedure does not involve a significant perversion of Clark's thinking.

What Clark appears to be proposing is an unstructured associative model of the lexicon in which words are paired with sets of perceptual features. The perceptual features give the meaning of the words and provide necessary and sufficient conditions for the application of a word to an instance. This is a proposal which we might represent as in Figure 3.1.

$$W_1 \longleftrightarrow FS_1$$
$$W_2 \longleftrightarrow FS_2$$
$$\cdots \cdots \cdots$$
$$\cdots \cdots \cdots$$
$$W_n \longleftrightarrow FS_n$$

Figure 3.1

Here the W_i ($1 \leqslant i \leqslant n$) represent the child's word-forms at the time in question[9] and the FS_i ($1 \leqslant i \leqslant n$) designate sets of perceptual features which constitute the meanings of the W_i. Obviously the feature sets will have members in common, and it is Clark's hope that a relatively small list exists out of which the word-meanings are formed, and which can be related to a set of universal semantic primitives such as is suggested by Postal (1966) or Bierwisch (1970).

In order to be clear on the developmental implications of the picture, we can consider a hypothetical example Clark uses to investigate her notion of 'restructuring'. Her version of a plausible path of development in that restricted part of the lexicon dealing with common animal names is presented in Table 3.2.

At Stage I the child is presumed to have learned the word *bow-wow* and to use it appropriately.[10] At Stage II the child overextends the use of *bow-wow* to include all common four-legged animals and it is suggested that a plausible candidate for the basis of the overextension is a feature to do with shape. The child is assumed to have sampled this feature, on acquaintance with an instance of a dog, from the total set of perceptual

Table 3.2. *Hypothetical instance of overextension and restructuring (reproduced from E. Clark 1973, p. 85)*

	Word	Semantic domain	Possible criterial features
Stage I	bow-wow	dog(s)	shape
Stage II	bow-wow	dogs, cows, horses, sheep, cats	shape
Stage III	(a) bow-wow	dogs, cats, horses, sheep	
	(b) moo	cows	sound (horns?)
Stage IV	(a) bow-wow	dogs, cats, sheep	
	(b) moo	cows	sound
	(c) gee-gee	horses	size (tail/mane?)
Stage V	(a) bow-wow/ doggie	cats, dogs	size
	(b) moo	cows	
	(c) gee-gee/ horsie	horses	
	(d) baa	sheep	sound
Stage VI	(a) doggie	dogs	
	(b) moo	cows	
	(c) gee-gee/ horsie	horses	
	(d) baa lamb	sheep	
	(e) kitty	cats	shape, sound

features available on that occasion. Elsewhere Clark talks about a feature + 4-legged, while admitting that this is not a plausible candidate for a primitive perceptual feature, so we can assume that at Stage II the relevant part of the child's lexicon is as in Figure 3.2.

$$bow\text{-}wow \quad \longleftrightarrow \quad + 4\text{-legged}$$
$$W_1 \quad \longleftrightarrow \quad FS_1$$
$$\cdots\cdots\cdots$$
$$\cdots\cdots\cdots$$
$$W_n \quad \longleftrightarrow \quad FS_n$$

Figure 3.2

An important point about this structure, which will receive extended discussion in Chapter 4, is that, in order for the feature $\pm$ 4-legged to have a coherent status, it is necessary for the negatively specified version $-$ 4-legged to appear somewhere in the FS_i ($1 \leqslant i \leqslant n$). This follows from viewing the features as *distinctive* semantic features.

At Stage III there is a restructuring of the system resulting in a reduction of the overextension associated with *bow-wow*, and the suggestion is that this is mediated by the child's use of a perceptual feature corresponding to the sound made by cows. For the sake of argument let us refer to this feature as $\pm$ moo and assume that no other lexical changes have occurred between Stage II and Stage III. At Stage III the relevant part of the lexicon will have the structure shown in Figure 3.3.

bow-wow	$\longleftrightarrow$	$+$ 4-legged, $-$ moo
moo	$\longleftrightarrow$	$+$ 4-legged, $+$ moo
W_1	$\longleftrightarrow$	FS_1
. . . .		
. . . .		
W_n	$\longleftrightarrow$	FS_n

Figure 3.3

Stage IV produces a further restructuring leading to another reduction in the overextension of *bow-wow*; this time the suggested criterial feature is based on the perceptual dimension of size. Unless we are to invoke such unlikely features as $\pm$ horse-sized, we shall have to admit a non-binary feature at this point, say, 1Size, 2Size, . . ., nSize, such that the child's lexicon at Stage IV is as in Figure 3.4.

bow-wow	$\longleftrightarrow$	$+$ 4-legged, $-$ moo, iSize
moo	$\longleftrightarrow$	$+$ 4-legged, $+$ moo, jSize
gee-gee	$\longleftrightarrow$	$+$ 4-legged, $-$ moo, jSize
W_1	$\longleftrightarrow$	FS_1
. . . .		
. . . .		
W_n	$\longleftrightarrow$	FS_n

Figure 3.4

Obviously, this sort of treatment can be extended to the later stages hypothesised by Clark, but there is little point in pursuing this here as the general lines of the argument are clear enough. As the child develops his lexicon in a semantic domain, he also extends his inventory of semantic features without (in early lexical development at any rate) going beyond perceptual features. If we have a set of word-forms, W_1, W_2, . . ., W_n, covering, in their applications, a particular conceptual field (see Lyons 1977b for some discussion of this notion), then the learning of an additional form, the application of which falls within the same conceptual field, involves the utilisation of at least one additional perceptual feature. This new feature, as well as providing part of the meaning of the new form, will also have a role to play in restricting the extension of a form already in the system. If, following the procedure of Chapter 1, we now consider theories being constructed at times t_1 and t_2, we can see that we are confronted with the general situation depicted in Figure 3.5.

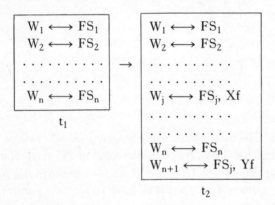

Figure 3.5

Here the W_i ($1 \leqslant i \leqslant n + 1$) designate the child's word-forms, the FS_i ($1 \leqslant i \leqslant n$) designate feature sets, W_{n+1} is the new form introduced at t_2, f is the new feature which allows for the introduction of W_{n+1} and contrasts it with the existing W_j, and X and Y are variables ranging over feature prefixes (i.e. over '+' and '−' for binary features and over 1, 2, . . ., n for n-valued features). In addition $X \neq Y$ in this schema.

This general formulation seems to cover the case discussed by Clark and to make clear the sense in which lexical learning proceeds by way of the accumulation of new perceptual features. It is this general formulation which must now confront the conditions of Chapter 1.

3.2 Evaluation of the semantic feature hypothesis

From the above presentation it is clear that the SFH is a competence theory with the sample lexicons of Figures 3.2–3.5 being models of lexical knowledge. The assumption is that these models will show up fairly directly in the child's naming behaviour but no attempt is made to specify operations on these lexicons which would put the theory within the more traditional boundaries for psychological explanation. I shall assume that an appropriate version of Condition I is satisified.

When we ask whether the SFH satisifies Condition II, the answer appears to be that in a sense it does and in a sense it does not. It does to the extent that the lexicon at each stage of development is constructed with reference to general considerations. These include claims that the meaning of a word consists of a set of features, that these features are perceptual features and so on. In accordance with these constraints, the theories constructed at various points will be of the same type and should be comparable, in the sense outlined in Chapter 1. If we pursue the analysis a little further, however, we realise that the features are not drawn from some antecedently defined set (cf. Jakobson's proposals in Chapter 2), the issue of whether all features are binary is not settled (see above), and the question of whether lexical entries consist only of conjunctive sets of perceptual features is not even raised. As far as the first of these problems is concerned, the fact that Clark insists that the initial features are *perceptual* is to her advantage and does constrain the theories in an intuitive way. One must be wary of the force of this, though, in the context of such *ad hoc* contenders as $\pm$ 4-legged and $\pm$ moo.

Turning to Condition III, the SFH appears to satisfy IIIa in a straightforward way. From t_1 to t_2 in Figure 3.5 there is a *complication* of the theory of the child's lexicon, a complication of an additive nature. And, in general, given a sequence of theories $(T_1, \ldots, T_n)$, it will be the case that T_{i+1} is more complicated (additively) than T_i ($1 \leqslant i \leqslant n - 1$), if the course of development suggested by Clark is being followed.[11] Most importantly, new features enter the system and, on the assumption that a richer set of features makes available a basis for more lexical items (cf. n. 8), we are justified in focusing on this aspect of the development. We have, then, a situation which can be depicted as:

$$X_1 \rightarrow X_1 \oplus X_2$$

where X_1 and X_2 refer to features or to sets of features.

Note now that we are not, as we were with Jakobson's theory, in a position to relate the SFH to other linguistic phenomena, e.g. distributional facts from the world's languages. The relevant analyses in terms of perceptual features do not exist, a fact which is related to the difficulty already mentioned concerning the lack of a fixed inventory of features. Apart from such remarks and speculations as can be found in Bierwisch (1967), semantic theorists have tended to eschew reference to perceptual properties of the human organism in formulating their proposals.[12] The conclusion of all this is that in this domain we do *not* have a rich set of linguistic phenomena which might be explicable within a single framework.

Regarding Condition IV, we can briefly consider the possibility of logical and environmental explanations. For the former there does not appear to be any relationship between particular features of the sort we need. If we examine the example discussed above (pp. 41–4), we can see that it demands a sequence of features:

($\pm$ 4-legged, $\pm$ moo, iSize, . . .)

and there is no logical reason why we should find this sequence rather than, say:

($\pm$ moo, iSize, $\pm$ 4-legged, . . .)

or any of the other numerous possibilities. Such an explanation might be forthcoming if the lexicons interacted with a set of semantic redundancy rules (see Kempson 1977 for some discussion), but this is not the case.[13] An environmental explanation would be available if there were reason to believe that the relevant perceptual features are presented to the child in a fixed order or that there are remarkable statistical imbalances across the set of features occurring in the child's perceptual environment. To my knowledge, we have no motivation for speculating in this direction.

This drives us in the direction of a reductive explanation, and, given that the features comprising the meanings of words are perceptual features, it might be felt that there should be no great problem in relating them, in a revealing way, to theories of perceptual development in the visual, auditory, and other sensory domains. That Clark sees this as a possibility is argued most fully in Clark (1974). There we find several references to research in sensory perception covering a number of modalities. For example, in connection with shape, Clark cites the findings of Gibson (1969) on the infant's attention to lines and vertices and tentatively relates this to Hubel and Wiesel's well-known work on the visual fields of cells in the cat's visual cortex (see, e.g., Hubel and Wiesel 1962). Evidence of a different sort is provided by Ricciuti's (1963) work showing that children in the 12–24 month age group used shape as their main criterion in a free sorting task. As for the auditory medium, we are directed to Kaplan (1969) and the conclusion that infants of four months can distinguish male and female voices, and to Eimas, Siqueland, Jusczyk and Vigorito (1971) and their claims concerning the infant's perception of speech sounds. Further evidence from the development of the perception of movement, of size and of texture bolsters the general position, but it is not my purpose to review this evidence in detail here. Rather, I wish to take the evidence at face-value and enquire into exactly what Clark shows by citing it.

Consider the example of sound. The pre-linguistic infant is shown as capable of some fairly sophisticated discriminations in this modality, discriminations which might, in principle, be conceptualised in terms of the child having available a set of auditory perceptual features. But there are three points I would like to make in this connection:

(a) All Clark's evidence concerns the child's perception of *linguistic* materials and, as she herself points out: 'The overextensions based on sound are mainly based on characteristic non-speech sounds, e.g. the sound of a train. However there has been much less research on the child's ability to identify or recognise these kinds of sound than there has been on speech sound' (1974, p. 35). In short, the evidence to which Clark draws our attention provides *no* support for the child controlling the features in his auditory perception with which she wishes to credit him in explaining his overextensions.

(b) Assume, contrary to what has just been suggested, that the evidence does argue for the existence of the required features in perception. Then we have to attend to the relative ordering of the appearance of the features in the perceptual theory and in the lexical theory. Some of the data presented by Clark come from children who are beyond the typical age-range for overextensions. Therefore, it can hardly be used in a reductive explanation for the order of acquisition of the features in the child's lexicon.

(c) Although there may be a chance of satisfying the necessary conditions on the reduction required by Condition IV there is little room for optimism as far as additional conditions put forward in Chapter 8 are concerned. It is not the case that a *sequence* of acquisition for perceptual features has been established.[14] To see this in its proper perspective we can imagine a set of findings which would strongly support Clark's position. Suppose that research on the development of form perception reveals that such perception is mediated by a set of features, the availability of which to the child is fixed in some ontogenetic sequence F_1, F_2, . . ., F_n. Suppose, further, that lexical development can be seen, as Clark would have it, in terms of the successive acquisition of perceptual features, say f_1, f_2, . . ., f_n. Finally, assume that the f_i can be systematically related to the F_i ($1 \leqslant i \leqslant n$) and that we find f_i being utilised in the lexical system *after* F_i appears in the perceptual system and *before* F_{i+1} is used in that system ($1 \leqslant i \leqslant n - 1$). That is, we would have a sequence of development which we could represent, collapsing the two domains as:

$$(F_1, f_1, F_2, f_2, . . ., F_i, f_i, F_{i+1}, . . ., F_n, f_n)$$

In such a situation, Clark's hypothesis would have extremely strong support (see Chapter 8 for extended analysis of this and similar states of affairs).

Compare this, then, to what we in fact have. We are offered some fairly fragmentary evidence that infants use perceptual features in a number of sensory modalities. None of this evidence points to a developmental sequence. *Ex hypothesi* we have the sequence f_1, . . ., f_n, this being what we are seeking to explain, but we do not have any systematic relationship between the perceptual features and the features used in the lexical system. Nor do we have any evidence of the required kind on the relative orderings of the perceptual and lexical features; the evidence we have indicates that a large proportion of the relevant perceptual features are used by the child in his perception long before he learns any lexical items at all. It appears that the SFH does not satisfy Condition IV.

Finally, what of Condition V? As mentioned previously, the claim that the child samples sets of features on acquaintance with instances could be seen as part of a theory of the data he has available at some stage in the learning process. However, Clark's work contains no discussion of how such data are evaluated in terms of an existing theory nor of how the existing theory may be modified on the basis of data which are inconsistent with it. The SFH does not satisfy Condition V.

By way of general conclusion, we can pin-point the weaknesses of the SFH. The features which it countenances are blatantly *ad hoc* within the constraint that they are perceptual. Two sets of undesirable consequences follow: first, the theory cannot be related to any general theory of semantic structure; second, it cannot be related to an independent theory of perceptual development. Coupled with the failure to produce any clear statement on learning, this explains our feeling of unease with the theory.

3.3 The functional core hypothesis

The FCH is put forward most forcefully in Nelson (1974). It is reaffirmed without modification in Nelson (1979) and empirical data supporting it appear in Nelson (1973a, 1973b). I shall focus here on the presentation in the 1974 paper.

Whereas E. Clark, in developing the SFH, saw overextensions as being of particular importance, Nelson wishes to accommodate other phenomena within a coherent framework. These are:

(1) the important commonalities between sets of lexical items which become apparent when the early vocabularies of a large number of children are examined;

(2) the readiness of a small child to invent a word for which he can find no linguistic expression in the adult language;[15]

(3) that words, once acquired, are subsequently generalised in their application. In this respect, Nelson has in mind a phenomenon which embraces overextension as a particular case.

The point of departure from Clark is indicated in Nelson's claim that the similarity which underlies generalisation need not be restricted to perceptual dimensions. 'Similarity may be based on many different dimensions of which the static perceptual dimension of shape is only one; others include function, action, or affect' (1974, p. 269).

It is intended that one of the main attractions of the FCH is that it is not an abstractionist theory of concept formation. The problem with such theories is that they presuppose the very concepts they are claimed to explain. This is because the concept learner will not know, in general, to compare instances of a concept, abstracting the appropriate similarities, unless he already knows that they are instances of a common concept. Without this knowledge, he is as likely to compare such instances with instances of different and distant concepts, modifying his set of concepts, after abstraction, accordingly. The result of such an unguided comparison process could, and, most likely, would, be a chaotic conceptual system. The SFH, interpreted as a theory of conceptual development,[16] is seen as an abstractionist theory and, hence, encounters difficulty.

There are, of course, additional, and not unreasonable assumptions which can be used to modify an abstractionist theory and insulate it against the criticism Nelson offers. One such assumption would be that some criterion is fixed which determines whether an instance shall be judged similar to another instance or not. A new instance, analysed into attributes, will be compared against the set of attributes constituting an existing concept. An uninformed comparison of the sort envisaged by Nelson will, in most cases, lead to a modified, and probably useless, concept, but a comparison using a criterion will yield a number either above or below that criterion. If the number is above criterion, the instance will be assigned to the concept, with an accompanying modification of the concept to take account of those properties which the original concept had and which the new instance lacks. In the event of the new instance not being assigned to the concept in question because of failure to reach criterion, further comparisons could be made, leading ultimately to a successful assignment or, in the limiting case, the establishment of a new concept corresponding, to begin with, to the new instance. Setting the criterion high would lead to a proliferation of concepts; setting it low would lead to a small number of very general ones. This idea clearly has much in common with Wittgenstein's (1953) notion of 'family resemblance' which, while introduced in an entirely different context, has recently been explored with regard to adult systems of categorisation (see, for example, Rosch and Mervis 1975).

A second assumption, also avoiding the thrust of Nelson's argument, is that certain dimensions may be picked out by the concept formation process as being particularly significant in determining similarities, whereas other dimensions are either ignored or given a very low weighting. For example, we might suggest that visual attributes of instances are what count in the establishment of concepts and, given access to a theory which made explicit the notion of 'visual attribute', an abstractionist theory could be maintained. What this amounts to is an assumption that the child comes to concept learning equipped with a tendency to compare instances along certain dimensions, an assumption which even a philosopher with the empiricist yearnings of Quine finds necessary, and which is encapsulated in his postulate, an 'innate quality space' (see Quine 1960).

Putting this to one side, let us examine how Nelson claims to avoid the pitfalls of abstractionist theories. She develops the notion of a 'functional core concept', arguing that 'analysis [into attributes – RMA] is not the *prerequisite* to the synthesis of concepts. Rather a dual process is found to be at work – first categorising according to some principle and *then* identifying common attributes' (1974, p. 276 – first emphasis is original, second emphasis mine – RMA). The question that immediately arises concerns the principle on which the initial categorisation is based. Nelson answers by suggesting that we consider instances, not in isolation, as abstractionist theories do but 'in the context of their relations to other instances and concepts' (*ibid.*). She claims further that 'Whole elements . . . take on definitions as concepts in terms of the synthesis of their functional or dynamic *relations*. Subsequently, other whole elements that enter into the same set of relations can be granted concept status within this previously defined concept. Analysis of parts of the whole is unnecessary to this initial concept formation process' (*ibid.*). The logic behind this move is clear, although the details of the move itself are murky. What is lacking, according to Nelson, in an abstractionist account of concept learning, is some parameter with respect to which instances can be compared which is distinct from concept-membership itself. She proposes to provide such a parameter in the 'functional and dynamic relations' of the whole to other wholes. Analysis of instances into their component attributes will only follow on this initial concept formation, and will have a part to play in concept identification when the functional and dynamic relations employed in the genesis of the concept are not apparent.

To illustrate, Nelson considers the hypothetical development of the concept 'ball'. She suggests that conceptual development begins with the child's first encounter with a ball, assuming that this is at an age when he is 'ready' to form concepts. This encounter may result in the schema of Figure 3.6 which is little more than a representation of the situations in

$$
\text{BALL}_1 \rightarrow \left\{
\begin{array}{l}
\text{In living room, porch} \\
\text{Mother throws, picks up, holds} \\
\text{I throw, pick up, hold} \\
\text{Rolls, bounces} \\
\text{On floor, under couch}
\end{array}
\right.
$$

Figure 3.6 (from Nelson 1974, p. 277)

which the child has met the ball. To be noted especially in connection with Figure 3.6 is the fact that the child is not presumed to control any lexical representation of 'ball' at this stage; BALL_1 is a concept and not a lexical item. What appears on the right of Figure 3.6 is intended to be relational and dynamic information, and this information is assumed to appear on the basis of the child's acquaintance with a single instance of a ball, i.e. the child experiences *one* ball in the living-room and on the porch which is thrown by mother, picked up by mother, etc. Nelson refers to this blending of experiences with a single ball as 'functional synthesis'.

Further development involves the child acquiring experience of another ball, leading to the functional synthesis which can be represented as in Figure 3.7. We now approach the crucial part of the argument. The two

$$
\mathrm{BALL}_2 \rightarrow \begin{cases} \text{On playground} \\ \text{Boy throws, catches} \\ \text{Rolls, bounces} \\ \text{Over ground, under fence} \end{cases}
$$

Figure 3.7 (from Nelson 1974, p. 277)

functional syntheses (Figures 3.6 and 3.7) are amalgamated. How is this effected? Nelson says:

Certain functions here [in BALL_2 − RMA] are the same as those for BALL_1: throwing, rolling and bouncing; although the relations of location and actor are different. *Boy* stands in the same relation to the function of *ball* as do *Mother* and *I*. Applying labels to these relationships yields the following scheme:

$$
\mathrm{BALL}_{1,2} \rightarrow \begin{cases} \text{Location of activity: living} \\ \text{room, porch, playground} \\ \text{Actor: Mother, I, boy} \\ \text{Action; throw, pick up, hold, catch} \\ \text{Movement of object: roll, bounce} \\ \text{Location of ball: on floor,} \\ \text{under couch, under fence} \end{cases}
$$

Some relations will eventually be identified as irrelevant to the defining functional core, for example, location of activity. The child must learn, therefore, which relations are concept *defining* and which are not. For some concepts the child may retain relations that the adult regards as superfluous . . . (1974, pp. 277–8)

But from this it is clear that Nelson is subject to exactly the same criticisms as she herself has levelled against the abstractionist theorist; she has provided no clear criteria for why the functional syntheses, BALL₁ and BALL₂, should be regarded, by a concept learner, as instances of the same concept. We are merely told that the synthesis proceeds on the basis of identity in 'certain functions', and, apart from a number of programmatic remarks, Nelson has said nothing about the identity of these functions.

The way out of the dilemma is, of course, perfectly clear. What Nelson must do is establish a criterion for matching instances of functional syntheses and, presumably, she would want this criterion to take account of certain aspects of the synthesis at the expense of others. But this was exactly the strategy adopted according to the second way of modifying an abstractionist theory mentioned above. Logically, there does not appear to be any difference between the SFH and the FCH in this respect (for similar remarks, see Bowerman 1976). Clark's theory is abstractionist, but includes the assumption that abstraction takes place along perceptual dimensions; Nelson's theory is abstractionist, and includes the assumption that abstraction takes place along certain dimensions specified in the functional synthesis.[17]

Having got this much clear, we can go on to consider how Nelson construes subsequent conceptual development and, more particularly, how language comes to be related to the developing concepts. She recognises that the functional core concepts will not serve the child to identify all instances of the concept. This is because it is necessary to identify a ball as a ball even when it is not partaking of the functional relationships which make up the core concept. Nelson says:

In order to do this, he needs to *analyze* the whole (object) into its relevant parts (attributes). It is assumed that this process begins to take place *any time* a concept is formed. Thus, although it is secondary, it is not discontinuous with the primary formation process. For this purpose, the child may pick out one or two salient static perceptual attributes and rely upon them. (1974, p. 278 – first emphasis in original, second emphasis mine — RMA)

But what we seem to have here is a weakening of the FCH to a point where, apart from a slant towards functional and relational attributes, it becomes indistinguishable from an unmodified abstractionist theory.

It is now permitted that perceptual features may be stored even when the concept is based on a single instance. If this is so, however, given that the child has eventually to work out the identifying attributes for a concept, there is nothing to prevent him discarding functional information and forming concepts on the basis of perceptual attributes. The FCH is weaker than the SFH in that it allows abstraction along both perceptual and functional dimensions. As the latter is rather vaguely specified anyway, it is not clear that the FCH disallows abstraction along any dimension. In order to prevent this collapse into an unmodified abstractionist theory, it is clear that Nelson must be far more precise in stating the form and role of the functional and relational properties which can enter into the functional core concept. This will become crucial in the next section.

Turning to the development of lexical items, Nelson suggests that the name of an object may, in certain cases, be attached to the structure corresponding to a concept. Again, it seems that what we have is an associative view of the lexicon where a lexical item is associated with a concept which corresponds to its meaning and has the sort of structure of the functional core concepts we have been investigating. Provision is made for the existence of concepts without attached lexical forms but not for lexical forms without attached concepts. Before turning to the explanatory adequacy of the proposals, we can briefly summarise the virtues Nelson identifies in her approach in terms of the phenomena she sees as important (p. 49 above).

The child's selectivity with regard to his first lexical items is explained as he can only use lexical items which correspond to his concepts. His first concepts are the functional core concepts which have, as their instances, objects which enter into dynamic relations with the child and others. Evidence on this is presented in Nelson (1973a).

The child's invention of lexical forms is explained by his having available some concept which does not correspond to a concept which is lexicalised in the adult language, or some concept, the lexicalisation of which the child is not familiar with. Nelson offers no new evidence on this and, as pointed out earlier, existing evidence is equivocal.

Generalisation to new instances is explained by the functional core concept not restricting the application of an item to a single instance but to anything which satisifies the properties contained in the concept. This leaves open the possibility of overextensions and suggests that such overextensions will be on a functional basis, at least in the early stages of lexical development. Later, they may shift to a static perceptual basis. However, on this question of the basis of overextensions, one obviously has to be cautious, given the remarks above and the fuller discussion in the next section. For evidence on this point, Nelson refers to her own work (Nelson 1973b), where she shows that small children's comprehension of *ball* was affected by the dynamic relationships which they had been allowed to enter into with a set of more or less ball-like objects. Some of Clark's overextensions are also cited in this connection, in particular, those which are based on movement and sound, which Nelson assimilates to her ideas of functional and dynamic relations.[18]

3.4 Evaluation of the functional core hypothesis

From the above, it is apparent that, as far as lexical development is concerned, the FCH can be cast in the same form as the SFH. At a particular time the child's lexicon will consist of a set of lexical items, each associated with a concept, which gives the meaning of the item. At a later time there will be an increase in the number of entries in the lexicon (ignoring lexical mortality) along with an increase in the associated set of concepts.

This proposal fares much as the SFH does with regard to Condition I. It seems most appropriately interpreted as a model of developing lexical competence and, accordingly, does not predict behaviour in any straightforward manner.

Condition II raises problems for the hypothesis. Obviously, at a suitable level of abstraction, two theories constructed according to the above outline will have general principles in common. Lexical forms are associated with concepts giving their meanings, the mode of association is consistent across theories and it is intended that the available concepts be specified by some general set of constraints. But it is with respect to this last claim that the most pertinent question arises. What is the form of the general theory which constrains the notion 'possible concept' in the acquisition model? It might be thought that an adequate formulation resides in Nelson's discussion of 'functional core concept', but, as the tenor of the previous section anticipated, a close examination of her work reveals no clear definition of this crucial idea. We are told that 'in order to form a concept of the ball or the "idea of ballness" rather than *ball* as many different objects in different relationships, the child must synthesise over time the various relations into which the ball enters. This functional synthesis is the core of the child's concept' (1974, p. 277). Further: 'Once functional synthesis has taken place with regard to an object, other objects may acquire status within the same functional synthesis or concept' (*ibid.*). Now, the functional core concept referred to in the first of these passages is the analysis of $BALL_1$ we are already familiar with from Figure 3.6. This contains a combination of locational, relational and predicative information about the ball in question, but nowhere is there any attempt to accurately delimit the information which might appear in the functional core. Reference to 'various relations' is hopelessly vague. As for the second passage, this leads into Nelson's analysis of $BALL_2$ and $BALL_{1,2}$ (see p. 52), but $BALL_2$, apart from displaying a rather sloppy structural similarity to $BALL_1$, hardly seems to require reference to the '*same functional synthesis or concept*' (my emphasis – RMA).

The upshot of this discussion, and, of course, it would be possible to raise further questions concerning the occurrence of 'non-functional' information along the lines of the previous section, is that Nelson appears to have no reasonably worked-out idea as to what a general theory of functional core concepts would look like.[19] In the absence of such a theory, Condition II can only be satisfied in a discursive and informal manner, i.e. we can examine purported instances of concepts and ask ourselves whether they 'feel' right, given the intuitions we are working from. Nevertheless, for the sake of discussion, I shall assume that Condition II can be met.

In order to consider Condition III, I shall assume that the information which can appear in a concept can be partitioned into sets corresponding, on the one hand, to relational and dynamic information and, on the other, to static information, i.e. I assume that we are equipped with a procedure for assigning information unambiguously to one of these categories. What Nelson appears to be saying in a number of places is that, *as far as the development of concepts is concerned*, it will be possible to find times, t_i and t_j, such that the information represented in the child's concepts at t_i is drawn exclusively from the set of dynamic and relational properties and that at t_j this information will not be restricted in this manner ($i < j$). Unfortunately, as should be clear from the previous section, it is far from obvious that Nelson is making a claim as specific as this. Sometimes she appears to suggest that there is a fixed order in the development of concepts:

(1) Use only relational and dynamic information in concepts.
(2) Supplement relational and dynamic information with static information.
(3) Attach names to concepts.

She says, regarding a slightly more elaborate ordering, the spirit of which is nonetheless the same as that of the above: 'the order in which these processes are listed implies a *usual temporal or sequential order* for initial concept formation and naming' (p. 276, my emphasis – RMA). But, if this is so, switching our attention away from concept development and towards the child's lexicon, the emphasis on relational and dynamic information is of no particular interest as, by the time lexical development gets started (stage 3 above), the relational and dynamic information in the concept is already supplemented, to an unknown degree, by static (presumably, including perceptual) information. However, an even more confusing picture can be deduced from the following statement.

It is important to bear in mind that this process is not proposed as a stage theory of development. Although language development may depend on the acquisition and elaboration of concepts . . . there is no 'functional stage' or 'attributive stage'. Rather all concept acquisition is assumed to involve both of these processes, whether the concepts are formed in infancy or childhood. (1974, p. 284)

One way in which we can reconcile the views expressed in the two most recently cited passages is to say that the first passage concerns the development of a *particular* concept, whereas the second embraces concept development *as a whole*. Thus, it is consistent to claim that, in the ontogeny of every concept, functional criteria for application to an instance precede attributive criteria, while maintaining that the child uses functional and attributive criteria simultaneously over the whole set of concepts. Accordingly, there would be no functional stage preceding an attributive stage.[20]

What is demanded, then, according to this interpretation and extending it into the domain of lexical development, is that we ought to be able to find lexical items which are initially associated with concepts including only relational and dynamic information; later these lexical items will be associated with concepts which admit static information. We ought not to be able to find forms initially associated with concepts including only static information which might later be extended to include information of the relational and dynamic type. If this turned out to be correct, what we would have is a spreading of non-relational and non-dynamic information over time in such a way that it plays an increasing and more systematic role in the structure of the lexicon. Of course, it may be that *new* non-relational and non-dynamic information is used at later stages and, if this were always true, we would have a clear case of satisfaction of Condition III. As it is, however, there is nothing in Nelson's discussion to indicate that it is true and, therefore, we must conclude that there is no reason to expect Condition III to be satisfied. Nor, of course, is it the case that Condition III is not applicable, as no new theoretical constructs are introduced at later stages at the expense of others from earlier stages. It looks as if Condition III should be applicable but, because of the inherent vagueness of the theoretical framework (stemming directly from failure to satisfy Condition II), we are in the position of not being able to apply it.

It follows from this that Condition IV cannot be addressed in a systematic fashion for the theory as a whole. It would do less than justice to Nelson, however, to leave off discussion at this point and we might consider restricting the domain of the theory in such a way as to make Condition IV applicable. This move involves focusing attention on the development of the lexical entry for a single lexical item, say W. With respect to W, given the assumption that functional criteria are always used before attributive criteria, Condition III could well be satisfied and lead to the formulation of the following question in connection with Condition IV: why do we find functional and relational criteria in the lexical entry for W before static criteria?

There is no readily available logical or environmental answer to this.[21] The possibility of providing a reductive explanation remains and it is reasonably clear from Nelson's writings that she is attracted by this strategy. She says (p. 279): 'It [the account she offers – RMA] is . . . in accord with what is known of the development of cognitive structures in infancy, for example, Piaget's account, *although much remains to be discovered about specific cognitive constraints and structures of the pre-language and beginning language periods*' (my emphasis – RMA). Certainly, the emphasis on action in Nelson's theorising is consistent with a Piagetian slant, but, at best, this is a vague statement of affiliation. More worrying is the fact that aspects of Nelson's proposal can be viewed as inconsistent with the Piagetian view on the cognitive structures of children at the relevant age. This can be easily seen. Most small children begin to use words and generalise their use early in the second year. According to Nelson's scheme, this assumes that the child is acquainted with a concept to which the word is related. The Piagetian period of sensori-motor intelligence is usually taken to extend up to about 18 months (Flavell 1963) and the *output* of this period is standardly taken to include a mature object concept, a concept of location, a concept of causality, etc. Before this period draws to a close, the child is assumed not to control mature versions of these concepts. Yet Nelson's functional core concepts appear to require an acquaintance with such concepts from at least the end of the first year. She herself says (1974, p. 277): 'The concept [BALL$_1$ – RMA] depends upon a prior notion of the boundaries of objects, events and their relationships. The ball is not confused with self, floor, mother or play-pen, nor is it seen as an unbound collection of attributes; identity as whole object has already been conferred upon it.' One can dispute the validity of Piaget's 'mature object concept' (Bower 1974) – perhaps Nelson's position does not require this but can survive via reference to a more primitive 'object concept' experienced by the child in the first eighteen months of life – but the first impression is one of contradiction. Thus, in a situation where Nelson turns to Piaget for support, that support is not readily forthcoming. The only conclusion is that Condition IV is not satisfied.

Finally, I have found no discussion of a mechanism of learning in any of the literature on the FCH. Condition V is also not satisfied.

In summary, it seems to me that the FCH says little of interest about lexical development.[22] By the time the child begins to acquire words the theory has become dangerously unconstrained. Even as a theory of concept development, the proposal is weak because of a failure to provide any clear discussion of the central theoretical notion, the functional core concept.[23]

3.5 The prototype hypothesis

The SFH and FCH share an important characteristic in their conceptualisations of word-meaning: both assume that the meaning of a word can be represented as a set of features. For the FCH it is, perhaps, necessary to be charitable in our interpretation of 'feature', but, as argued by Barrett (1978) and Bowerman (1976, 1978), it is difficult to construe the theory in any other way. The sets of features are seen as providing necessary and sufficient conditions for the application of a word. This general view has recently come under attack from a number of diverse directions. Thus, experimental work with adults has suggested that semantic categories, rather than having their membership defined in an all-or-none fashion by satisfaction of a set of critical features, admit degrees of membership. This requires that they are viewed as internally structured, having instances which are more or less good members of the category (see, e.g., Rosch 1973, 1975a, 1977, Rosch and Mervis 1975, Rips, Shoben and Smith 1973, Smith, Shoben and Rips 1974, Rips 1975). Linguists too have been attracted to this idea, although their work has been less systematic than that of the psychologists (see Fillmore 1977, Chafe 1977), and, from a philosophical perspective, Putnam (1970, 1975) has argued for views which, while different in point and emphasis from the above, have something of the same spirit. Work on the acquisition of language bearing on these issues has begun, but, at the moment, forms a rather amorphous collection of positions rather than a unified and cogent hypothesis. Nevertheless, the increasing importance of the basic idea of prototypes demands that some discussion be included here, aimed at achieving a measure of unification.

The earliest work with which I am familiar in this connection is that of Heider (1971).[24] In a series of studies she examined the developmental implications of Berlin and Kay's (1969) work on basic colour terms.[25] The first of these involved the child (aged 2; 11 to 3; 10) in choosing, from a small array of colours, one to show to an experimenter who has her eyes covered. The arrays were constructed so that each contained a single focal chromatic colour embedded in a set of colours which differed from it either in brightness or saturation. Such arrays were constructed for the eight Berlin and Kay chromatic basic colour terms, *red, yellow, green, blue, brown, pink, orange*, and *purple*. For the second experiment children (aged 3; 11 to 4; 10) were asked to match a coloured chip with one from a set of chips in an array constructed in such a way that the to-be-matched chip appears only once in it. The arrays again included one chromatic focal colour and the chips constituting the rest of the array differed from it either in terms of brightness or saturation. The chip which the child had to match could be focal, boundary (falling on the edge of those areas in the colour space which were innominate in the Berlin and Kay study) or internominal (falling in the centre of an innominate area). Matching accuracy was the variable in which Heider was interested. Neither of these experiments explicitly involves the child's lexical knowledge but in the third study the child's task (aged 3; 0 to 4; 7) was to choose from an array of coloured chips varying in hue and containing one chip corresponding to a focal instance of the chromatic basic colour term X, in response to the question 'Which is the X one?' or the instruction 'Show me the X one'. Adults had previously judged that there were a number of chips in each array that could be appropriately referred to as 'X'.

The results of the series of experiments were quite clear-cut. In the first study children exhibited a significant tendency to choose focal chips. In the second experiment children were more accurate in matching focal colours than either boundary or internominal colours (there being no significant difference between the latter pair), and, in the final task, many more children chose the focal example of X in response to 'Which is the X one?' than would have been expected by chance, given that there was more than one adult-correct response in these cases.

What this research appears to show is that focal colours tend to control a child's attention, are easier to match (although this is probably not independent of the first result), and that, once children are familiar with a colour term, this term is attached to a focal instance of the colour, rather than having an unstructured extension over the whole range covered by the colour term in the adult language. Heider is at pains to argue that it is the perceptual salience demonstrated in the first two experiments which accounts for the phenomenon encountered in the third study, although she admits that, because of ignorance about the child's previous experience with colour terms, parental tuition, etc., it is impossible to isolate perceptual salience as *the* causal factor.[26]

These results, then, are consistent with the view that, in the restricted case of the development of colour terms, each basic colour term is initially attached to a representation of its focal instance which, to all intents and purposes, gives its meaning at this stage. Subsequently, the child develops additional representational machinery which will enable him to apply the colour term beyond focal instances and to approximate the poorly defined boundaries of adult usage. During this subsequent development he retains his representation of the focal instance in the role of a prototype which, while no longer determining the extension of the colour term, functions as a cognitive reference point (see Rosch 1975b for an explication of this notion).[27] Such a view can be seen as involving claims about the development of single lexical items and also about development within the set of colour terms. I shall return to these considerations in the next section.

If the domain of the PH were restricted to colour terms, it would be of limited interest. Griffiths (1976) is an attempt to establish the position that a theory of lexical development employing some notion of 'prototype' is of more value, when studying early 'referential' vocabulary, than is a theory using 'critical features' or 'criterial attributes'. Most of the evidence he cites is not easily given a developmental interpretation; the fact that it might be possible to demonstrate that a child is making crucial use of a prototype at a certain stage does not tell us anything about the genesis of that prototype nor about its subsequent development. More relevantly, Griffiths cites Reich (1976) who claims that his son's understanding of *shoe*, when he first showed any comprehension of the word, was restricted to it referring to a particular pair of shoes in a particular location. Of course, this is nothing more than an extreme case of overrestriction and, while it is difficult to demonstrate the existence of this phenomenon with certainty, it has achieved a degree of acceptance amongst people working on early vocabulary growth. Reich's conclusions, cited approvingly by Griffiths, are that (1976, p. 120) 'the very first word-meanings are formed by associating a sequence of sounds with essentially everything that is perceptually and functionally salient about the objects or actions in the environment that co-occurs with that word'.

While this is consistent with the point of view being advanced, it hardly bears on the subsequent development of the term in question and, in particular, on how the suggested prototypicality manifests itself. For this we can turn to some recent evidence provided by Bowerman (1978). She presents a number of examples of the 'complexive' use of vocabulary, where the application of a lexical item to new referents is based on these referents sharing one or more attributes with a prototype. Normally, this prototype is determined by the child's first use of the word, but, whereas in the SFH the set of features associated with a word is taken as criterial, Bowerman allows for subsequent usage to be determined on the basis of partial matching to the prototype. An example is provided by one of her children's use of *kick*. This lexical item, she claims, is associated with a prototype involving (1) a waving limb, (2) a sudden sharp contact and (3) an object propelled. It is extended and used in situations where the child is watching a fluttering moth (involves (1) but not (2) or (3)), where she is about to throw something (involves (1) and (3) but not (2)), where she is pushing her chest against a sink (involves (2) but not (1) or (3)) and several others. It is evident from such examples that none of the features associated with the prototype can be regarded as criterial. The discussion appears to require that the initial meaning of a word be a set of features characterising a prototype.[28] Whether this set is later extended or modified is not made clear by Bowerman and I shall return to this in the next section.

Finally, it has been argued by Rosch, Mervis, Gray, Johnson and Boyes-Braem (1976) that prototypes may play a role in explaining aspects of the child's choice of early words (cf. Nelson's treatment of this issue). They suggest that 'categories within taxonomies of concrete objects are structured such that there is generally one level of abstraction at which the most basic category cuts can be made. In general, the basic level of abstraction in a taxonomy is the level at which categories carry the most information, possess the highest cue validity and are thus the most differentiated from each other' (1976, p. 385). Rosch *et al.* do not provide detailed numerical computations of cue validity in their paper (for some

Table 3.3. *Concrete nouns used in Stage I of language acquisition (from Rosch et al. 1976, p. 425)*

Category	Superordinate Tokens	Superordinate Types	Basic Tokens	Basic Types	Subordinate Tokens	Subordinate Types
		Taxonomic level of word used				
	NONBIOLOGICAL					
Musical instrument	0	0	13	6	0	0
Fruit	0	0	7	3	0	0
Tool	0	0	37	13	0	0
Clothing	2	1	91	18	4	1
Furniture	0	0	75	16	1	1
Vehicle	0	0	50	11	3	2
	BIOLOGICAL					
Tree	0	0	0	0	0	0
Fish	19	1	0	0	0	0
Bird	13	1	0	0	0	0

The distinction between biological and non-biological categories is motivated by the earlier experiments reported by Rosch *et al.* where it became obvious that adults treated the superordinates, *tree, fish* and *bird* as if they were basic-level names, with the result that the biological taxonomies are only of depth 2. Similarly, the categories used in this table are derivative on the experimental studies of Rosch *et al.*

fairly informal discussion, see Atkinson 1978) but, having conducted several experiments which persuaded them of the viability of the 'basic object concept', they studied the vocabulary of Brown's subject, Sarah, categorising her Stage I (see Brown 1973) concrete nouns in terms of whether they were 'superordinate', 'basic' or 'subordinate'. The results appear in Table 3.3 and led Rosch *et al.* to conclude: 'basic level names were essentially the only names used by Sarah in Stage I' (1976, p. 425). The relevance of this to a discussion of prototypes is that if we assume that prototypes play a significant role in the representation of word meanings, it is possible to approach an explanation for why basic-level names are learned first. This argument properly belongs in an evaluation of the whole approach to which I now turn.

3.6 Evaluation of the prototype hypothesis

As already mentioned in the previous section, Heider's work on the perceptual salience of colours and the ontogenesis of colour terms can be viewed as involving a claim about the development of the extension of a single term. This claim is that such a term is initially 'attached' to a representation of the focal colour corresponding to the term, and only later is it associated with a lexical entry which specifies an approximation to the adult extension of the term, i.e. schematically, we have the development:

$$CT \longleftrightarrow P \rightarrow CT \longleftrightarrow P \oplus X$$

where CT designates the colour term in question, P is a representation of the focal instance of CT and X refers to whatever representational machinery is necessary to fix the extension of CT.[29] Now, it is clear from the vague nature of this characterisation that, as a developmental theory, even in this restricted domain, it leaves a great deal to be desired. Nevertheless, being charitable with respect to Conditions I and II, we can see that Condition III is satisfied with the machinery designated by X being added to the system in the course of development, and we can enquire why we find this order of acquisition rather than:

$$CT \longleftrightarrow X \rightarrow CT \longleftrightarrow P \oplus X$$

We can note immediately that a language-internal explanation (1.8) follows from Berlin and Kay's work. Focal colours enjoy a status in the languages of the world which is not shared by whatever principles fix the boundaries of colour terms (but, see Kay and McDaniel 1978 for a cautionary note). Thus, it would follow from the correctness of Berlin and Kay's original views that one could formulate implicational universals from boundaries of colour terms to foci, although not vice versa. As we have seen, such implicational statements are what we need if we are to explicitly relate facts from language acquisition to facts concerning the distribution of properties in the world's languages. Further, and more importantly, Heider, in her attempt to relate the results of her third experiment to those of the first two, can be credited with the postulation of a reductive explanation which might accommodate both the developmental and distributional phenomena. Just as in lexical structure focal colours enjoy a privileged status, so it is in visual perception, where Heider's experiments have demonstrated the extent to which they control a child's attention and facilitate his performance on a matching task. It seems likely that, in a theory of perceptual development, there will be constructs related to focal colours, and it may be possible to formulate the necessary correspondence rules between such a theory and our current theory of lexical development in a satisfactory way. For the moment, though, such suggestions must remain speculation.[30] It is hardly necessary to point out that there is no discussion of Condition V in this area.

There is another aspect of Heider's work which is suggested by Berlin and Kay's hypothesis and which deserves brief comment. Berlin and Kay (1969), as well as stressing the role of foci in colour categories, postulate a partial ordering on a set of eleven basic colour terms, which is intended to characterise the basic colour vocabularies of the world's languages. This partial ordering can easily be re-cast as a set of implicational universals, and we might look for correspondences between these and the order of acquisition of colour terms. Heider is conscious of the possibilities in this regard but points out that her study says nothing about the actual order in which lexical items are acquired. She feels, however, that it might still turn out that the Berlin and Kay ordering will be matched by the performance of the children in her experiments, an outcome which, while not establishing that the ordering is reflected in order of acquisition, would, nevertheless, be consistent with such a claim and lend it plausibility. Unfortunately, this is not what the author found. In her own words (1971, p. 454):

Neither the saliency order of the focal colours in Experiment I, the matching accuracy order from Experiment II, nor the frequency with which focal colours were chosen to represent the category name in Experiment III matched Berlin and Kay's proposed evolutionary order. Only one measure of the present study, the number of subjects who knew each colour name, did not, with the exception of orange, contradict the proposed evolutionary order.

Thus, all we can conclude in this case is that evidence, which it was hoped might be supportive, is not forthcoming.[31]

When we turn to general referential vocabulary, we can again focus on a single lexical item. Bowerman (1978) sees prototypes as represented by sets of features, and it is necessary to assume that the child will eventually develop a lexical representation which will fix (perhaps, incorrectly or fuzzily) the extension of the term while continuing to contain a prototype, i.e., schematically, we have:

$$T \longleftrightarrow P \ (= F_1 \ \& \ \ldots \ \& \ F_n) \rightarrow T \longleftrightarrow P \ (= F_1 \ \& \ \ldots \ \& \ F_n) \oplus X$$

where T designates the term in question, P and X are as above in the discussion of colour terms and $F_1, \ldots, F_n$ are the features associated with the prototype.[32] Obviously, Condition III is satisfied by this development and we can ask why it is found rather than:

$$T \longleftrightarrow X \rightarrow T \longleftrightarrow P \oplus X$$

It is apparent that we cannot, at this point, formulate any language-internal explanation, as we could for the restricted case of colour terms. The relevant comparative data do not exist and, while the possibility of some systematic correspondences of foci in certain areas of vocabulary across the languages of the world cannot be ruled out *a priori*, there is currently no reason to believe that these correspondences will be extensive. Bowerman herself speculates in the direction of both environmental and reductive explanations, saying (1978, p. 281):

the prototypical referent was present from the beginning and constituted the core around which the subsequent category grew, rather than being an induction made later on the basis of diverse exemplars of the category. It is difficult to assess the relative importance of language-independent cognitive activity vs. linguistic input (e.g. frequency of exposure) in drawing a child's attention to particular objects or events such that they become the growing point or prototype for a category.

To my knowledge, no substantive claims concerning a cognitive basis for general prototypes have been made and there are too few data on which to assess the environmental claim (but, see Ferrier 1978, Braunwald 1978 for data which I believe can be interpreted as supporting this position). However, the problems appear to be reasonably defined in this area and we might anticipate some progress during the next few years.

Assuming now that early lexical development can be construed, at least partly, in terms of the acquisition of a set of prototypes, we can examine development within this set, and it is in connection with this issue that the work of Rosch *et al.* (1976) is most relevant. Recall that Rosch *et al.* claim that basic-level names are learned first, i.e., for the child's concrete referential vocabulary, we have:

$$B \rightarrow B \oplus X$$

rather than:

$$X \rightarrow B \oplus X$$

where B designates the set of basic-level names and X designates the set of non-basic-level names. Why should this be so?

Interestingly, Rosch *et al.* provide some language-internal evidence to support this ordering. If there were languages which were impoverished as far as taxonomic depth is concerned and, if, furthermore, the levels in taxonomies which were absent in such cases were never the basic levels, we would have the required sort of evidence. In the final study of their paper, Rosch *et al.* investigate American Sign Language with this point in mind and what they found was that it was deficient at the superordinate and subordinate levels to a much greater extent than it was at the basic level. American Sign Language could thus be cited as the first step in an argument towards a language-internal explanation for the claimed ordering. It remains to be seen whether there are 'standard' languages which exhibit the same behaviour (see Berlin, Breedlove and Raven 1973, Berlin 1977 for some relevant observations).

Perhaps more significant is Rosch *et al.*'s attempt to establish the primacy of the cognitive categories corresponding to basic-level names. As far as the development of these categories is concerned, a series of experiments was conducted showing that children as young as 3 years were capable of sorting objects into basic-level categories, while it has been known for some time that children of that age do not exhibit control of superordinate categories in sorting tasks. It seems, therefore, that there is an important parallel between cognitive and linguistic development with, on the one hand, basic-level concepts preceding superordinate concepts and, on the other, basic-level names preceding superordinate names. Unfortunately, the ages of the children involved create difficulties for this route to reductive explanation. Sarah, the slowest of the children studied by Brown in this respect, left Stage I at about 35 months (see Brown 1973, p. 80 for details) and this means that she was already displaying the appropriate linguistic behaviour before the youngest children in the Rosch *et al.* study were indicating that they controlled the relevant concepts in the sorting task. It is, of course, quite conceivable that children considerably younger than 3 years would be capable of evidencing the control of basic-level categories through some means other than their language, but, for the moment, it is necessary to conclude that the reduction cannot be successfully carried out.

'Basic objects' seems to me to be an exciting and useful construct. The major difficulty confronting it right now, as with all the proposals we briefly examined in 3.5, is that of specifying the exact nature of the theory. Clark and Nelson have put forward reasonably articulated theories, although examination has demonstrated crucial inadequacies. It is more difficult to pin-point inadequacies in the ideas I have considered in this and the previous section, and this could be a direct reflex of the fact that the exact nature of prototypes is never spelled out. Until Condition II can be seriously directed against some version of the PH, it will remain necessary to temper any enthusiasm we may feel for this position.

4 The acquisition of relational terms

One of the attractions of the SFH which has not emerged from the discussion in the previous chapter is that, using essentially the same conceptual machinery, i.e. conjunctive sets of semantic features, Clark feels that she can account for a number of phenomena from later development, which have been studied with some intensity during the last ten years or so. At the outset we should note that the features employed in the analyses which follow are not *perceptual* features and that the interplay between perceptual and non-perceptual features in an overall theory of lexical development has not been the subject of systematic speculation.

The work I wish to consider in this chapter concerns the development of *comprehension*, in experimental situations, of such relational adjective pairs as *more* and *less* and *same* and *different*, of antonymic dimensional adjective pairs such as *big* and *small, fat* and *thin* and *wide* and *narrow*, of the temporal conjunctions, *before* and *after* and of the deictic verbs of motion, *come* and *go* along with their 'causative' counterparts, *bring* and *take*.[1]

4.1 Empirical work on relational terms[2]

Donaldson and Balfour (1968) showed, in a seminal study, that Scottish nursery school children between the ages of 3;5 and 4;1 appeared to go through a stage where they understood *less* as having the meaning of *more* while understanding *more* correctly. Their technique involved confronting children with two cardboard apple trees on which metal apples could be hung. For one set of questions, conditions were arranged so that the trees held different numbers of apples and the children were asked either 'Does one tree have more?' or 'Does one tree have less?' They were almost 100% correct in producing affirmative answers to these questions. However, when subsequently asked either 'Which tree has more?' or 'Which tree has less?', the children remained substantially correct for the first question, while a large proportion of responses to the second question consisted of choosing the wrong tree, i.e. the one which had more apples. These results were consistent with the children understanding *more* correctly and understanding *less* as if it had the meaning of *more*.[3] The possibility that the subjects simply did not understand *less* is argued against by the fact that they did respond to questions involving *less* rather than look baffled and, furthermore, they responded quickly and confidently. This main result of the original experiment has been reproduced under several different sets of conditions and various difficulties pointed out by H. Clark (1970), not taken account of by Donaldson and Balfour, have been accommodated (see the work of Palermo and his associates, particularly Palermo 1973, 1974 and Holland and Palermo 1975). As we shall see in 4.3, E. Clark, using the SFH, has considered two alternative explanations for this phenomenon.

Similar results were obtained in a later study by Donaldson and Wales (1970) concerning the child's comprehension of the pair *same* and *different*. In situations in which children of nursery school age were asked either to give the experimenter an object which was the same as some specified reference object, different from that object, the same as that object with respect to some particular attribute, or different from that object with respect to some attribute, the investigators found that, while apparently understanding *same* perfectly, children understood *different* as if it had the meaning of *same*. Without being very explicit, E. Clark proposes that the same general principles as she invokes to explain the data from the *more* and *less* studies will serve for explanation in this case too, but as we shall see this lack of explicitness covers up a serious gap in the argument.[4]

Donaldson and Wales (1970) also examined children's ability to comprehend the antonymic adjectives, *big* and *wee*,[5] *thick* and *thin, tall* and *short* etc. The situation they used was one in which children were presented with an array of objects varying along the appropriate dimension and were asked to comply with a series of instructions which included 'Show me the X-est one', 'Show me one that is X-er than that', etc. Two findings are of particular interest to the subsequent discussion:

(1)   Children responded more accurately to instructions involving the 'general' pair, *big* and *wee*, than they did to the more specific adjective pairs (but see Maratsos 1973 for caution in this regard).

(2)   Children responded more accurately to instructions involving the positive member of the pairs, showing a tendency to interpret the negative member as if it had the meaning of the positive member.[6]

The second result is of more general interest to the discussion which follows, but the former result can be related to a study by E. Clark (1972b), which she again sees as providing support for the SFH, and which is interesting because it employs a very different experimental paradigm from most of the studies reviewed in this section. Rather than having the child perform some non-linguistic action on the basis of his understanding a request or instruction, Clark's study introduces a game to the child where his task is to supply the antonym of the form provided by the experimenter. These forms are drawn from the set of adjectives under discussion and may be either positive or negative instances from this set.[7] What Clark found was that responses to the 'general' forms, *big* and *small*, were more accurate than responses to the more specific items but that these latter items could be ranked in a way which accorded with an analysis in terms of semantic features. Further, she found that 'errors' tended to be in the direction of the more general terms (e.g. *big* being supplied in response to *short*), and this was viewed as consistent with the sort of incomplete feature specification countenanced by the theory.

Results from a different domain have been interpreted in similar fashion (E. Clark 1970, 1971, 1973). This work has investigated the child's understanding of sentences involving the temporal conjunctions *before* and *after* and has required the acting out, using farm animals, of sentences of a small number of specified types. These are: 'P before Q', 'Before P, Q', 'P after Q' and 'After P, Q', where 'P' and 'Q' refer to linguistic encodings of events which the farm animals can be made to instantiate, e.g. 'The dog jumped over the gate before the old woman sat down.' The results of this work are quite complicated and certain aspects of Clark's interpretation are questionable, but one claim which does emerge clearly is that children appear to go through a stage where they interpret *after* as if it meant *before*. Accordingly, they consistently get right instructions including *before* and equally consistently, get the wrong order of events for instructions including *after*.[8] This is to be compared with what one might expect if the children simply did not understand *after*, namely, a good deal of confusion, non-responding and randomness in response. Again, this phenomenon proves amenable to an analysis in terms of features which I shall discuss in detail in 4.4. In connection with her work on *before* and *after*, however, Clark has introduced a further concept into the discussion, which has subsequently been widely employed to approach phenomena which were originally treated exclusively in terms of semantic features. This concept is that of a non-linguistic strategy in one of the several senses in which that phrase has been used in recent years (see Cromer 1976a for a review). Briefly, and in general terms, if we have two linguistic forms, X and Y, and the child consistently understands sentences involving X and consistently misunderstands sentences involving Y as if they involved X, there are at least two approaches that the theorist can adopt. He may, as has been implicit so far in this section, assume that the child has a fully specified (from the point of view of the adult lexicon) meaning for X which is also attached to Y. Alternatively, he can assume that, in the experimental situation, the child responds on the basis of applying a non-linguistic strategy in conjunction with meanings of X and Y, neither of which is fully articulated. This leads the child to behave, *in that situation*, as if he fully understood X and understood Y as having the meaning of X. This recourse to non-linguistic strategies has found further application in Clark's work on the comprehension of simple spatial prepositions (E. Clark 1972a, 1974) and in her interpretation of the *more/less* findings described above, as well as in work reported below.

To conclude this brief resumé of some of the major research relevant to the topic of this chapter, I shall discuss the claims of a paper which relies, almost exclusively, on the coherence of the notion of non-linguistic strategy. The study of Clark and Garnica (1974) uses requests to children between the ages of 5;6 and 9;5 to identify the speaker or addressee of utterances involving the verbs *come, go, bring* and *take*. These utterances are presented to the child as being uttered by one of a number of potential speakers to one of a number of potential addressees in a carefully constructed situation. The results of the experiment bear out the following conclusions:

(1) Children perform more accurately on utterances containing *come* than they do on utterances containing *go*.

(2) Children perform more accurately on utterances containing *bring* than they do on utterances containing *take*.

(3) The pair, *come* and *go*, are responded to more accurately as a pair than the pair, *bring* and *take*.

(4) It is not the case that, when the child is performing more accurately on, say, *come* sentences than *go* sentences, this is because he

understands *come* and fails to understand *go*. Rather, a detailed analysis of the results (see 4.5) suggests to the experimenters that the child should be credited with a developing set of non-linguistic strategies which, interacting with a partially specified lexicon, can lead to the impression that he understands *come* and is either performing at random on *go* or is understanding *go* as if it had the meaning of *come*.

Enough has been said now to give the reader an impression of the large amount of work which has been done in the last few years in these related areas and also some idea of the tendencies which have repeatedly emerged in the results. I now wish to consider the explanatory value of the SFH in these domains. In addition, when non-linguistic strategies have been introduced into the discussion, I shall consider the status of theories which embrace them. I shall begin by considering the development of antonymic spatial adjectives, as the discussions we meet in this area raise most of the problems we shall meet in later sections.

4.2 Antonymic dimensional adjectives

Above it was pointed out that the work of Donaldson and Wales (1970) led to the formulation of two conclusions which are of interest in the present context and it is the first of these, concerning children's better performance on the 'undifferentiated' adjective pairs, *big* and *wee* (*small*), that I wish to take up first.[9]

E. Clark provides the following account of this phenomenon (1973, p. 93):

The data on dimensional terms can also be represented in terms of components of meaning known by the child at different stages in the acquisition process. *Big* is substituted for other unmarked dimensional terms because it is specified (like them) as + Dimension (3) and + Polar but the child at this stage has not yet worked out how many dimensions are necessarily presupposed by the other terms such as *long* and *tall*. He has yet to differentiate between the dimensional properties of linearity, surface and volume. While *big* simply applies to three dimensions, *tall* is more complex since it supposes that all three dimensions are present and then talks about one specific dimension: + Vertical. The child appears to learn first the feature of dimensionality, then, later on, he specifies further what kind of dimensionality he is talking about; for instance whether the dimension is + Vertical as in *tall* or *high* or − Vertical as in *long, deep, far* etc.

While some of the phrasing in this passage is bizarre, the nature of the proposal and the way in which it can be cast to make the framework of Chapter 1 applicable is clear enough. The domain of enquiry, I shall regard as a part of the child's lexicon which is implemented in his ability to produce and comprehend simple sentences including dimensional adjectives as well as his ability to produce and comprehend these forms in isolation (E. Clark 1972b). The data relevant to the domain are, in the case of Donaldson and Wales (1970), instances of comprehension or non-comprehension of sentences having a limited set of structures and, in the case of E. Clark (1972b), instances of the comprehension and production of isolated forms.[10]

Calling this domain of enquiry D, one can say that Clark is claiming that at least the following two stages can be isolated in D, where each of the stages is represented by a theory of the relevant part of the child's lexicon. For the first stage, at t_1, the theory is something like what we have in Figure 4.1, ignoring differences between positive and negative adjectives

$$
\begin{array}{lll}
big - wee \ (small) & \longleftrightarrow & [+ \text{Dimension (3)}, \pm \text{Polar}] \\
long - short & \longleftrightarrow & [+ \text{Dimension (3)}, \pm \text{Polar}] \\
high - low & \longleftrightarrow & [+ \text{Dimension (3)}, \pm \text{Polar}] \\
wide - narrow & \longleftrightarrow & [+ \text{Dimension (3)}, \pm \text{Polar}]
\end{array}
$$

Figure 4.1

which will be discussed later. Figure 4.1 makes explicit the claim that at t_1, all dimensional adjectives are synonymous (ignoring polarity) and all have the meaning of the undifferentiated pair, *big* and *wee* (*small*). By t_2 the picture is changed and we now have the situation depicted in Figure 4.2. Obviously further stages would be necessary in order to chart the full course of development in this domain, but the general picture is sufficiently clear from this simple case.[11] What happens between t_1 and t_2 is that the child begins to use an additional feature, $\pm$ Vertical, enabling him to make new distinctions in his lexical system. In this case, unlike the situation for

$$
\begin{array}{lll}
big - wee \ (small) & \longleftrightarrow & [+ \text{Dimension (3)} \pm \text{Polar}] \\
long - short & \longleftrightarrow & [+ \text{Dimension (3)} \pm \text{Polar} - \text{Vertical}] \\
high - low & \longleftrightarrow & [+ \text{Dimension (3)} \pm \text{Polar} + \text{Vertical}] \\
wide - narrow & \longleftrightarrow & [+ \text{Dimension (3)} \pm \text{Polar} - \text{Vertical}]
\end{array}
$$

Figure 4.2

early referential vocabulary growth discussed in Chapter 3, the additional feature is not accompanied into the system by a new lexical item utilising that feature in its lexical entry. Rather, it is accompanied by an enriched ability to understand a particular form in a way more appropriate to the adult norm. This form is, however, assumed to exist in the earlier system. Thus the SFH applied to dimensional adjectives does not make any predictions about the appearance of *forms* in the lexicon but only about the order of development of understanding of these forms.

It is time now to confront this strand of the SFH with the conditions of Chapter 1, and I shall assume, without further discussion, that some version of Condition I can be satisfied.[12]

Condition II is problematic as there is no generally accepted feature theory which addresses the analysis of dimensional adjectives. Clark relies heavily on the work of Bierwisch (1967), but, while this work is significant and tackles a number of fundamental problems in an interesting way, it does not provide a well-motivated inventory of features to be used in the analysis of dimensional adjectives. Such an inventory would appear to be one necessary component of a general theory of the required sort. The extent of the problem can be easily appreciated by citing a passage from Bartlett (1976) which should be compared with the quotation from Clark (1973) on page 72. Bartlett says (p. 206):

The SFH bases its predictions about the acquisition of these features on the notion of feature generality. Thus it predicts that the dimensional feature [size] will be acquired first since it can be applied without restriction to any of the terms in the domain. While E. Clark (1973) makes no further explicit predictions about the acquisition of other dimensional features, she does refer to the analysis of these features in H. Clark (1973). According to this analysis, the feature [dimension] (corresponding roughly to the notion of 'extended edge' or 'extension along one dimension') will be acquired next, followed by features which express orientation of extension (i.e. [verticality]) and relative length of the edge to which the adjective applies (i.e. [secondary] which refers to the second-most extended edge of an object.

Questions which immediately arise are whether the feature [± Dimension (3)] in Clark's discussion is to be identified with the feature [size] in Bartlett's, whether Clark's 'feature of dimensionality' is intended to capture the function of Bartlett's [dimension], and exactly what confusion is lurking under the qualification, 'corresponding roughly to the notion of "extended edge" or "extension along one dimension" ' in the Bartlett passage. If something is going to correspond to both an edge and an extension along a dimension the correspondence must indeed be rough. Contrary to what I believe to be the case, I shall assume, for the sake of further discussion, that the proposal does make reference to a coherent general theory.

Condition III is applicable and satisfied in a straightforward additive fashion; in the passage from t_1 to t_2 we have one feature added: [± Vertical].

We approach Condition IV and ask whether the theory admits analysis in terms of any of the three possibilities mentioned in this connection.[13] Is there any reason for finding the development which we can schematise as $X \rightarrow X \oplus Y$ rather than the development, $Y \rightarrow X \oplus Y$ where, in this case, X denotes the feature [+ Dimension (3)] (or [size]) and Y denotes the feature [+ Vertical]?

Consider whether we have a teleological explanation for this order of development; here the interpretation of the features becomes crucial. The passage cited from Clark is of little help in this regard, although she can be seen as suggesting otherwise when she says: 'While *big* simply applies to three dimensions, *tall* is more complex since it supposes that all three dimensions are present and then talks about one specific dimension: + Vertical.' As it stands, this statement is false as is witnessed by the existence of tall rectangles but, presumably, what Clark is striving towards is the claim that anything to which the contrast *tall/short* is applicable must also be amenable to description in terms of the contrast *big/small*. Bartlett's choice of terminology is more transparent in this respect. We can see that having a vertical dimension 'presupposes' having size and we can, therefore, suggest that there is the sort of relationship we are looking for between the features [size] and [verticality]. It seems, then, that aspects of the development of dimensional adjectives may have a teleological explanation within the SFH, but, clearly, the lack of a well-formulated general theory is detrimental to any confidence we may place in this assertion. Neither of the other possibilities mentioned in Condition IV, reductive explanation and environmental explanation, provides any additional leverage on the issue at this point, and we are left with Condition V. I am aware of no systematic discussion relevant to the existence of a mechanism for lexical growth in this area and this must be seen as a major inadequacy in the theory. As we shall see, the SFH is not alone in this respect.

Turning now to the second major finding of Donaldson and Wales (1970), that unmarked dimensional adjectives appear to be acquired before their marked dimensional counterparts, E. Clark (1973), largely following H. Clark (1970), offers an account along the following lines. For the pairs of adjectives in question, the positive member is unmarked according to a number of criteria.[14] In particular, the positive member, as well as being used in explicit or implicit comparison (e.g. 'x is taller than y', 'x is tall'), also has a non-comparative use, when it can be seen as simply identifying the relevant dimension. Thus we find such phrases as '6 feet tall', '5 miles wide', etc. but not, without special assumptions about the context of utterance, phrases such as '6 feet short', '5 miles narrow', etc. The non-comparative interpretation can be viewed as including one less feature than the comparative interpretation and, at this point, Bartlett can take up the story (1976, p. 207):

> Thus, the SFH predicts that initially both terms in a pair [of antonymic dimensional adjectives – RMA] will have a nominative [*sic*] meaning which indicates the appropriate dimension of comparison, without regard for polarity (e.g. both *long* and *short* will mean 'having some length'). For any given pair, the SFH further predicts that the [+ pol] feature will be acquired prior to its [− pol] counterpart, a prediction based on the assumption that children have a bias towards picking the greater of two objects and that this bias makes it easier for children to acquire meanings which encode 'greater' relationships.[15]

From this it is clear that at least three stages are envisaged in the development of the relevant part of the child's lexicon, the domain of enquiry not having changed from that specified earlier in this section. At t_1, and using Bartlett's terminology, we have the situation represented in Figure 4.3. The important fact to note about this partial lexicon is the

tall	⟷	[+ size, + vertical]
short	⟷	[+ size, + vertical]
wide	⟷	[+ size, − vertical]
narrow	⟷	[+ size, − vertical]
big	⟷	[+ size]
small	⟷	[+ size]
	etc.	

Figure 4.3

synonymy of each of the antonymic pairs. Furthermore, there is no feature corresponding to their comparative senses in the analyses, which amounts to the claim that information about dimensionality is acquired before information about polarity. At t_1 we have a transition to the lexicon depicted in Figure 4.4.[16] Again, here the antonymic pairs are treated as synonyms but now they are intended to have an explicitly comparative

tall	⟷	[+ size, + vertical, + pol]
short	⟷	[+ size, + vertical, + pol]
wide	⟷	[+ size, − vertical, + pol]
narrow	⟷	[+ size, − vertical, + pol]
big	⟷	[+ size, + pol]
small	⟷	[+ size, + pol]
	etc.	

Figure 4.4

sense, encoded in the feature [+ pol]. Furthermore, this comparative sense is restricted to that of saying that something exceeds the norm for the dimension(s) in question. By t_3 the system will approximate to the adult lexicon and we shall have the structure shown in Figure 4.5.[17] So, we appear to have a developmental theory (T_1, T_2, T_3) and similar comments

tall	⟷	[+ size, + vertical, + pol]
short	⟷	[+ size, + vertical, − pol]
wide	⟷	[+ size, − vertical, + pol]
narrow	⟷	[+ size, − vertical, − pol]
big	⟷	[+ size, + pol]
small	⟷	[+ size, − pol]
	etc.	

Figure 4.5

are applicable to this proposal, regarding Condition II, as have already been raised earlier in this section. There is, however, one additional point for concern. If the authors of the theory have a standard version of a feature theory in mind, the role of semantic features must be to *distinguish* the meanings of lexical items. It follows that, in a system countenancing only binary features, each such feature will occur somewhere in the system with both a positive and a negative value. Unfortunately, in the theory T_2, the feature [pol] occurs but only positively specified and it has no distinguishing role to play in this part of the lexicon (nor, presumably, in any other part). Thus, T_2 is not a theory utilising semantic features in the 'normal' way and the suspicion is aroused that no cogent general considerations are informing theory construction.

This last point has an immediate reflex as far as Condition III is concerned, because we cannot see either the transition from T_1 to T_2 or the transition from T_2 to T_3 in terms of the addition of *features*. Rather, we must talk about the addition of *values* of features. I shall assume, however, that this way of talking is not too misleading and move on to a discussion of Condition IV.

For the transition from T_1 to T_2, we are asking why the child acquires the feature value [+ pol] after he has acquired the features [size] and [vertical], rather than the other way round. Subject to the qualifications expressed in my earlier discussion of differentiated and undifferentiated adjectives concerning the difficulties of interpretation attached to the features, it would appear that the same sort of considerations as arose in the earlier context could lead in the direction of a teleological explanation. The feature value [+ pol], interpreted as something like 'having more than average extent', assumes some dimension along which extents are being compared and the feature [vertical] refers to just such a dimension. Therefore, although the theoretical term [+ pol] does not rely specifically on the term [vertical] for its intelligibility, it does rely on *terms of this type*, and, given the tentative nature of the data and the early stage of enquiry, this seems good enough. Palermo seems to have this in mind when he says (1976, p. 251): 'On invoque, par exemple, l'idée que le trait d'extension est acquis avant les traits de polarité qui permettent la distinction entre "extension plus" et "extension moins", ce qui permet de distinguer "plus" de "moins".' Consideration of the other possibilities under Condition IV adds little to the discussion at this point, and, opposing the above teleological interpretation, we should note that Carey (1978b) manages to find 'polarity before dimensionality' intelligible (see below, 4.6).

Consider now the transition from T_2 to T_3. In this case, there is no logical reason why we should find the development schematised as $X \rightarrow X \oplus [- \text{pol}]$ (where X includes the feature value [+ pol] rather than the development schematised as $Y \rightarrow Y \oplus [+ \text{pol}]$ (where Y includes the feature value [- pol]). E. Clark is aware of the problem here and introduces an assumption made by H. Clark (1970, p. 274) that 'the best exemplar of a dimension is an object with the most extent'.[18] H. Clark refers to this as possibly 'a perceptually motivated fact', and so, to the extent that it can be used to explain the appearance of [+ pol] before

[$-$ pol], it can be seen as an attempt to reduce the transition from T_2 to T_3 to one that is explicable in perceptual terms. It is not my intention here to examine the status of this assumption in the light of what is known about the development of perception. What interests me is the nature of the theory which is supported by such an assumption. It is clear from H. Clark's discussion that he sees his principle as operative *before* the child controls the comparative sense of the dimensional adjectives. It is a principle which can be seen as causing the child to act as if he understood both adjectives as having the comparative sense of the unmarked member of the pair when, in fact, he understands both adjectives as being non-comparative in sense (cf. the discussion of non-linguistic strategies in 4.1). So, for example, in the situation devised by Donaldson and Wales, given an instruction to the child to show the experimenter the tallest or the shortest from a set of rectangles, the child at the appropriate stage is going to understand either of these non-comparatively, i.e. as something like 'show me the one with vertical extent'. Coupled with the principle suggested by H. Clark, the child's partial lexicon will lead to correct responding to instructions including *tallest* and incorrect responding to instructions including *shortest*. But now we have a different theory to the one originally put forward by E. Clark and it is not a theory which recognises a stage at which the child's lexicon includes the feature value [$+$ pol] but not the feature value [$-$ pol]. This theory suggests that there will be a stage at which the child simply understands all adjectival forms non-comparatively and controls no principles for suggesting that this is not so (to my knowledge, there is no evidence in the literature for such a stage), a later stage where his lexical understanding is unchanged but Clark's principle makes it appear as if the child understood the unmarked form correctly and understood the marked form as having the meaning of the unmarked form, and a third stage, mediated by the introduction of the feature [pol] (both positively and negatively specified), at which the child fully understands the comparative senses of the adjectives. It seems to me that something like this is the position towards which E. Clark is moving, although I have found it impossible to find a clear statement of it in her work. For such a position the transition from the second to the third stage could be given a teleological explanation along the lines already suggested (comparison presupposes a dimension of comparison), and the transition from the first to the second stage would be marked by the emergence of H. Clark's principle and we would expect to look to a theory of perceptual development for reassurance in this regard.

It is not my purpose here to draft alternatives nor, indeed, to tease out what may be implicit in the literature I am examining, but to take what I find at face-value. Such an activity leads to the conclusion that the formulations of the SFH in Clark (1973) and Bartlett (1976) are inadequate in several crucial respects: they do not satisfy Condition II, they struggle promisingly with Condition IV rather than meeting it head-on and they never even raise Condition V.[19]

4.3 *More* and *less*

A similar conclusion is justified for the SFH analysis of the data cited on the acquisition of *more* and *less*. Again the domain of enquiry D is fixed as a section of the child's lexicon, and data relevant to the investigation of D include the child's ability to comprehend simple instructions involving *more* or *less* as well as, somewhat anecdotally, the child's spontaneous use of these forms. Clark is more explicit than she is for dimensional adjectives when she says (1973, pp. 90–1):

First the child uses *more* and *less* in the nominal non-comparative sense only. Next, since the nominal term refers to extension rather than to lack of extension, the child will use both *more* and *less* to refer to the extended end of the scale, and finally, he will distinguish *less* from *more* and use it contrastively to apply to the less extended end of the scale. At the first stage, therefore, *more* is simply taken to mean 'amount' or 'quantity of' and its comparative nature is not understood. . . . While this nominal interpretation of both words would explain why *more* and *less* are treated as synonyms, it does not account for why *more* and *less* both mean 'more' . . . one has to make one assumption at this point: that the notion of 'having extent' is always best exemplified by the object with the *most* extent . . . . At the last stage *more* and *less* will be used comparatively in their contrastive sense and *less* is then differentiated from *more*.

Here we have a direct analogue to Clark's theorising in connection with dimensional adjectives and we can represent her claims as a three-stage theory as in Figure 4.6. Exactly the same set of problems as arose in the previous section appear again, when we attempt to analyse this proposal in terms of my conditions, and, again, it is possible to formulate a less problematic theory by introducing a non-linguistic principle to account for the child's behaviour at t_2. There is no point in repeating these considerations here.

There is, however, an additional problem concerning the supposed non-comparative use of *more* at t_1 which deserves brief discussion. While it is possible to argue a weak case for *more* being unmarked relative to *less* on

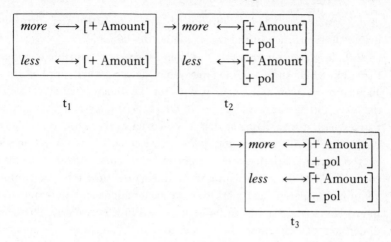

Figure 4.6

the basis of its relatedness to *much* (versus *little*), it is not the case that *more*, unlike the unmarked dimensional adjectives, has the specialised task of naming a dimension. To my way of thinking, there is nothing marked about the phrase '15 less' when compared with the phrase '15 more'.[20] And what exactly is the non-comparative use of *more* to which Clark refers? She cites no source, but Bloom (1973) (see also Brush 1976) provides extensive and relevant discussion of the use of *more* in the speech of her own daughter. She suggests that in the earliest stages *more* has two distinct uses. In the first use an instance of a category exists in the environment, ceases to exist and then reappears (or a new instance of the category appears) to be designated *more*. According to the second usage, an instance of a category is joined in the environment by another instance of the same category which is designated *more*. These are to be contrasted with a third usage, which Bloom did not find in the early stages of language development, and which she refers to as 'comparative'. For this two instances of a certain stuff together make more of that stuff and this result of putting the two instances together is referred to as *more*. Without wishing to quibble with Bloom's interpretation of the phenomena, it seems to me that the choice of the term 'comparative' for the third usage is unfortunate. It carries the implication of 'non-comparative' onto the first two usages and to refer to them in this way is misleading; they do involve comparison and it is certainly not the case that they can be seen as examples of *more* which refer simply to amount or extent. If it is this sort of usage to which Clark is alluding, I do not feel that it is sufficient to justify the first stage in the theory under discussion.[21]

Without going into more details, then, it seems reasonable to conclude that the SFH suffers from the same defects when applied to the acquisition of *more* and *less* as it does for the dimensional adjectives. To the extent that the explanation it offers depends upon the notion of markedness, it would appear that it is on even weaker ground in this case.

Turning briefly to *same* and *different*, we come across a situation which is even worse. Clark does not even begin to speculate on what the feature composition of these words might be during the time they are confused, and it is transparent that markedness considerations and non-comparative interpretations are going to be of little use in this respect. There is no dimension of 'sameness' for *same* to name, and *same* is inherently relational. As far as my judgements are concerned, there are no situational variables rendering the question 'Are X and Y different?' somehow specialised, when compared with the question 'Are X and Y the same?' I conclude that the SFH has nothing to say about the acquisition of *same* and *different*.

4.4 Temporal conjunctions

The work which E. Clark has done on the comprehension of *before* and *after*, when used as temporal conjunctions, provides an explicit example of the interplay of the acquisition of semantic features and non-linguistic strategies. She claims to discern four stages in this development, using the experimental technique briefly described in 4.1.

Using Clark's numbering, at Stage I the child, while comprehending that *before* and *after* involve the ordering of events in time, formulates his actions on the basis of an order-of-mention strategy: whatever is mentioned first happens first.[22] The conjunction of these two hypotheses leads to the child apparently comprehending utterances of the form 'P before Q' and 'After P, Q' and consistently getting wrong his attempts to act out utterances of the form 'Before P, Q' and 'P after Q'. At Stage IIa the child understands utterances containing *before*, the lexical entry for *before* is now complete, but *after* continues to have its Stage I entry and is still responded to using the order-of-mention strategy. In terms of performance on the experimental task, what this means is that the child now correctly acts out all utterances including *before*, irrespective of the position of *before* in the utterance but still shows Stage I behaviour for *after*-utterances. For Stage IIb *after* is more fully specified but incorrectly, so that the child interprets it as if it had the meaning of *before*. Thus, the child is now consistently correct on *before*-utterances and consistently incorrect on *after*-utterances. With this more complete specification of *after*, the order-of-mention strategy is dropped (but see below). Finally, at Stage III the child is able to distinguish *before* from *after* and consistently responds correctly in the experiment.

Before going on to examine in detail Clark's proposals, it is necessary to make two related observations. The first is that I have described the children's behaviour at the different stages as if it were completely clear-cut. This is not true, of course, and in some cases the figures cited by Clark are not totally convincing. The second point is that children were assigned to groups *post hoc* on the basis of trends which became apparent in the results.[23] Group IIb had only three children in it, and what this amounts to is an indication that the empirical support for the stages is not compelling.

The domain of enquiry D can again be fixed as a part of the child's lexicon, but this time, we must also consider the strategies to which the child resorts in cases of partial understanding and the interaction of these strategies with the lexicon. Behaviour which is relevant to D is restricted to the child's comprehension of sentences involving *before* and *after* used as temporal conjunctions (cf. Coker 1978), as evidenced by his ability to act out the events depicted by the sentences.

$$\begin{array}{ll} \textit{before} & \longleftrightarrow \quad [+ \text{Temporal}, \ - \text{Simultaneous}] \\ \textit{after} & \longleftrightarrow \quad [+ \text{Temporal}, \ - \text{Simultaneous}] \end{array}$$

Figure 4.7

At Stage I one may infer, following Clark's informal remarks, that the part of the lexicon in which we are interested will have the structure represented in Figure 4.7. Another component of the overall theory is something like the following strategy:

S_T: when presented with a structure of the form
$$(P) \ (+ \text{Temporal}, \ - \text{Simultaneous}) \ (Q)$$
or a structure of the form
$$(+ \text{Temporal}, \ - \text{Simultaneous}) \ (P) \ (Q)$$
assume that the event referred to by 'P' precedes the event referred to by 'Q)

T_I (the theory for Stage I) is thus a two-component theory $L_I + S_T$ where L_I designates the relevant part of the lexicon at Stage I.

At Stage IIa the lexicon changes to L_{IIa}, represented in Figure 4.8. S_T will be unchanged, assuming some convention to prevent it applying to utterances with *before*, so $T_{IIa} = L_{IIa} + S_T$.

before   ⟷   [+ Temporal, − Simultaneous, + Prior]

after   ⟷   [+ Temporal, − Simultaneous]

Figure 4.8

For Stage IIb we have another change in the lexicon to L_{IIb}, as in Figure 4.9. At this stage S_T is dispensed with.[24] Thus, $T_{IIb} = L_{IIb}$.

before   ⟷   [+ Temporal, − Simultaneous, + Prior]

after   ⟷   [+ Temporal, − Simultaneous, + Prior]

Figure 4.9

Finally, at Stage III the lexicon reaches its putative adult state as in Figure 4.10. Again, no non-linguistic strategies play a role at this stage.

before   ⟷   [+ Temporal, − Simultaneous, + Prior]

after   ⟷   [+ Temporal, − Simultaneous, − Prior]

Figure 4.10

It is clear, then, that we have a sequence of theories (T_I, T_{IIa}, T_{IIb}, T_{III}) and we can consider the various transitions in this sequence with regard to Conditions I–V.

Condition II is complicated by the fact that some of the theories in the sequence are hybrid, consisting of lexicons and non-linguistic strategies. As far as the lexicons are concerned, there are similar reservations to those we have met in the two previous sections. But also we must attend to the notion of 'strategy', i.e. we need some general formulation of what can count as a strategy in this context and of how such strategies can interact with partially specified lexical information, resulting in a form of comprehension. Clark provides no insights from this general perspective, and, as is clear, the sequence of theories under consideration draws its members from two types, involving a discontinuity between Stage IIa and Stage IIb, which we might expect to produce problems in the application of Condition III.

Consider, then, the transition from T_I to T_{IIa} in the light of Conditions III and IV. This transition is accompanied by the introduction of a *feature value* ([+ Prior], cf. discussion in 4.2) as part of the meaning of *before* and there is no change in the set of strategies at the child's disposal. If we are prepared to admit the introduction of single feature values, this looks like straightforward addition, thus satisfying Condition III. Furthermore, the sequence of features and feature values ([± Temporal], [± Simultaneous], [+ Prior]) appears to be teleologically explained in much the same way as was the sequence ([size], [vertical], [+ pol]) of 4.2 (using Bartlett's notation). That is, the feature [± Simultaneous] only becomes intelligible in the context of temporal notions and the feature value [+ Prior] 'presupposes' lack of simultaneity. There is nothing of value to be gained by considering the other possibilities under Condition IV here.

The transition from T_{IIa} to T_{IIb} is problematic, as we might expect, given that theories of distinct types are involved. The strategy S_T is lost in the transition and this might appear to be a straightforward violation of Condition III. Of course, the way is open to suggest that the strategy is a performance constraint which the child has to overcome, in which case part of the theory under consideration would be negatively construed in the manner outlined in Chapter 1. However, the fundamental point is that the status and formulation of the strategy is not made clear, and, until it is, there is little point in further discussion.

Finally, consider the transition from T_{IIb} to T_{III}. It is easy to see that the crucial factor here is the introduction of the feature value [− Prior]. Accordingly, we have satisfaction of Condition III additively. As far as Condition IV is concerned, however, there is no logical reason why [− Prior] should enter the system after [+ Prior]. Looking to the child's linguistic environment provides no obvious leads, and we are left with the possibility of a reductive explanation for this transition.

Attempts to provide such an explanation can be gleaned from the work of the Clarks (see particularly, H. Clark 1973, pp. 48–52). These attempts proceed from the view that the system of prepositions, conjunctions, etc. encoding temporal concepts in English is based on a spatial metaphor and they employ the 'equations':

before (temporal) = *before* (spatial) = *in front of* (spatial) and

$$after \text{ (temporal)} = after \text{ (spatial)} = behind \text{ (spatial)}$$

These 'equations' establish correspondences between the lexical items in which we are interested and lexical items which encode spatial concepts. Now, the argument goes, in the domain of the child's developing perceptual space, it is reasonab'ᵉ to assert that his concept of the space in front of him develops more quickly and is more elaborate than his concept of the space behind him. In addition, the space in front of the child can be viewed as positive, when compared to the space behind him, thus establishing links between the pair *before/after* (positive and negative) and pairs of words discussed earlier in this chapter. Whether this argument matches up to the rather strong constraints on reduction introduced in Chapter 1 and developed more fully in Chapter 8 is debatable, but I believe that there is at least the beginning of a sound case here. It is to be noted, however, that it is a case for the child learning *before* before *after* and, strictly speaking, does not address directly the perceptual or cognitive primacy of [+ Prior] (versus [− Prior]).

In summary, we can see that the SFH fares badly in the domain of temporal conjunctions, the major reason for this being the lack of a general theory incorporating a lexicon and interacting strategies. Against this substantial flaw, the success in reduction which I have discussed is, perhaps, of marginal significance.

4.5 *Come* and *go*

Many of the comments from the previous section can also be applied to Clark and Garnica's (1974) treatment of the child's acquisition of *come* and *go*.[25] The data obtained in the study justified the setting up *post hoc* (cf. 4.4) of four developmentally ordered groups. The task the children faced was that of identifying the speaker or addressee of an utterance containing either *come* or *go*, and the results for the four groups were distributed as in Table 4.1.

An examination of the means in the right-hand column of Table 4.1 might suggest the conclusion that Groups A and B were performing at chance level and knew nothing about the meanings of *come* and *go*, and that Groups C and D knew the meanings of both words. A somewhat less gross analysis, averaging responses to *come*-sentences and to *go*-sentences, might lead to the following conclusions for each group:

A: understands *come* and consistently goes wrong on *go*.

B: performs at chance level on both *come* and *go*, i.e. does not understand either.

C: understands *come* and performs at chance level with *go*.

D: understands both *come* and *go*.

Table 4.1. *Percentage of semantically correct responses produced by each group (modified from Clark and Garnica 1974, p. 566)*

Group	Speaker to be identified		Addressee to be identified		Mean
	Come	*Go*	*Come*	*Go*	
A	90	24	100	1	54
B	30	80	73	23	52
C	76	87	94	33	73
D	83	90	94	70	84

Clearly, insofar as Groups A–D are roughly ordered with respect to chronological age, what we have above, with the odd development between A and B, would be difficult to make sense of in terms of the child's gradual acquisition of the meanings of the items. Clark and Garnica claim, however, that by taking account of the detailed structure of the results, as presented in Table 4.1, and introducing strategies, it is possible to reconstrue the development in such a way that it becomes more readily intelligible. The strategies they propose appear in Table 4.2.

Following these rules will enable the child in Group A to be correct in his responses to utterances containing *come* and consistently incorrect to those containing *go* – he acts as if such utterances contain *come*. For a child in Group B, following the rules will lead to correct identification of speakers for *go*-utterances and addressees of *come*-utterances and misidentification of speakers of *come*-utterances and addressees of *go*-utterances. The child in Group C will identify correctly both speakers and addressees of *come*-utterances; in effect, he now controls the adult procedure. The addressee of *go*-utterances will, however, continue to be misidentified. Finally, Group D children have the adult rules and perform correctly under all conditions.

Two remarks need to be made immediately in connection with this way of looking at things. The first is that the strategies or rules must be

Table 4.2. *Rules used to identify speaker and addressee (from Clark and Garnica 1974, p. 566)*

Group	Speaker to be identified	Addressee to be identified
A	Choose goal	Choose goal
B	Choose nongoal	Choose goal
C	1. If *come*, choose goal	Choose goal
	2. If *go*, choose nongoal	
D	1. If *come*, choose goal	1. If *come*, choose goal
	2. If *go*, choose nongoal	2. If *go*, choose nongoal

presumed to operate on partially specified semantic entries for *come* and *go* (but cf. n. 22). Thus, this wholesale resort to strategies does not imply complete abandonment of the SFH, although this latter has a very attenuated role to play in the present context. The second point is that it is difficult to be confident that the study tells us very much about children's knowledge of the *meanings* of the verbs. The child has a problem to solve, a problem which a mature acquaintance with the verbs *come* and *go* will render transparent, but we cannot conclude from the child's inability to solve the problem and his resort to strategies that he does not control the meanings of *come* and *go*. A similar point is made by Richards (1976) who shows that, in what he regards as more natural and child-oriented surroundings, it is possible to demonstrate the control of *come* and *go* at ages considerably younger than those studied by Clark and Garnica. This control demands that the child be credited with some deictic information in his lexical entries for *come* and *go* (cf. also Macrae 1976). This position is supported by a recent paper of Shatz (1977) where the author points to consistent variations in children's performances according to task demands. Thus, there is a substantive and difficult issue concerning the nature of the domain of investigation in this case. Presumably, Clark and Garnica would say that they are studying the interaction of incomplete lexical knowledge with strategies, but the alternative that they are discovering problem-solving strategies, which are highly task-specific and which make minimal reference to the contents of the lexicon, cannot be lightly dismissed.

With these qualifications in mind, then, we have a sequence of theories (T_A, T_B, T_C, T_D), where each of the T's is a hybrid theory consisting of a partial lexicon, a set of strategies and a statement of the interaction of these two components.

Condition II leads to no new questions for such a sequence. Consider Condition III for each of the transitions in the sequence. The change from T_A to T_B, although involving no alteration in feature composition of *come* and *go*, does introduce a new strategy: 'Choose non-goal.' Similarly, for the transition from T_B to T_C, in the latter we find two conditional strategies which do not appear in the former. In addition, however, the strategy 'Choose non-goal', which plays a role in T_B, does not appear in T_C, and we appear to have this 'simple' strategy being replaced by the two conditional strategies. While it might be tempting to resort to an intuitive sense of simplicity here, the safest conclusion is that Condition III does not apply in this case. Finally, the transition from T_C to T_D is not marked by the development of any new strategies and what we find is an extended use of the two conditional strategies from T_C together with the dropping of the 'simple' strategy 'Choose goal.' On the face of it this looks like a failure to satisfy Condition III, although the tactic of interpreting the strategies as constraints remains to be explored (cf. p. 85 above). This tactic would, of course, have difficulties when confronted with the transition from T_A to T_B. Condition IV gives rise to interesting problems in connection with the transition from T_A to T_B. The question this condition poses can be formulated as follows: why is it that we find the developmental sequence $X \rightarrow X \oplus$ 'Choose non-goal', where X includes 'Choose goal' rather than the sequence $Y \rightarrow Y \oplus$ 'Choose goal' where Y includes 'Choose non-goal'? In other words, why does the goal of movement have ontogenetic priority over the non-goal? Clark and Garnica are aware of this issue and they say (1974, p. 570): 'The goal however, plays a basic role in the child's strategies from the beginning. This could be because the goal was always named in the deictic utterances. In addition the one animal at the goal may have been more salient because the goal was a distinct location.' In this passage we can dimly discern two of the possibilities offered by Condition IV, environmental and reductive, but Clark and Garnica present no general considerations from outside their experimental context to render either of these more plausible. In fact, the passage also reveals the limitations of this study for semantic development. If we are interested in the acquisition of *come* and *go* in quite general terms, it is not the case that goals are always mentioned in utterances containing these verbs, nor is it always the case that the goal constitutes a definable location. This strengthens the view that Clark and Garnica's strategies are created by children to handle a particular problem situation and tell us little about lexical development. Even putting this aside, there is no theory (perceptual or cognitive) with which I am familiar to play the role of reducer if this is the explanatory path that Clark and Garnica wish to follow.

It is possible, then, to give the authors the credit for realising that there is a problem here, but nothing they say can be seen as a satisfactory solution to this problem. The transitions from T_B to T_C and from T_C to T_D fare no better than that from T_A to T_B (see Atkinson 1978 for discussion), and, summarising, it seems clear that the SFH and its association with strategies does no better in the area of the acquisition of *come* and *go* than it does elsewhere. To the extent that the domain of enquiry cannot be established with confidence, it is tempting to conclude that it does worse. It is less distressing to know what you are doing and that you are doing it badly than not to know what you are doing.

4.6 Haphazard examples

While many findings have been reported which are difficult to accommodate within the SFH, several of them referred to in previous sections of this chapter, alternative theories of comparable scope have been rather thin on the ground. One exception to this is outlined in Carey (1978b), and I would like to conclude this chapter by briefly examining her ideas.

There are two major differences between Carey's proposals and those of the SFH. The first is that she is convinced that the child acquires semantic information about polarity before he acquires information about dimensionality, and there are various pieces of evidence in favour of this. One is that provided by Brewer and Stone (1975) that, given the array of Figure 4.11 and asked to choose the shortest one, children's errors respect polarity but not dimensionality, i.e. the erring child will choose D rather than A.

A second sort of evidence comes from using an array, the spatial properties of which are questioned, using inappropriate dimensional adjectives (e.g. *fat* and its related forms *fatter* and *fattest* when members of the array differ only in terms of height). Responses in these circumstances appear to indicate that children use polarity information in the inappropriate adjectives. Finally, the behaviour of children in the task which has them supply the opposite to a test adjective already described in 4.1 (Clark 1972b) is consistent with Carey's position. Thus, the learner is viewed as first acquiring the dimensionally undifferentiated adjectives *big* and *little* providing what Carey calls a 'core comparative structure'. Because the differentiated adjectives are syntactically similar to *big* and *little*, it is suggested that this core comparative structure is overgeneralised to these adjectives before the appropriate dimensionality features are acquired. This leads to a situation where *big* is synonymous with *tall*,

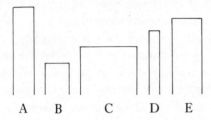

Figure 4.11

wide, fat, etc. and *small* is synonymous with *short, narrow, thin,* etc. which will produce the sort of error described above.

It is apparent then that, in terms of features, Carey sees $[\pm \text{pol}]$ as an early acquisition and must, therefore, face the issue of why this is so. Of course, this is exactly the question raised by Condition IV. Carey says (1978b, p. 282): 'This explanation of why polarity might be more learnable than dimensionality depends upon the child's mastery of the syntax of comparative constructions and of the lexical entries for *big* and *little* prior to his acquisition of the specialized spatial adjectives.' But the mastery of comparative constructions in no way contributes to the explanation of the early development of $[+\text{pol}]$, but rather to an explanation of the child's errors in certain experimental tasks. So, we are left with the early acquisition of *big* and *little* as the basis for the argument and on this we are told that 'The child's original, and early, learning of *big* and *little* has not been explained' (*ibid.*). How could it be explained? 4.2 argued that, if we examine the logical relations between features, it is most appropriate to view polarity as 'presupposing' dimensionality. To attempt to construct an argument for the reverse relation would be perverse in this context.[26] No reductionist explanation suggests itself, leaving the possibility of an environmental approach. Carey moves in this direction when she suggests that the child, by acquiring *big* and *little* with the associated polarity features, will minimise production and comprehension errors.

What is wide is also big, and understanding *wide* as *big* will not often lead to a breakdown of communication. Additionally, one might speculate that parental speech to children of the relevant age is not rich in differentiated dimensional vocabulary, the child simply does not receive enough information to induce a lexical representation for *tall, short, wide, narrow*, etc. This possibility deserves systematic investigation.

The second divergence between Carey's and Clark's views is more radical and concerns the nature of the child's lexical entries. Carey feels that if, say, *tall* had an entry making it synonymous with *big*, one should find more consistency within children on a battery of tasks than she in fact found. She is led to the view that 'immature lexical entries for spatial adjectives might contain information about some particular objects to which each adjective applies' (1978b, p. 286), and as a schematisation, she offers Figure 4.12. A child equipped with these entries, confronted with

tall: [Adj] [comparative] [+ pole] [—building, ground up;
    — person, head to toe]
short: [Adj] [comparative] [− pole] [— person, head to toe;
    — hair, root to end; — distance, direction of motion]

Figure 4.12 (from Carey 1978b, p. 286)

an array of people differing in height and girth will perform correctly, when questioned on tallness. However, if the stimuli are changed to, say, rectangles, the child may resort to treating *tall* as a synonym of *big*.

While there is much that remains unclear in this proposal, it is evident that it bears some resemblance to the PH discussed in Chapter 3, *tall* and *short* are first learned in application to specific situations and will only be used for novel situations if these bear some (but, perhaps, not fixed) resemblance to the original context of learning. From this it would seem to follow that the ontogenesis of the structure of lexical entries, far from being explicable in perceptual or cognitive terms, is very much at the mercy of chance encounters with the relevant lexical items. There are a number of interesting questions that such a view raises. For example, and again making contact with the discussion of Chapter 3, we might suppose that there are 'natural categories' of objects such that, if a child learns that a certain spatial adjective applies to one exemplar of the class, then he will be in a position to generalise its application throughout the category.

According to this suggestion, learning that *tall* and *short* apply to a dimension of people may be sufficient to enable the child to know that these adjectives also apply to a dimension of trees or buildings. Conversely, to use Carey's own example, if a child learns how to apply *deep* and *shallow* in the context of swimming pools, he may not be in a position to use these adjectives correctly in connection with bowls, holes or puddles. Further, we might speculate on parental usage of these terms and wonder whether parents initially avoid usages which might confuse the child, e.g. 'deep drawers'. These two tentative suggestions are, of course, no more than a recommendation that future research should examine the two possible sources for prototypes mentioned by Bowerman (1978) and discussed in 3.5. To my knowledge nothing is known on these matters.

My discussion of the 'haphazard example theory' has been less structured, in terms of the framework of Chapter 1, than that of the SFH. This is inevitable, as Carey's proposal is not systematically worked out and is in the early stages of development. However, it appears to be provoking a number of interesting and challenging questions and the inadequacies of the SFH are such that an alternative approach is to be welcomed.

5 The development of formal grammar

Between the early 1960s and early 1970s a number of attempts were made to write complete or partial grammars which were intended to capture a child's developing syntactic competence. While the role of what the child might mean by his utterances became more important in constructing and evaluating such attempts throughout this period, it was not intended that these grammars would contain any explicit indication of semantic structure. It is in this sense that the present chapter is concerned with formal grammar; the issues surrounding more semantically-based notions of grammatical development will be taken up in Chapter 6.

The emphasis in most of the work I shall focus on here was on the description of a system which was neutral between comprehension and production, and which was intended to characterise the knowledge underlying these abilities. However, with isolated exceptions such as Shipley, Smith and Gleitman (1969), the data used in the construction of such systems were the productions of the child. The actual form of grammatical theory employed typically owed something to one or another version of transformational grammar, and, of course, Chomsky's influence in this matter cannot be over-emphasised.

From this perspective, then, the child's developing knowledge of syntax can be represented by a sequence of grammars $(G_1, G_2, \ldots, G_n)$, where he is credited with G_1 as soon as he manifests behaviour which indicates *any* grammatical knowledge. This has usually been taken to be when he first employs two-word utterances, although, if the well-subscribed view that comprehension precedes production is correct, the child may possess grammatical knowledge before this time.[1] In the interests of general presentation, we can assume that G_n is a theory of adult syntactic competence and that $G_2, \ldots, G_{n-1}$ represent grammars at arbitrary sampling points in the passage from G_1 to G_n. In practice, most people working in this domain have restricted themselves to a small number of points in the sequence, often concentrating their attention on the earliest stages of development.

The sense in which linguistic theory has informed theory construction in this area can be rapidly spelled out. An adequate linguistic theory, according to the Chomskyan conception, supplies, among other things, a definition of the notion 'possible grammar of a language' (and, consequently, 'possible human language') and can be seen as restricting the space of grammars through which the child has to search in order to arrive at the grammar of his linguistic environment (cf. Chapter 10). The child's 'transition grammars', the guesses he makes as to the grammar of his native language as he learns it, must, then, be seen as constrained by the same general theory. The exact nature of an adequate general linguistic theory has, not surprisingly, resisted discovery, although a large number of more or less tentative suggestions in this direction are available in the literature. Clearly, however, compliance with a coherent set of such suggestions on the part of the child-language theorist will go a long way towards the satisfaction of Condition II.[2]

The proposals which I shall consider in this chapter are, perhaps more than any others discussed in this book, out of date and no longer subscribed to by their authors. This is largely irrelevant to my purposes, as it could turn out that such proposals have highly desirable features distinct from their empirical adequacy or inadequacy and, if they have, it will be instructive to discover them. Where appropriate in what follows, I shall adopt the practice of compartmentalising syntactic development, considering such questions as the order of development of grammatical classes, grammatical rules or grammatical rule-types, rather than considering grammatical development *in toto*. On occasions this coincides with the interest of the proposal under discussion; in other cases it simply facilitates exposition and does not, in my view, lead to serious distortion.

5.1 McNeill on grammatical classes

The characteristics of pivot and open grammars and the extent and manner of McNeill's manipulation of the concept in adapting original suggestions of Braine (1963), Brown and Fraser (1963) and Miller and Ervin (1964) and synthesising them are too well-known to merit more than the briefest statement here (see McNeill 1966 and, for detailed discussion and criticism, Park 1970, Bowerman 1973, Brown 1973 and many other places). According to McNeill, at the beginning of syntactic development, it is possible to define, on purely formal, distributional grounds, two, or sometimes three, grammatical classes. If the distributional analysis yields two such classes, they are referred to as the pivot class and the open class;

if three classes emerge, they are the first-position pivot class, second-position pivot class and open class. Distributional and statistical criteria come together in such a way that the classes have the characteristics exhibited in Figure 5.1 (restricting ourselves from now on to the situation

Pivots	*Open-class words*
Occur frequently in a corpus (some arbitrary criterion of frequency has to be fixed)	Occur infrequently in a corpus
Always occur in first position in two-word utterances	Occur in variable position in two-word utterances
Never occur in single-word utterances	Sometimes occur in single-word utterances
Never occur in construction with another pivot	Sometimes occur in construction with another open-class word

Figure 5.1

in which there are only two classes and assuming that all pivots are first-position pivots). These distributional facts can be summarised by saying that, at the stage in question (for McNeill, the very beginning of syntactic development), say at t_1, the child has a grammatical competence which recognises two grammatical categories other than Sentence, which can be referred to as 'P' and 'O' and which are organised according to the grammar of Figure 5.2 (ignoring the introduction of lexical items). From

$$S \rightarrow \begin{Bmatrix} (P) + O \\ O + O \end{Bmatrix}$$

Figure 5.2

our point of view, it is most important to note that membership of the categories P and O is claimed to be typically heterogeneous with respect to adult grammatical categories.

At a later stage of development it will be necessary to postulate a different grammar to account for the child's syntactic knowledge, and we might expect that such a grammar, while being related to the grammar of

t_1, will bear a closer resemblance to the adult grammar than does the earlier system. As far as grammatical categories are concerned, this expectation might be realised by our being able to credit the child with one or more grammatical categories which *can* be identified with those from the adult set. As a hypothetical example, we can imagine postulating the grammar of Figure 5.3 for the child at t_2 to account for the observations

$$S \rightarrow \begin{Bmatrix} (P') & +O' \\ (Adj) & +O'' \\ \begin{Bmatrix} O' \\ O'' \end{Bmatrix} & +\begin{Bmatrix} O'' \\ O' \end{Bmatrix} \end{Bmatrix}$$

Figure 5.3

that a class of morphemes including only adult adjectives now has privileged distributional properties, that a modified pivot class P' (which will not contain any adjectives) can only provide the first member of two-member constructions (just as for P at t_1), that members of P' are restricted to the extent that they can only occur in construction with members of O' (a modified open class) and that members of O' and O'' can occur freely together as well as occurring alone. This developmental process, or something like it, will, presumably, continue until the child controls the adult grammar and, in particular, employs the full set of adult grammatical categories S, NP, VP, Det, N, V, etc., where we can assume that this set is supplied by an appropriate linguistic theory.

In general, then, what we have is a developmental sequence of grammars $(G_1, G_2, \ldots, G_n)$ where G_1 is as in Figure 5.2, G_2 is, hypothetically, as in Figure 5.3 and G_n is a grammar of adult English. It is a sequence such as this and, in particular, the sets of grammatical categories in each G_i ($1 \leqslant i \leqslant n$) that I wish to submit to Conditions I – V.

Condition I is worth mentioning if only because McNeill and others working in this area have always been explicit on the point that they are attempting to characterise the child's syntactic competence and are not producing a model which will predict what the child will say on a particular occasion. Workers in other domains have been less explicit in this regard, although it seems that, on the whole, they too are not interested in predicting behaviour in any familiar sense. Obviously, the cogency of McNeill's (and others') position depends upon our abilities to make sense of competence explanations in psychology. For small children the immediate problem is whether one can make sense of some proposed grammar as a theory of syntactic knowledge and not whether the concept of syntactic knowledge itself makes sense in the context of psychological explanations.[3]

Turning to Condition II, the close relationship between linguistic theory and language acquisition is emphasised by McNeill when he says (1966, p. 15):

The intention of this paper is to examine [the intersection of linguistic theory and empirical studies of language acquisition – RMA] in an effort to interpret empirical studies in the light of linguistic theory. The aim is to develop a theory of language acquisition that will be consistent with linguistic theory and will cover the facts of acquisition as they are now known.

To what extent can we see the sequence of grammars $(G_1, G_2, \ldots, G_n)$ as being constructed in accordance with the general principles of some theory of language structure? To approach this question we can note a relevant passage from a work of Chomsky with which McNeill was familiar and which can be seen as hazarding suggestions as to the contents of a general linguistic theory. Chomsky says (1965, p. 28–9):

Traditional universal grammar was also a theory of substantive universals . . . [It] advanced the position that certain fixed syntactic categories (Noun, Verb etc.) can be found in the syntactic representations of the sentences of any language and that these provide the general underlying syntactic structure of each language.

According to this view, we can hope to find a universal inventory of grammatical categories in general linguistic theory; this inventory will inform the child's guesses as he constructs the grammar of his native language.

Now, taking account of the above, it is immediately obvious that G_1 in our sequence has a strange look, recognising the categories S, P and O, which, with the exception of S, are foreign to the grammar of adult English and, so far as I know, to the grammar of any human language.[4] Similar remarks can be made in connection with the hypothetical G_2 except that there we find a move towards the set of adult categories via the introduction of the category of adjectives. Therefore, we can conclude that, within the set of developing grammatical classes, we have a discontinuity: the child begins with the grammatical categories P and O (thereby, we may presume, violating the prescriptions of the general theory which is supposed to be constraining his hypotheses), subsequently dropping them to take over the set of adult grammatical classes, going through stages where he uses categories which are also heterogeneous with respect to adult categories and equally alien to the grammars of the world's languages, e.g. P', O', O'' in G_2. As pointed out in Chapter 1, such a discontinuity does not necessarily amount to a demonstration of incorrectness, but it does deserve discussion and argument. McNeill does not argue for the discontinuity but, significantly, claims that what we have is an *apparent* discontinuity which analysis will reveal as quite benign. His treatment of this problem, later abandoned on empirical grounds, is well known. Briefly, he claims that, while it is true that the categories P and O are heterogeneous with regard to the adult grammatical categories, nevertheless, they honour those categories generically. What this amounts to is the claim that there is no pair of morphemes X and Y, such that X and Y both belong to the same adult category, X belongs to P and Y belongs to O. This view would be supported by the hypothetical development we are considering from t_1 to t_2, where the pivot class at t_1 would simply lose the class of adjectives at t_2. Obviously, if development were to proceed along these lines, McNeill would have solved the discontinuity problem by showing that, in effect, the discontinuity does not exist. The problematic categories P and O are just our familiar categories in disguise. What is important from my point of view is to see this analysis as inspired by an implicit recognition of the necessity of satisfying Condition II.

For the sake of completeness, we may quickly consider NcNeill's proposals with regard to Conditions III and IV. He presents as an example of development within the set of grammatical categories, the tree-structure of Figure 5.4. We can note that there is a gradual increase in

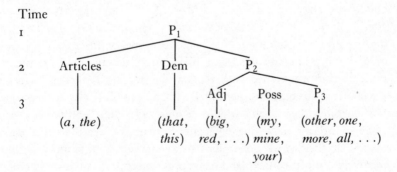

Figure 5.4 (from McNeill 1966, p. 27)

the number of grammatical classes from t_1 to t_2 and from t_2 to t_3 and this might lead us to think that Condition III is satisfied. But, because of the modification of the original pivot class, this conclusion is not justified. We do not get the categories Articles and Dem *added* to P_1 in the transition from t_1 to t_2. Rather, these categories appear along with another new category P_2, and P_1 disappears from the grammar. So, unless we have some independent way of evaluating the complexity of the set {Articles, Dem, P_2} against the single category P_1, we are forced to conclude that Condition III is not applicable.

Consultation of Figure 5.4 does not suggest any teleological explanation for why the categories enter the system in the order McNeill offers, nor does any environmental account emerge as plausible. McNeill makes no attempt to relate the emergence of categories to some other aspect of development, and so, the possibilities under Condition IV are exhausted. We are led to the conclusion that, even if McNeill's theory in this area were descriptively correct, it would still leave the level of explanatory adequacy unexplored.

5.2 The grammar of negation

Klima and Bellugi (1966) is the first systematic attempt to investigate the development of the expression of negation in English.[5] It is explicitly modest in aims and restricted to considerations of form, entirely leaving aside questions of meaning and the interaction of form and meaning. As far as their aims are concerned, Klima and Bellugi have this to say (1966, p. 191): 'It should be understood that when we write rules for the child grammar it is *just a rough attempt to give substance to our feeling about*, and general observations demonstrating, the regularity in the syntax of the child's speech' (my emphasis – RMA). As for the neglect of semantic considerations, we find (*ibid.*): 'We want to emphasise here that we are not dealing with the expression of semantic concepts on the part of the child, or of basic grammatical notions like subject function and transitivity; rather we are concerned with the way he handles lower-level syntactic phenomena like position, permutability and the like.' Given these qualifications, it is questionable whether Klima and Bellugi's proposals deserve to be considered as serious explanatory theories. Nevertheless, a consideration of their work does point to a number of difficulties within a relatively simple context and may prove useful as an introduction to similar difficulties which we shall meet within more complex frameworks later in this chapter.

The authors claim to discern three stages in the development of the syntactic expression of negation.[6] Typical of the data produced at Stage 1 are the utterances 'No . . . wipe finger', 'more . . . no', 'No singing song' and 'Not a teddy bear'. The generalisation which emerges is that there are no sentence-internal negative elements nor are there any auxiliary verbs. Formalising this generalisation leads to crediting the child with a grammar-fragment along the lines of Figure 5.5.[7] At Stage 2 a more complex

$$S \rightarrow \left\{ \begin{matrix} \begin{Bmatrix} no \\ not \end{Bmatrix} + \text{Nucleus} \\ \text{Nucleus} + no \end{matrix} \right\}$$

Figure 5.5

picture presents itself, evidenced by the following sample: 'I can't catch you', 'you can't dance', 'I don't want it', 'No pinch me', 'This is a radiator no', 'Don't bite me yet', 'That not "O", that blue', 'That no mummy'. As well as finding the patterns of Stage 1 persisting into Stage 2, we now also find sentence-internal negative elements, which may take the form of a simple negative such as *no* or *not* or may be a negated auxiliary verb. An important point for Klima and Bellugi is that there are no occurrences in their Stage 2 corpus of non-negative auxiliary verbs. In summarising these facts, they say (1966, pp. 194–5):

Let us begin with a basic structure something like:

$$S \rightarrow \text{Nominal} - (\text{Aux}^{\text{neg}}) - \begin{Bmatrix} \text{Predicate} \\ \text{Main verb} \end{Bmatrix}$$

. . . This first rule can be related to the shape of sentences by the following rules:

$$\text{Aux}^{\text{neg}} \rightarrow \begin{Bmatrix} \text{Neg} \\ \text{V}^{\text{neg}} \end{Bmatrix}$$

$$\text{Neg} \rightarrow \begin{Bmatrix} no \\ not \end{Bmatrix}$$

$$\text{V}^{\text{neg}} \rightarrow \begin{Bmatrix} can't \\ don't \end{Bmatrix} \quad \text{V}^{\text{neg}} \text{ restricted to non-progressive verbs}$$

where the particular selection of the negative is determined by the Main Verb with *don't* and *can't* restricted to occurrence before instances of non-progressive main verbs.

All of this is reasonably clear and the last rule could easily be converted to a context-sensitive phrase-structure rule if we are allowed reference to a subcategory of verb, say V^{prog}. These rules, along with the rule from Stage 1, comprise the relevant part of the child's grammar at Stage 2.

The major development at Stage 3 is that auxiliaries now occur unnegated as well as negated. Along with more detailed observations of a sample of negative utterances, this leads Klima and Bellugi to the following conclusions (1966, p. 197):

so we can now begin with a basic structure like:

$$S \rightarrow \text{Nominal} - \text{Aux} - \begin{Bmatrix} \text{Predicate} \\ \text{Main Verb} \end{Bmatrix}$$

and suggest such rules as follows:

$$\text{Aux} \rightarrow T - V^{aux} - (\text{Neg})$$

$$V^{aux} \rightarrow \begin{Bmatrix} do \\ can \\ be \\ will \end{Bmatrix}$$

where *be* is restricted to predicate and progressive and is optional, *can* and *do* to non-progressive main verbs.

Transformations
 I. Optional *be* deletion
  $NP - be \Rightarrow NP$
 II. *Do* deletion
  $do - V \Rightarrow V$

The details of much of this need not concern us. We assume, perhaps contrary to Klima and Bellugi's intentions (see above) that the three grammar-fragments, illustrated in Figure 5.5 and in the two cited passages, are to be interpreted as theories of a domain D, the child's syntactic knowledge of negative structures, i.e. we have a sequence of grammar-fragments (G_1, G_2, G_3) which can be analysed in terms of the conditions of Chapter 1.

Condition II is, as it was in 5.1, perhaps the most interesting. The theories we are considering are presented in the form of grammars with the linguistic influence being clearly Chomsky's, although Klima's (1964) pioneering work on the syntax of negation in English supplies some of the more detailed concepts. Concentrating first on rule-format, the sequence

(G_1, G_2, G_3) appears to satisfy the minimal requirements that all rules are either phrase-structure rules (or translatable into phrase-structure equivalents) or transformational rules. To the advantage of the theories is the observation that the transformational rules in G_3, while deletion rules, do not fail to satisify the recoverability of deletions condition on such rules. This condition, first formulated in Chomsky (1965) and subsequently extensively discussed, allows for the deletion of specified lexical material and in both I and II of G_3 this is what we find (cf. in this respect remarks made in connection with deletion rules formulated by Bloom and by Bowerman which are discussed in 5.3).

Turning to grammatical categories, however, things are not so clearcut. The inventories of categories used by the sequence of grammars is as follows:

G_1: Sentence, Nucleus

G_2: Sentence, Nucleus, Nominal, Aux^{neg}, Predicate,
Main Verb, Neg, V^{neg}

G_3: Sentence, Nominal, Aux, Predicate, Main Verb,
T, V^{aux}, Neg.

Now the trouble with these categories is that, with one or two exceptions, they are not candidates for inclusion in anyone's general theory of grammar. This is particularly true for Nucleus, Aux^{neg} and V^{neg}, and what this amounts to is the fact that Klima and Bellugi must subscribe to one or more discontinuities in the set of grammatical categories as the child learns the system of negation. McNeill, encountering a similar situation, attempted to argue the problem away. Klima and Bellugi neither adopt this strategy nor make any attempt to insulate their analyses against this sort of problem. It appears, then, that we can conclude, with some justification, that the Klima and Bellugi analysis of the development of negation fails Condition II with respect to the inventories of grammatical categories employed at the various stages. Given this, there is little point in pushing further to see how it matches up to Conditions III and IV. However, it is worth pointing out that, in the aspect in which it satisfies Condition II (with regard to rule-types, it also satisfies Condition III (although not, of course, for *particular* rules), and this satisfaction of Condition III can be explained in terms of the logical structure of transformational grammars – structure-deformation rules 'presuppose' structure-building rules.

5.3 Bloom's grammars

Lois Bloom's work (1968, 1970) represents the first attempt to write complete grammars for a number of children and to trace the detailed development of these grammars. It can also be seen as containing the first efforts to codify children's utterances in terms of the context in which they occur, according to an argued scheme of categorisation, and to integrate the results of this into a developmental syntactic theory relating to the then current views on syntactic structure. Because of this primacy, I shall take her work as representative of a number of studies which have undertaken similar programmes (most notably, Bowerman 1973, Brown 1973). Arguably, in terms of the critical points I shall raise, Bloom's work is not the strongest in this area. However, I would contend that other work shares most of the defects we shall discover, and that there is some virtue in raising these defects in a context in which they are most transparent.

Bloom presents a total of five complete grammars for different stages in the development of the three children she studied, one for Kathryn, two for Gia and two for Eric. Obviously, from the point of view of the present enterprise, the one grammar for Kathryn is of little consequence, as no developmental conditions can be tested against it.[8] Accordingly, I shall discuss Gia's grammars in some detail and summarise some conclusions which arise from a similarly detailed study of Eric's grammars. All page references in this section are to Bloom (1968).

The sample on which Gia's first grammar was based was collected when the child was 19 months and 1 week old with an MLU of 1.12 morphemes. The grammar which Bloom writes for this sample contains phrase-structure rules and 'lexicon feature' rules and is shown in Figure 5.6. A few clarificatory comments are in order in connection with the relationship between this grammar and the framework introduced in Chapter 2 of Chomsky (1965). The single phrase-structure rule is straightforward enough; but the lexicon-feature rules contain a number of peculiarities. (i) is a simple subcategorisation rule but (ii) violates the condition that only lexical categories appear on the left-hand side of such rules. Chomsky (1965, p. 112) contains a discussion of this restriction arguing that 'it may be a bit too severe', but it is not insignificant that already we come up against one of the less well understood aspects of the general theory that Bloom is taking for granted. (iii) is also a subcategorisation rule and does have a lexical category on its left-hand side, but the right-hand side suggests that not being able to follow a particular morpheme (*hi*) is an inherent feature of verbs. No rule of this sort, mentioning a particular

Phrase structure rules

1. $S \rightarrow \begin{Bmatrix} N \\ Q \\ Hi \end{Bmatrix} + \begin{Bmatrix} VB \\ N \end{Bmatrix}$

Lexicon feature rules

   i. $N \rightarrow [+ N, \pm \text{animate}]$
  ii. $[+ \text{animate}] \rightarrow [+ — N]$
 iii. $VB \rightarrow [- Hi —]$
 iv. $Q \rightarrow [+ \text{quantifier}]$
  v. $[+ \text{quantifier}] \rightarrow$ *more, 'nother*

Figure 5.6 (adapted from Bloom 1968, p. 165)

lexical item, figures in the theory Chomsky proposes. (iv) is again a subcategorisation rule of the type found in (i), except that, in this case, it does not subcategorise. To be told that the syntactic category Q (= quantifier) has the feature [+ quantifier] is not to be told anything, although syntactic features of this sort may be necessary *as part of a larger enterprise* within a theory achieving lexical insertion via matching of features. Finally, the last rule, (v), seems to be an attempt to incorporate an aspect of lexical insertion into this component of the grammar, a move which is quite at variance with the general theory.

Along with these rules goes a lexicon which has the entries shown schematically in Figure 5.7 among others. It is difficult to see exactly how

baby [+ N]	*Gia* [+ N, + animate]
bag [+ N]	*away* [+ VB]
fly [+ N, + animate]	*go* + [— Part]

Figure 5.7 (adapted from Bloom 1968, p. 437)

this lexicon interacts with the other parts of the grammar but two points are sufficiently obvious to be noted:

(1)   There is no reason why the quantifiers should be given their privileged status within the lexicon-feature rules rather than appearing in the lexicon with simple entries of the form:

     more [+ quantifier]

(2)   The verb *go* will never be inserted into a phrase-marker as it requires the presence of a following particle (= Part) and particles are not introduced in the phrase-structure component of the grammar.

As far as points such as these are concerned, it is perhaps best to leave the last word to the author who, when presenting her first lexicon for the grammar she wrote for Kathryn says (p. 431): 'The form in which the lexicons are presented may be considered unorthodox, but there does not appear to be a consensus regarding the form for lexical entries in a dictionary. Moreover, the form of the lexicon is not the issue; attention has been given to the children's use of words – in syntactic contexts and in isolation.' It is possible to agree with the sentiments expressed in this passage regarding the lack of an accepted view of the lexicon and still demand a more cogent treatment than Bloom offers. These, by no means trivial, problems aside, what are the characteristics of the first Gia grammar?

The phrase-structure component of the grammar lacks recursive rules and, hence, generates only a finite number of structures. There were, in the corpus, instances of $\mathrm{\vartheta} + \mathrm{N}$, $\mathrm{\vartheta} + \mathrm{VB}$, $\mathrm{Q} + \mathrm{N}$, $\mathrm{Q} + \mathrm{VB}$, $\mathrm{N} + \mathrm{N}$, *Hi* $+ \mathrm{N}$ and $\mathrm{N} + \mathrm{VB}$. There were no occurrences of *Hi* $+ \mathrm{VB}$ and this is accounted for by (iii) in the lexicon-feature rules. In cases of $\mathrm{N} + \mathrm{N}$ constructions, the first N could usually be categorised as an animate noun and (ii) accounts for this. Only a small number of utterances in the corpus are outside the scope of the grammar.

The second sample for which a grammar was written was collected from Gia when she was 20 months and 2 weeks old and the MLU for this sample was 1.34 morphemes. The second grammar consists of a phrase-structure component, lexicon-feature rules and a transformational component and appears as Figure 5.8. Again, before proceeding further, some comments are in order. The phrase-structure rules of Figure 5.8 are unobjectionable but the lexicon-feature rules and the transformational rules have several worrying aspects. As for the former, similar remarks apply to (i)–(vi) as have already been made for the corresponding rules in Figure 5.6. This leaves (vii) and it is difficult to make any sense of this, as Bloom offers no discussion of its function. Strictly speaking, in order to be intelligible at all, it must assume that 'ə' is either a syntactic category or a complex symbol; it is self-evidently neither of these. What seems to be the most likely interpretation of the facts leading to the formulation of (vii) is that we find /ə/ and /də/ in free variation, except that /də/ never follows a quantifier. But, if this is correct, is this sort of information appropriately

Phrase structure rules

1. $S_1 \rightarrow N + (Q) + \begin{Bmatrix} NP \\ VP \end{Bmatrix}$

2. $S_2 \rightarrow Hi + N$

3. $VP \rightarrow VB + NP$

4. $NP \rightarrow (\partial) + (N) + N$

Lexicon-feature rules

   i. $N \rightarrow [+ N, \pm \text{animate}]$

  ii. $[+ \text{animate}] \rightarrow + [- VB]$

 iii. $Q \rightarrow [+ \text{quantifier}]$

 iv. $[+ \text{quantifier}] \rightarrow more$

  v. $VB \rightarrow [+ VB]$

 vi. $[+ VB] \rightarrow \pm [- NP]$

vii. $\partial \rightarrow + [/d/ -], - [Q -]$

Transformational rules

(1) $T_{\text{placement}}$ (optional)

    S.D.: *away* + X

    S.C.: $x_1 - x_2 \Rightarrow x_2 - x_1$

(2) $T_{\text{reduction}}$ (obligatory)

    S.D.: $\# - X - Y - Z$, where X, Y, Z are category symbols

    S.C.: $\# - x_1 - x_2 - x_3 \Rightarrow \# - x_i - x_j$, where $0 < i < j \leqslant 3$

(3) $T_{/\partial/\text{Placement}}$ (optional)

    S.D.: $X - VP$, where X may be Q or null

    S.C.: $x_1 - x_2 \Rightarrow \partial - x_1 - x_2$

Figure 5.8 (adapted from Bloom 1968, pp. 185–6)

represented in this component of the grammar? I know of no framework which would subscribe to such a view, and one can only conclude that (vii) is fundamentally misconceived.

The transformational rules also contain some mysteries. (1) is a permutation transformation designed exclusively to make sure that *away* can occur in both utterance-initial and utterance-final position. Permutation transformations are deemed undesirable in the theoretical literature since Postal (1964), because of the absurdities they lead to in derived constituent structure, and so, the rule would have to be recast as an amalgam of deletion and adjunction to accord with the canons of the theory. What implications this might have for derived constituent structure, one can only wonder at. Much more interesting is the case of (2), the reduction transformation. The motivation for it is that, with a small number of exceptions, Gia's utterances were restricted in length to two morphemes. Yet, there was evidence, based on adults' interpretations of what the child was 'meaning', that she controlled structures which could only be clearly expressed in utterances which were three morphemes long. Briefly, the corpus of 1015 utterances, containing 451 that were two or more morphemes in length, included 15 interpretable as subject-verb strings, 23 interpretable as subject-object strings and 38 interpretable as verb-object strings. These interpretations are reflected in the theory of the child's syntactic competence by crediting her with the phrase-structure rules 1 and 3 in Figure 5.8, which allow the construction of derivations like that in Figure 5.9. This can be associated, by well-known principles,

S_1
N VP
N VB VP
etc.

Figure 5.9

with trees like that in Figure 5.10 from which the functional notions, 'subject-of', 'main verb-of' and 'direct object-of' can be derived as in Chomsky (1965).[9] The reduction transformation is then seen as operating on structures like Figure 5.10 and getting rid of one of the categories, while maintaining, in the theory of the child's competence, a level of representation at which it makes sense to credit her with these functional notions. The trouble is that, from the point of view of the general theory, the reduction transformation is not a possible transformational rule,

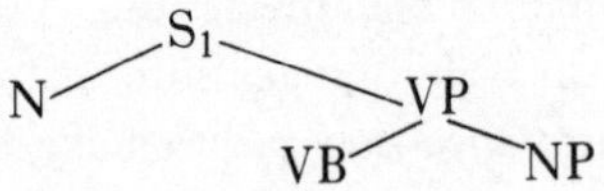

Figure 5.10

violating, as it does, the condition of recoverability of deletions (cf. 5.2). Informally, this condition states that material deleted by a transformational rule must either be specified lexical material or must leave a copy behind, thus being recoverable. Whether the condition is one which linguistic theory must insist upon is not a question to be settled here.[10] All I am anxious to point out is that, in embracing a rule which blåtantly violates this important condition, Bloom calls into question her interpretation of the theoretical literature on which she is, supposedly, basing her acquisition model. This leaves (3) for discussion and, so far as I can make out, this is a permissible format for a transformational rule, merely involving the adjunction of new material on the left of a category node.[11] The importance of the above remarks cannot be over-emphasised. The theoretical machinery being adopted cannot be manipulated at will and still inspire confidence. Whatever plausibility Bloom's suggestions get by virtue of their allegiance to the standard theory of transformational grammar must be vigorously disputed.

The grammar accounts for almost all the utterances in the second Gia corpus, exceptions being a number of three-term strings and some N + N constructions which were not consistent with any of the structures available from the grammar. With this success in mind, we can now turn to a consideration of my conditions with regard to the sequence of grammars (G_{G1}, G_{G2}).

One comment is worth making in connection with Condition I. If G_{G1} and G_{G2} are intended to be theories of the child's syntactic knowledge, then it might be more appropriate to remove the reduction transformation from G_{G2} and include it, or some analogous device, in a theory of linguistic performance, where it could be interpreted in terms of planning constraints or some similar notion.[12]

Condition II has already been discussed in some detail. Whether one agrees with the theory or not, Chomsky (1965) advances a consistent set of views on the nature of general linguistic theory, including speculation on the identity of syntactic categories and the types of rules to be found in grammars. Adopting the strategy of compartmentalising grammars, consider first syntactic categories.

Bloom's grammars are on firmer ground than Klima and Bellugi's in this respect. Gia's development can be represented by two inventories of syntactic categories:

G_{G1}: S, N, Q, VB
G_{G2}: S_1, S_2, N, Q, NP, VP, N, VB

and with the possible exception of the reference to two sentence-types in
G_{G2} these inventories are impeccable. The categories are all to be found in
respectable theoretical proposals and would probably be on most lists of
universal syntactic categories.[13]

Again, in the case of syntactic features, there seems to be little to take
exception to, apart from some of the obscurity already discussed, and we
have the following inventories for the two grammars:

G_{G1}: ± N, ± animate, ± quantifier (and, presumably, though
     Bloom does not mention it, ± VB)
G_{G2}: ± N, ± animate, ± quantifier, ± VB

In addition, the two grammars use the following sets of contextual
features:

G_{G1}: ± ____ N, ± *Hi* ____
G_{G2}: ± ____ VB, ± ____ NP, ±/d/ ____ , ±Q ____

and, as has already been made clear, problems arise here, because
included are feature-types which it is difficult to see having a place in any
general theory of grammar. I refer here, particularly, to the types
exemplified by ± *Hi* ____ and ±/d/ ____ , which surely go beyond the
bounds of what Chomsky had in mind for a set of contextual features. In
general, however, embracing a principle of charity, we might be tempted
to conclude that, such aberrations aside, G_{G1} and G_{G2} are constructed in
accordance with the general principles of Chomsky (1965), at least as far
as syntactic categories and syntactic features are concerned.

What now of syntactic rules? Here the position is much less encouraging. There are three rule-types to consider: phrase-structure rules,
lexicon-features rules and transformational rules. No problems arise with
the first type, rules of the second type are very heterogeneous with no clear
principles being evident in their construction,[14] and serious questions have
been raised above in connection with the examples of the third type
employed in the grammars. For rule-types, G_{G1} and G_{G2} are *not*
constructed in accordance with Chomsky (1965), nor, so far as I can see,
with any other set of well-articulated principles. The overwhelming
impression created by a close examination of the rules is that they are
purely *ad hoc* and motivated simply by a desire to accommodate as much
of the data as possible, while paying lip-service to the familiar theoretical
notions.

Given this damning diagnosis, it is, perhaps, unnecessary to pursue

Conditions III and IV in detail. It is, however, interesting that, in comparing G_{G1} and G_{G2}, Bloom feels that she can provide an affirmative answer regarding the satisfaction of Condition III. She says (p. 187): 'The Gia II grammar is more complex and reflects syntactic maturity in a number of important aspects – although the grammars are also similar in a number of important ways.' It should be apparent that, given the failure to adhere to any consistent theoretical framework, this is more a statement of faith based on intuition than a reasoned conclusion, and the extent to which this is true can be seen by again considering the grammars in terms of their different components. We find that Condition III applies and is satisfied in just those cases where departure from general theory is not radical.

Consider sets of syntactic categories in G_{G1} and G_{G2}. There is a simple increase in membership of these sets from the earlier to the later grammar with the exception of the replacement of S by S_1 and S_2. But the distinction between S_1 and S_2 is not vital to the proposals – it could be replaced by having optional expansions of a unitary S – and so, for sets of syntactic categories, Condition III applies and is satisfied.

Nor do syntactic features present any problems, as membership of this set remains static between G_{G1} and G_{G2}. Predictably, however, the contextual features are a complete mess. G_{G2} has more of these than G_{G1}, but any hopes we might have of comparing the two sets beyond this gross numerical measure founder on the peculiarities of the items involved. The kindest conclusion we can draw is that Condition III does not apply.

For rule-types, we can diagnose satisfaction of Condition III as G_{G2} contains 'transformational rules' and G_{G1} does not. I suspect that it is possible to make similar claims for the sets of *particular* phrase-structure rules involved in the two grammars, although Bloom does not present the grammars in a way which makes this easy to see.

To explore this matter a little further, consider the possibility of replacing rule 1, in the phrase-structure component of G_{G1}, with something like:

$$1'. \quad S \rightarrow \left\{ \begin{array}{c} \left(\binom{N}{Q} \right) + \left(\binom{NP}{VP} \right) \\ (Hi) + (N) \end{array} \right\}$$

and adding to the grammar the rules:

$2'. \quad NP \rightarrow N$

$3'. \quad VP \rightarrow V$

removing (iii) from the lexicon-feature rules. If we then amalgamate rules 1 and 2 from the phrase-structure component of G_{G2}, we get:

$$1''. \quad S \to \left\{ \begin{matrix} N + (Q) + \begin{Bmatrix} NP \\ VP \end{Bmatrix} \\ \\ Hi + N \end{matrix} \right\}$$

However, $1''$, like 1 in G_{G2}, does not allow for the possibility of utterance-initial *more*, which does occur in the corpus. So, better would be:

$$1'''. \quad S \to \left\{ \begin{matrix} \begin{Bmatrix} N + (Q) \\ Q \end{Bmatrix} + \begin{Bmatrix} NP \\ VP \end{Bmatrix} \\ \\ Hi + N \end{matrix} \right\}$$

Now, $1'''$ is simply $1'$ with the addition of the option of the generation of structures of the forms $N + Q + NP$ and $N + Q + VP$, i.e. $1'''$ can be seen as additively more complex than $1'$. It seems to me that a similar case could be made for the relationship between $2'$ and $3'$, on the one hand, and 3 and 4 from G_{G2}, on the other, but Bloom does not present enough data to make consideration of these possibilities worthwhile. All we are justified in concluding, therefore, is that, regarding particular phrase-structure rules, the case for increasing complexity between G_{G1} and G_{G2} is not clearly established.

The lexicon-feature rules only allow us to say that there are more of them in G_{G2} than in G_{G1} but the relationship between the two sets is not an additive one, and, finally, Condition III is vacuously satisified by 'transformational rules' as none of these occur in G_{G1}.

Do we approach explanation for any aspect of the transition between G_{G1} and G_{G2}? I shall restrict my consideration of this question to those parts of the development for which Condition III is satisfied: syntactic categories and syntactic rule-types.

For syntactic categories we are concerned with the question as to why we find the development schematised as:

$$\{S, N, Q, VB\} \to \{S, N, Q, VB\} \oplus \{NP, VP\}$$

rather than the development schematised as:

$$\{NP, VP\} \to \{S, N, Q, VB\} \oplus \{NP, VP\}$$

continuing to ignore differences between S_1 and S_2. Condition IV can be seen as partially satisfied via certain notional reflections on the status of the syntactic categories, and we might want to go so far as to call this a partial teleological explanation. Thus, we can argue that the phrasal categories (NP and VP) 'presuppose' their heads (N and V) and, therefore, that there are theory-internal reasons for why N precedes NP and V, VP developmentally. Such reasoning is not, of course, available for other pairs of categories in the inventories, hence the reference to 'partial' teleological explanation.

Again, we have a positive answer to the question raised by Condition IV in connection with rule-types because, as has been spelled out already, transformational rules assume the presence of phrase-structure rules in the theory and, therefore, the latter should appear developmentally before the former.[15]

In both cases, then, where Condition III is satisfied we can see at least a partial explanation for the order of development in terms of the logical structure of the theory. The fact remains, however, that Condition III is not satisfied in general and, more importantly, Condition II is also severely strained. The grammars Bloom presents for Gia have about the same status as the partial descriptions of stages of negation discussed in 5.2 – they are crucially weak in detail, although the broad outline appears to comply with established linguistic techniques.

When we turn to the two grammars Bloom offers for Eric, we find a similar set of problems to those discussed in detail above. I content myself here with merely listing some of the most obvious points which emerge from a detailed analysis. The interested reader can consult Atkinson (1978, pp. 229–41) for justification of these points.

(1) The lexicon for the first Eric grammar uses syntactic features. However, there are no rules introducing features in this grammar.

(2) One lexical entry, that for the verb *turn*, mentions a syntactic category which is nowhere introduced in the categorial part of the grammar.

(3) The lexicon provides no way of inserting lexical material under Pivot nodes which are introduced in the categorial part of the grammar. Thus, the lexicon both needs information which is *not* provided by the categorial part of the grammar and ignores information which *is* included in this component.

(4) The second Eric grammar contains a reduction transformation which has the same problems associated with it as that in the second Gia grammar. This remains true despite the fact that Eric's reduction transformation is restricted to operating only in negative sentences.

(5)   Lexical insertion is not handled uniformly in the second Eric grammar. Sometimes lexical items are introduced by phrase-structure rules and sometimes they come from the lexicon.

(6)   One of the alternatives Bloom offers for the second Eric grammar uses a 'feature representation'. This contains four rules, two of which are phrase-structure rules introducing lexical items in the manner of Chomsky (1957), one of which is a context-sensitive phrase-structure rule which should be in the phrase-structure component of the grammar (except that the remaining phrase-structure rules will never produce an appropriate context for it to operate in!) and the last of which appears to involve the contextually specified re-writing of a schwa-vowel as a lexical item.

(7)   On the basis of (6) it is clear that Condition II is not satisfied for the sequence of Eric's grammars.

(8)   By expanding the conventions used in the phrase-structure components of the two grammars, it is possible to see an approximate additive relationship between the two sets of phrase-structure rules, i.e. Eric simply adds to his stock of phrase-structure rules between the two samples and Condition III is satisfied with regard to this component of the grammars.

(9)   There is, however, no obvious way in which Condition IV can be satisfied for the sets of rules mentioned in (8). For example, there are no intrinsic ordering relationships in the rules which could be used to provide a teleological explanation.

As mentioned at the beginning of this section, other work of a similar nature to Bloom's does not appear to have as many obvious deficiencies. Atkinson (1978) examines in detail some of the proposals in Bowerman (1973) and concludes that, while there is room for discussion of Condition II, the author does pay more attention to general theory than does Bloom. Even given this, though, there is nothing in Bowerman's work to suggest that she has any interesting approach to Condition IV, either for those aspects of the development which satisfy Condition III or for those which do not, and this leaves her work in an unsatisfactory state, although, perhaps, descriptively sound.

5.4 Derivational complexity and the acquisition of transformations

Brown and Hanlon (1970) is an attempt to interpret the derivational theory of complexity, suggested and extensively investigated in experimental psycholinguistics, in a developmental context. At its crudest this theory claims that the more grammatical 'operations' there are involved in the generation of a sentence in a grammar, the more complex that sentence will be psychologically. Psychological complexity, typically, is indexed by some measure like time to respond with a truth-value judgement for a generic sentence, time to respond in a task of matching sentence content to picture content, ability to remember a sentence *verbatim*, etc (for an exhaustive survey of work in this area, see Fodor, Bever and Garrett 1974). In this crude form the derivational theory of complexity requires the assumption that each grammatical 'operation' contributes equally to psychological complexity, in order to give rise to experimental predictions, and this assumption has not been an attractive one for psycholinguists. Because of this, a more sophisticated version of the theory, the version investigated by Brown and Hanlon, was formulated which may be referred to as the derivational theory of *cumulative* complexity. According to this theory, a sentence S_1 is predicted to be psychologically more complex than a sentence S_2, if the generation of S_1 in the grammar requires all the operations employed in the derivation of S_2 plus some additional ones. This move to the more sophisticated version of the theory can be compared to my discussion of simplicity in Chapter 1, which gravitated towards the additive notion, because there is no way of weighing the relative simplicity of distinct theoretical entities.

Brown and Hanlon are concerned with eight sentence-types which are listed in Figure 5.11. In connection with these sentence-types and positive and negative tag questions, the authors formulate a set of transformational rules, which, while not identical to those found in any linguistic treatment of the sentences, acknowledges such works as Klima (1964), Katz and Postal (1964) and Chomsky (1965). No particular set of phrase-structure

1. SAAD   – *We had a ball*
2. Q   – *Did we have a ball?*
3. N   – *We didn't have a ball*
4. Tr   – *We did*
5. NQ   – *Didn't we have a ball*
6. TrQ   – *Did we?* (also used in positive tag questions)
7. TrN   – *We didn't*
8. TrNQ   – *Didn't we?* (also used in negative tag questions)

Figure 5.11 (adapted from Brown and Hanlon 1970, pp. 18–19; SAAD is simple active affirmative declarative, Q is question, N is negative and Tr is truncated) rules is assumed and the seven transformational rules which Brown and Hanlon deem necessary are:

TI.   Tag-question formation (optional)
TII.   Predicate truncation schema[16] (optional)
TIII.   Preverbal placement of *neg* (obligatory)
TIV.   Question transformation (obligatory)
TV.   Affixation (obligatory)
TVI.   *Do*-support (obligatory)
TVII.   Negative contraction (optional)

The reader is referred to p. 22 of Brown and Hanlon's article for a detailed presentation of each of these rules. In introducing them, they say (p. 21): 'We . . . offer these rules as a set of imperfect rules based on what we have been able to work out on our own.' A word or two of amplification is in order with respect to their status.

TI has two parts, both of which are essentially copying rules, with one being responsible for the generation of negative tags and the other for positive tags. As well as copying the original sentence, the rule introduces a feature [+ pro] to the subject NP in the new portion and, if a main verb is present, it is deleted in the tag. TII has already been mentioned (n. 16), but I might also point out that its optional status is problematic, given that it contains a term in the structural analysis of the rule (Pro) which is a trigger for the rule. TIII is a version of the familiar rule of *Neg*-placement, but the formulation leaves open the question of exactly how the *neg* is adjoined to the right of the auxiliary.[17] TIV is intended to be a version of subject-auxiliary inversion but is odd in that Q should not survive on the right-hand side of the rule as this amounts to allowing it to appear in terminal strings. TV is based on the well-known rule of affix-hopping, identical in most respects to the version formulated in Chomsky (1957), except that the *-en* suffix of perfect aspect is missing from the structural analysis of the rule.[18] The rule of *Do*-support is the well-known one and, finally, TVII, the rule of negative contraction, while clear enough in function, does not give us any reason why it should work. What the rule does is move a negative element out of one term of the structural analysis and adjoin it to the right of the Tense morpheme, but there is no indication in this description that the negative will thereby be contracted. TI – TVII thus contain some obscurity, but putting this aside for the moment, what can we say of the role they play in the generation of the eight sentence-types of Figure 5.11 plus positive and negative tags?

Brown and Hanlon suggest that the transformations involved in the generation of each sentence-type are as shown in Figure 5.12. From these analyses it is possible to derive a number of predictions concerning relative psychological complexity, in accordance with the derivational theory of cumulative complexity.[19] The psychological measure which Brown and Hanlon adopt is the age at which children show sufficient evidence to credit them with control of the grammatical knowledge involved in each of

SAAD TV
Q   TIV, TVI
N   TIII, TVI, TVII
Tr   TII, TVI
NQ   TIII, TIV, TVI, TVII
TrN   TII, TIV, TVI
TrQ   TII, TIV, TVI
Tag   TI, TIII, TIV (twice), TVII
TrNQ   TII, TIII, TIV, TVI, TVII
NTag   TI, TIII, TIV, TV, TVI, TVII

Figure 5.12

the sentence-types, and the claim is, to take a particular example, that TrNQ will be acquired later than N because, in their grammatical derivation, the former involve every rule involved in the generation of the latter plus some additional ones. These predictions are spectacularly confirmed by an analysis of the data collected from the three children in Brown's longitudinal study. Nineteen predictions are made for each child and, of 57 individual predictions, 47 are confirmed, 6 cannot be evaluated and only 4 go in the wrong direction.[20]

Brown and Hanlon's views can be seen as imposing a partial ordering on the eight sentence-types as shown in Figure 5.13. What this amounts to is a constraint on the possible orders of acquisition of sentence-types, such that the ordering:

(SAAD, Q, N, Tr, TrQ, NQ, TrN, TrNQ)

is possible, whereas the ordering:

(SAAD, Q, N, TrQ, Tr, NQ, TrN, TrNQ)

is not, because Tr is ordered before TrQ in Figure 5.13. The theory which is to explain this constraint is one which assumes as a domain of enquiry the child's syntactic knowledge and that the possession of syntactic knowledge can be explicated in terms of the child controlling, in some sense, transformational rules. It is sets of transformational rules which comprise the (partial) theories in which we are interested and it is

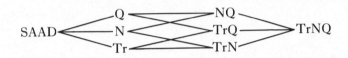

Figure 5.13

necessary to work out exactly what Brown and Hanlon's proposal amounts to in this connection. It might be thought likely that they are committed to a fixed linear order of acquisition of their seven rules, but, in fact, no such strong position emerges.

Under all possible orders of acquisition permitted by Figure 5.13, SAAD is acquired first. SAAD requires the operation of only one transformational rule, TV, and so we can say that there is a time t_1 at which the transformational component of the child's grammar contains only TV. Next, however, given Figure 5.13, the child may acquire *any* of Q, N and Tr and, depending on which he does acquire, he begins to use the transformational rules, TIV and TVI (for Q), TIII, TVI and TVII (for N) or TII and TVI (for Tr). But, of course, these possibilities exhaust the set of transformations under discussion except for TI.[21] So, all we can conclude is that there is a time t_2 at which the child not only uses TV but also TII, TIII, TIV, TVI, and TVII (I omit further discussion of TI), and we have development which can be schematised as:

$$TV \rightarrow TV \oplus \{TII, TIII, TIV, TVI, TVII\}$$

The reason we get this rather unexciting outcome is that the three sentence-types, Q, N and Tr, are not ordered relative to each other, in accordance with the theory of cumulative derivational complexity, and that, in their derivations, they use the full set of transformations under discussion. Unexciting or not, we have a developmental theory against which to test my conditions.

Condition II has already been discussed in some detail above.

Although several difficulties of detail were alluded to there, the only urgent question, to my mind, surrounds TII and its violation of the condition of recoverability of deletions. TIV, as presented, looks like a permutation transformation, but, generally, there appears to be somewhat closer adherence to standard practice than in the previous instances we have discussed. Condition III, the one which first impressions suggested might prove very interesting with a complex ordering of particular rules, is satisfied in a rather dull fashion as the above schema demonstrates.

What about Condition IV? The question it raises is why we find TV appearing before the rest of the transformational rules. It is difficult to imagine a perceptual or cognitive explanation for the primacy of this rule – the formal operations it employs are not remarkably simple when we compare it to other rules in the set. Nor are there many intrinsic ordering relations between the appropriate pairs of rules and so we cannot expect to find more than a partial teleological explanation. Brown and Hanlon *do* note a correlation between frequency of parental usage of the various sentence-types and order of development, suggesting this is a confounding factor for their 'transformational explanation' of this order. Of course, the line I am pursuing here does not accept the 'transformational explanation' as explanatory, but demands that we find some basis for it. Therefore, from my perspective, it is legitimate to view Brown and Hanlon's remarks on frequency of parental usage as constituting the first steps towards an environmental explanation of the acquisition of transformations. However, frequency of usage is a gross variable to base this sort of speculation on and whether there is enough structure in parental usage to make this sort of approach feasible remains unclear. (See Chapter 10 for more systematic discussion.) In paying attention to parental usage, Brown and Hanlon can also be seen as being sensitive to Condition V, although a much more detailed analysis of the input to the child would be necessary to tackle this problem with any confidence.

The conclusion is clear. Brown and Hanlon's theory concerning the development of a restricted set of sentence-types, interpreted as a theory of the successive acquisition of transformational rules, while, perhaps, satisfying Conditions I – III in a more or less convincing fashion, says little to inspire confidence in connection with Condition IV. As far as the theory is concerned, it would be equally plausible for the child to learn most of the transformations in the set under discussion before learning TV.[22]

5.5 Fourteen grammatical morphemes

Exhibiting a similar logic to that of the Brown and Hanlon study is Brown's analysis of the acquisition of a set of fourteen 'grammatical morphemes' (Brown 1973). Cumulative complexity (although not exclusively concerned with transformations) occupies a central place throughout the discussion (Brown 1973, 289ff). The fourteen morphemes investigated are:

(i)   present progressive inflection
(ii)   regular past tense morpheme
(iii)   irregular past tense morpheme
(iv)   regular third person singular present indicative morpheme
(v)   irregular third person singular present indicative morpheme
(vi)   regular plural inflection
(vii)   the possessive morpheme
(viii) the preposition *in*
(ix)   the preposition *on*
(x)   the 'article morpheme' (does not distinguish definite and indefinite articles)
(xi)   the uncontracted copula
(xii)   the contracted copula
(xiii) the uncontracted auxiliary
(xiv)   the contracted auxiliary

The constitution of this list and the arguments for splitting up some categories while leaving others intact will not concern me here (see Brown, pp. 300–13, for details).

Given a criterion for acquisition, whereby a morpheme is judged to be acquired when it appears in 90% or more of obligatory contexts, Brown, averaging rankings over three children, produced the summary of order of acquisition shown in Figure 5.14. Brown considered three possible determinants of this ordering: frequency of the morphemes in parental speech, semantic complexity of the morphemes and grammatical complexity of the morphemes. It is clear that the first of these is in the direction of an environmental explanation, and, at the outset, we can note that Brown found no basis for believing that frequency in parental speech was a determinant of acquisition order. Accordingly, it will receive no further discussion in this section. Each of the other two was a reasonably successful predictor, and I shall here restrict attention to Brown's semantic analysis. To take full account of the syntactic proposals, using Jacobs and Rosenbaum's (1968) grammar would be time-consuming and

Morpheme		Average Rank
1.	Present progressive	2.33
2–3.	*in, on*	2.50
4.	plural	3.00
5.	Past irregular	6.00
6.	Possessive	6.33
7.	Uncontractible copula	6.50
8.	Articles	7.00
9.	Past regular	9.00
10.	Third person regular	9.66
11.	Third person irregular	10.83
12.	Uncontractible auxiliary	11.66
13.	Contractible copula	12.66
14.	Contractible auxiliary	14.00

Figure 5.14 (from Brown 1973, p. 317)

tedious. Atkinson (1978, pp. 289–301) contains the first steps in such an analysis.

Brown's limiting himself to cumulative complexity restricts the scope of his investigation of the semantic determinants of order of acquisition in a way which is not necessary within my framework. I am anxious that the scope should not be restricted in this way and it will become apparent that Brown's considerations of cumulative complexity emerge as special cases in the treatment I shall give. The important thing to be clear about is that many of the suggestions I shall discuss are not Brown's but represent the sort of claim that someone, adopting his semantic proposals, would have to make, if they were to argue that those proposals provide *full* explanations of the order of development in Figure 5.14. Brown explicitly refuses to speculate along these lines on a number of occasions.

The nature of the semantic theory Brown resorts to is obscure. It appears to consist of little more than a set of notional semantic categories which play a loose role in characterising the meanings of the morphemes. Within the full set of morphemes, there are four pairs which do not involve any semantic contrast: regular and irregular past, contractible and uncontractible copula, regular and irregular third person, and contractible and uncontractible auxiliary. Taking the view that the acquisition of one member of each of these pairs should signal the acquisition of the relevant semantic notions which are vital to both members of the pair, we reduce the number of morphemes in the developmental order to ten, with each of the above pairs being represented by the morpheme which is acquired earlier as in Figure 5.15.[23] For each of these ten morphemes, Brown

1.	Present progressive
2.5.	*in*
2.5.	*on*
4.	Plural
5.	Past irregular
6.	Possessive
7.	Uncontractible copula
8.	Articles
9.	Third person regular
10.	Uncontractible auxiliary

Figure 5.15

provides a discussion of their semantics, essentially trying to isolate the dimensions of meaning which they encode. This discussion leads to Figure 5.16, where each morpheme is paired with its notional semantic definition. Development, in this domain of grammatical morphemes, can therefore be seen, partially, at any rate, as involving the successive acquisition and combination of semantic dimensions (cf. Chapters 3 and 4). We can represent this as a nine-stage process – not ten because *in* and *on* occupy the same position in the ranking – as in Figure 5.17. The development is now represented in a form to which my conditions can apply, and we presumably regard the domain of enquiry as something like the semantic knowledge (in the form of a partial lexicon) which makes the child's production and comprehension of the fourteen grammatical morphemes possible.

Condition II, not surprisingly as we return to semantics, is not satisfied in any clear way. We are not provided with anything like a theory of possible semantic dimensions, which could be seen as informing the child's progress from T_1 to T_9. Nevertheless, because of the extremely simple relationship between the successive theories in the sequence, it is possible to compare them and investigate the satisfaction of Condition III.

A moment's inspection reveals that Condition III is satisfied over the whole sequence, as each T_{i+1} contains everything in each T_i ($1 \leqslant i \leqslant 8$)

and, in addition, something else. The nature of what is added in the transition varies. It may, as in the transitions from T_1 to T_2, from T_2 to T_3, from T_3 to T_4, from T_4 to T_5 and from T_6 to T_7, involve a new semantic dimension. Alternatively, it may simply involve the novel combination of semantic dimensions which are already used in the system. This possibility is demonstrated by the transitions from T_5 to T_6, from T_7 to T_8 and from T_8 to T_9. We can anticipate that Condition IV will be approached differently under these two sets of circumstances.

Consider, then, those transitions which introduce a new combination of semantic dimensions already present in the system. It might be thought that these transitions can be teleologically explained but, while it is true

Morpheme		*Meaning*
1.	Present progressive	Temporary duration; (process-state)
2.5.	*in*	Containment
2.5.	*on*	Support
4.	Plural	Number
5.	Past irregular	Earlierness
6.	Possessive	Possession
7.	Uncontractible copula	Number; earlierness
8.	Articles	Specific-nonspecific
9.	Third person regular	Number; earlierness
10.	Uncontractible auxiliary	Temporary duration; number; earlierness; (process-state)

Figure 5.16 (from Brown 1973, p. 240). *Note.* The child's usage is taken as the yardstick against which the various dimensions are matched and the entries we have in the 'Meaning' column should be taken as based on this usage and not adult usage. So, for example, as well as signifying 'Earlierness' the past tense morpheme can be used in English to indicate 'Hypotheticalness' or some such when it is used in conditional clauses. However, there were no conditional clauses in the speech of the children at this time, and so this aspect of the past tense morpheme's meaning was not credited to the child. For the present progressive morpheme there was clear evidence that the child intended to refer to the temporary duration of events but no clear evidence that he controlled a semantic distinction between processes and states, although this additional possibility could not be ruled out. *In, on,* Plural and Possessive are self-explanatory. For the uncontractible copula the claim is that it encodes number (redundantly, this being marked in almost all cases in the subject of the sentence) and 'Earlierness' because there is a contrast between the present and past tense forms of the copula. Therefore, appropriate use of the copula presupposes acquaintance with these two semantic dimensions. Drawing heavily on the work of Karttunen (1968) and Maratsos (1976), Brown suggests that the children's use of articles demands that they be credited with knowledge of the specific-nonspecific dimension and, finally, the entries for third person regular and uncontractible auxiliary can be analysed and justified in the same way as for the uncontractible copula

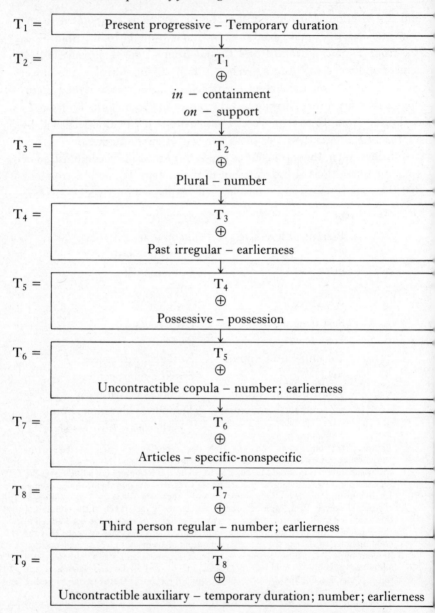

$T_1 =$ | Present progressive – Temporary duration

$T_2 =$ | T_1
$\oplus$
in – containment
on – support

$T_3 =$ | T_2
$\oplus$
Plural – number

$T_4 =$ | T_3
$\oplus$
Past irregular – earlierness

$T_5 =$ | T_4
$\oplus$
Possessive – possession

$T_6 =$ | T_5
$\oplus$
Uncontractible copula – number; earlierness

$T_7 =$ | T_6
$\oplus$
Articles – specific-nonspecific

$T_8 =$ | T_7
$\oplus$
Third person regular – number; earlierness

$T_9 =$ | T_8
$\oplus$
Uncontractible auxiliary – temporary duration; number; earlierness

Figure 5.17 *Note.* I have ignored the possibility of including Process-State as a semantic dimension as it has no bearing on subsequent discussion. It should be pointed out that the reason a stage-type theory like this can be constructed in this case whereas it could not for cumulative transformational complexity in 5.4 is that Brown does supply a near total ordering for the grammatical morphemes averaged across children, whereas Brown and Hanlon did not do this for the sentence-types they were interested in

that for the child to use a combination of semantic dimensions he must, in some sense, be acquainted with each of the components, it does not follow that he needs to have put them to use singly in his semantic system. This is, of course, a very general problem for teleological explanations and it seems reasonable to make the additional assumption that the child must *use* dimensions singly before he uses them in combination. Then, the transition from, say T_5 to T_6, can be explained in terms of the logic of the theory, and it is significant that it is this sort of case which lends itself to analysis in terms of cumulative semantic complexity. Because of this, Brown feels able to conclude that the fact that the Uncontractible copula follows Plural and Past irregular in the acquisition order is determined by semantic complexity. Much the same goes for the transition from T_8 to T_9, where it is necessary to assume that the child can only use combinations of three dimensions after he has used combinations of two, but the transition from T_7 to T_8 is rather more problematic. The combination which appears in T_8 is a combination of Number and Earlierness, but this same combination has already appeared in T_6. Thus, there is nothing in the logic of the theory to explain why one morpheme, involving this combination of semantic dimensions, should be acquired later than another which involves exactly the same combination, a fact which Brown is well aware of and which arises anyway in connection with the reduction of the original list of fourteen morphemes to ten.

Consider next those transitions where it is the addition of a new semantic dimension which is crucial, rather than a novel combination of previously acquired dimensions. On whether the theory has any explanatory status in this situation, Brown is pessimistic. He says (p. 421):

There is no general theory of semantic complexity that makes it possible to assign complexity values to the seven independent unitary meanings. It is my impression that Specific-nonspecific is the most complex of these, in some sense or other, and so perhaps the fact that it is the last of the meanings to be acquired is an indication that semantic complexity is a determinant of acquisition order. Without a theory of complexity, however, which predicts the difficulty of the Specific-nonspecific meaning, no real importance attaches to this result.

We can see exactly what would be involved in diluting Brown's pessimism if we consider the transition from T_1 to T_2 in connection with the satisfaction of Condition IV. We are required to provide an explanation for why we get the development schematised as:

Temporary duration $\rightarrow$ Temporary duration $\oplus$ {Containment, Support} rather than the alternative:

{Containment, Support} → Temporary duration ⊕ {Containment, Support}

and there is nothing in the notional theory of semantics Brown adopts to provide such a reason. If there were, this would be an answer to Brown's plea for a theory of semantic complexity, but, whereas some sort of theory-internal explanation appears to be the only type he considers, in the scheme I am using there are two others. Unfortunately, however, there is no reason to believe that the pursuit of either of them would be rewarding in our current state of ignorance. Brown himself argues against a simple environmental approach and, while an attempt to reduce the development of semantic dimensions to, say, a theory of cognitive development may lead to the formulation of interesting questions, we are unlikely to be able to make much progress in answering them for the moment.[24]

6 *Semantic approaches to syntactic development*

During the first half of the 1970s there was a significant move away from a formal emphasis in studies of the acquisition of grammar. There are at least three identifiable reasons for this.

First, workers in this area were becoming increasingly aware of the difficulties involved in representing the child's syntactic knowledge without taking account of what he meant by his structured utterances. This was already apparent in the work of Bloom, discussed in the previous chapter, but, whereas she remained within a formal framework, merely demanding that her syntactic representations be rich enough to capture the relevant semantic distinctions, others were more radical, demanding that processes should make direct reference to semantic representations. An intermediate position in this regard was adopted by some, most notably Bowerman (1973) in her adaptation of Fillmore's (1968) case-grammar framework, whereby, although the child was credited with representations which were more obviously semantic than those arising in the context of the standard theory, formal criteria were systematically used to justify those representations. As is well known, doctrinaire support for this sort of move became available in the theoretical literature with the shift away from standard theory (Chomsky 1965) towards case grammar and, more centrally, generative semantics (McCawley 1968, Postal 1970, Lakoff 1971, 1972).

It is important at the outset to distinguish two strategies which were adopted within this change of emphasis. On the one hand, such scholars as Bowerman continued to attempt to produce complete statements of the child's grammatical competence, i.e. rules which determined well-formedness conditions on semantic structures and additional rules which converted these into the child's output, these latter being based on transformational formalism. On the other hand, workers were content to list a number of semantic relations, often drawing their theoretical vocabulary from case grammar. The claim that small children, in some sense, controlled these semantic relations was not backed up by an explicit treatment of how the relations were converted to surface utterances. Representative of this sort of work are Slobin (1970) and Bloom, Lightbown and Hood (1975), and the correspondences across studies emerging from these enterprises are examined and summarised by Brown (1973) and Bowerman (1976).

A second major stimulus, taking the study of developmental syntax in the direction of semantics, was the necessity, felt by some, to render more comfortable the competence–performance distinction. Intuitively, it is clear that, when a small child (or an adult) utters something, he begins with an intention to convey a certain message, rather than with an abstract symbol in a formal grammar. Therefore, a theory which is to mirror the child's syntactic performance must begin with a representation of the child's intended meaning. Formal processes operating upon this representation will convert it to something resembling the child's utterance but there is no necessity for these formal processes to resemble the linguist's transformational rules (Schlesinger 1971, 1974, 1975). The role of a theory of syntactic competence, as a psychological model, within this approach is opaque; arguably, it is non-existent.

Finally, the third reason for incorporating semantic considerations into syntax concerns one-word utterances. Once the domain of semantic relations is available, it becomes possible to re-open the holophrase question: can the child's one-word utterances (or even his pre-linguistic vocal behaviour) be seen as involving sentence-like structures? Here much will depend on how the theorist construes his task in terms of the distinction drawn earlier between merely specifying semantic relations and not only doing this but also attempting to define processes operating on these representations. If he adopts the latter, more ambitious position, he is likely to be committed to the holophrase position (e.g. Ingram 1971). If, however, he is content to merely list relational meanings occurring in single-word utterances, his position is more flexible in this respect (see, e.g., Dore 1975, Greenfield and Smith 1976, Greenfield 1978a for relevant discussion).

Not suprisingly, as we return to semantics, the availability of a general theory of relational meanings becomes an overriding consideration. Against this, however, it was generally felt that the problems surrounding the acquisition of syntax would become more readily intelligible in terms of the child's general cognitive development; the mystery of how the child acquires abstract deep-structures which are never available to him in his environment would be removed, and with this one of the strongest arguments for linguistic nativism would be de-fused. The extent to which this optimism was justified will be of central concern in this chapter (see also Chapter 8).

6.1 Inventories of relational meanings for two-word utterances

There are available in the literature a fairly large number of suggestions for inventories of semantic relations encoded by the small child. Some of these are intended to apply, not only to structured utterances, but also to single words and this will be my concern in 6.3; others constitute the input to a set of rules which map them onto child forms and I shall not explicitly consider them here.[1] There are, however, proposals which are less ambitious in these respects, limiting themselves to structured utterances and remaining aloof from the 'mapping problem'.[2] It is this sort of proposal with which I shall be concerned here.

One of the earliest suggestions of this type with which I am familiar appears in Slobin (1970). There, in the course of a discussion of universals of language development and a presentation of data from English, German, Finnish, Russian, Samoan and Luo, he offers the following semantic categories from Stage I (Brown 1973) speech:

(i) ostension or naming (*that car*)
(ii) demand or request (*more milk*)
(iii) negation (*not eat*)
(iv) possession (*my shoe*)
(v) question (*where ball?*)
(vi) subject-verb (*Bambi go*)
(vii) subject-object (*mommy book*)
(viii) object-verb (*hit ball*)
(ix) subject-locative (*baby highchair*)
(x) modify, qualify (*pretty dress*)

All of these categories are illustrated with examples from the six languages from which Slobin had data, and, at the time of presenting these findings, Slobin contented himself with description, although he does propose that the relational meanings have their source in the child's general cognitive development. It is, of course, readily apparent that the vocabulary used in describing the relations (i)–(x) is a pastiche of syntactic and semantic terminology and Slobin himself would admit that there is little theoretical foundation for this particular set. Also, he does not propose any order of development within (i)–(x) and, while we might remark that there are obvious omissions which, presumably, only appear later (e.g. verb–indirect object, verb–locative), I do not intend to pursue this analysis in detail. Brown (1973) offers a much fuller treatment in similar terms.[3]

Brown distinguishes *operations of reference* from *minimal two-term semantic relations*. Operations of reference are characterised by the presence (in a two-word utterance) of one word, the sense of which can be seen as operating on the sense of the other. Thus, for the utterance *more shoe*, intuitively we feel that we do not have here the encoding of a semantic relation between two entities, but rather a modification of the sense of one of the expressions, viz. *shoe*. *More shoe* illustrates one of the operations of reference, *recurrence*, and the others are nomination (e.g. *that car*) and nonexistence (e.g. *no dolly*). Together these three operations account for a large proportion of the words which occur most frequently in combination with other words in Stage I speech.

Minimal two-term semantic relations do not have the asymmetry of operations of reference – they do appear to be genuinely relational. The list of such relations which Brown found to be prevalent in Stage I speech runs to eight items: (1) Agent–action; (2) Action–object; (3) Agent–object; (4) Action–locative; (5) Entity–locative; (6) Possessor–possessed; (7) Entity–attributive; (8) Demonstrative–entity. There are a number of remarks to be made in connection with this set.

(a) Along with the operations of reference, there is a good deal of notional overlap between Brown's categories and Slobin's. In fact, identifying Slobin's Subject with either Agent or Entity, the overlap is almost total, except that Brown has no Question category and Slobin does not recognise a Recurrence category, assimilating instances of recurrence to Demand or Request.[4]

(b) It is a *semantic* inventory, carrying no implications for the mode of expression of a particular relation. So, for example, the order in which the *relata* are mentioned in the list is not significant.

(c) There is some overlap in the assignment of instances to operations of reference and minimal two-term semantic relations. For example, instances of *more* + N will be treated as manifesting both Recurrence and Entity–attributive. Thus, the two schemes of categorisation are not exclusive and should not be viewed as alternatives.

(d) The minimal two-term relations exhausted some 70% of Stage I speech in Brown's data.

(e) The remainder of Stage I two-word utterances are made up of: (i) low-frequency semantic relations (e.g. instrumental, benefactive); (ii) infrequent and apparently uncomprehending use of forms; (iii) idiosyncratic and inflexible terms. From the point of view of the theory Brown offers, (i)–(iii) are ignored.

(f) Later development consists of concatenation of three terms (e.g. Agent–action–object) or embedding of a complex NP term inside another relation (e.g. (Entity–attribute)–locative).

What are we to make of Brown's proposals as part of a developmental theory? First, it is clear that he does not present a developmental theory in an explicit fashion (contrast the discussion in 6.3 below in this respect). He limits himself to noting that there are certain things which adults talk about but which are not taken account of by the inventory he provides (e.g. hypothetical situations, temporal relations). Presumably, he could also be seen as committed to the view that the marginal semantic relations mentioned above under (e) develop later than the eight in his chosen set, but Brown himself is eager to point out the likelihood of this relative infrequency arising from other sources (e.g. sampling). Finally, Brown does discuss the phenomenon mentioned under (f) above in terms of cumulative complexity (cf. 5.5) and I shall return to this briefly below.

It follows from this discussion that the developmental conditions of Chapter 1 are not going to be applicable to Brown's proposals in any general fashion. However, there is, perhaps, some benefit to be gained from examining their applicability, even if this is somewhat attenuated.

Condition II was presented as a developmental condition in Chapter 1, involving the comparison of *two* theories in the light of some general theory in the relevant domain. One sense in which a developmental theory could fail to satisfy Condition II arose if there were *no* general theory informing theory construction, and, clearly, this can be examined in a non-developmental way. Looking to Brown's two inventories, it is apparent that there is no general theory of semantic relations to which he subscribes. For the minimal two-term semantic relations, there are similarities between some of the terms employed and the vocabulary of case grammar, as developed, for example by Fillmore (1968) and Chafe (1970), and Brown is quick to point this affiliation out. But the similarities cannot be pushed too far and a number of items which appear in the eight relations are not primitives in case-grammar systems. So, for example, Fillmore would not distinguish an object in an Agent–object relation from an entity in an Entity–locative relation. Again, Possessor–possessed would translate into Fillmore's system as Dative–Objective and similar remarks apply to others of the minimal two-term semantic relations. Of course, there is no reason why Fillmore's system should be able to be taken over and applied, without modification, to developmental problems. But, if we adopt a modification-strategy, we must maintain awareness of how the system is thought to develop and, if we find ourselves in a situation where recognition of the parent linguistic theory is no more than token, we cannot look to this linguistic theory for respectability. We are left with a notional set of semantic relations and their plausibility emerges primarily from their appropriateness in *describing* data.[5]

Strictly speaking, no further conditions can be tested against Brown's theory, but it would be doing less than justice to his position to let matters rest here, for he believes that he has an *explanation* for the make-up of his two inventories. This explanation, while clearly not an explanation for why a particular item precedes another in development, does attempt to say why we find just *these* operations of reference and minimal two-term relations as the first in language development. It does *not* address other possible relations and operations which do not appear at this stage and provide a reason for relative late emergence. The argument involves a cognitive reduction and reference to the Piagetian sensori-motor period.

Note, first, anticipating the discussion of Chapter 8, that to argue from a set of meanings to cognition is not, in itself, of much interest. If the child controls a particular meaning in his semantic system, and if we believe that an intelligible distinction can be drawn between meanings and concepts, it would seem to follow automatically that he also controls the relevant concept. This concept, presumably, is the product of general cognitive development. However, this is not to say that we have an appropriate *theory* of cognitive development which recognises the concept in question and to which we can relate the semantic development. The strength and interest of Brown's proposal is that he believes that, in this case, there is such a theory available, that of Piaget.

Let us attempt to see what is involved in Brown's claim. The semantic theory which he adopts has a number of primitives but very little formal structure; therefore, we focus attention on the primitives. Brown has this to say (pp. 236–8):

Nomination and recurrence both presume the ability to recognise objects and actions. Nonexistence presumes the ability to anticipate objects and actions. . . . Recognition, anticipation based on signs, the concept of an enduring object . . . are all developed in the period of sensori-motor intelligence . . . The productive, freely combinatorial use of agent, action and object constructions would seem, minimally, to presume the ability to distinguish an action from the object of the action and the self from other persons and objects. Piaget judges that mental life begins with an undifferentiated world in which none of these distinctions is made. The Stage I [Piagetian stage – RMA] infant's reflexes are exercised on objects but not clearly distinguished from them. The object begins to emerge as an independent entity only when it becomes co-ordinated with multiple action schemas.

There are at least three points which suggest that Brown's argument achieves less than he hopes for.

(a) The sort of reduction which Brown attempts cannot, in itself, constitute an *explanation* for why we find the linguistic categories we do in Stage I. What Brown does is identify prerequisites for the relevant semantic relations in the sensori-motor period but a prerequisite is not an explanation. A similar point is made by Edwards (1973) and, in a different context, by Dore (1978).

(b) It is not clear that the categories with which the child emerges from the sensori-motor period are at the appropriate level of generality for Brown's argument, i.e. Brown requires a general category of agent, a general category of object, etc. and not a child who knows that a *particular* individual is capable of initiating action or that a *particular* object endures through space-time. This, of course, raises the question as to whether the categories recognised in the minimal two-term semantic relationships are, themselves, at the appropriate level of generality for capturing what the child knows (see Bowerman 1976).

(c) There are, in the set of minimal two-term relations, some which are not discussed by Brown. It follows from this that the attempted cognitive reduction is, at best, partially successful. In particular, I would draw attention to the relations, Possessor–possessed and Entity–attribute, which are not approached by anything Brown says in his discussion.[6]

Of course, none of these points is sufficient to demonstrate the incorrectness of Brown's claim. However, it should be apparent that a more sophisticated argument than any Brown presents will be necessary to establish the position.

Before leaving this discussion of Brown's work, I would like to briefly mention his treatment of cumulative complexity in Stage I speech. Very simply, a three-term relation such as Agent–action–object is seen as composed from (and, thereby, 'presupposes') two two-term relations, Agent–action and Action–object. Therefore, the prediction, based on the logical structure of the theory, is that the three-term relations will follow, developmentally, appropriate pairs of two-term relations. This prediction is borne out and, thus, the order of development can be seen as teleologically explained.

6.2 Early grammar from a generative semantics perspective

Of the semantic treatments of early grammatical development which not only pay attention to the meanings which the child's structured utterances convey, but also take some view on how these meanings are mapped onto surface forms, Schlesinger's 'intention-marker and realisation rule' model has already been mentioned (see n. 1). Many other proposals of this nature operate within a case-grammar framework (e.g. Bowerman's grammar for Seppo at MLU 1.42 and Brown's case grammar for late Stage I English) and generally the agreement between these suggestions and the general theory on which they are based is reasonably close (although cf. Bowerman's use of verbless propositions and subsequent reconstrual of case-relations). Unfortunately, neither Bowerman nor Brown presents us with a series of case grammars against which my conditions could be tested. Further, as already mentioned, the inadequacies of these theories are of a similar type to those covered fully in the previous chapter. For these reasons, I have decided to concentrate, in this section, on some ideas which have a rather different 'flavour', the treatment of early syntactic development using a generative semantics model, put forward by Antinucci and Parisi (1973, 1975).

Antinucci and Parisi's model consists of three components: a specification of a set of well-formed semantic structures in predicate–argument form, a lexicon which is involved in the substitution of lexical material for semantic configurations, and a transformational syntax. In their 1975 paper the authors present the set of data given in Figure 6.1, along with contextual information to aid interpretation. The data come from a six-month period in the development of an Italian child.[7] They then suggest, taking account of contexual information, that all of these utterances have the same meaning, which can be represented as in Figure 6.2. The argument slots, in each case, are filled by appropriate representations of subject, direct object and indirect object, e.g. *Claudia, pencil* and *mother* for (1) in Figure 6.1. What are the important features of this account?

First, Antinucci and Parisi appear to subscribe to the view that, throughout the six-month period under discussion, there is *no* semantic development in the child. The structure of Figure 6.2 is available to the

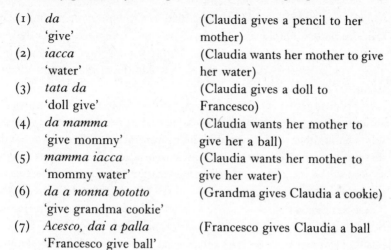

(1)	*da* 'give'	(Claudia gives a pencil to her mother)
(2)	*iacca* 'water'	(Claudia wants her mother to give her water)
(3)	*tata da* 'doll give'	(Claudia gives a doll to Francesco)
(4)	*da mamma* 'give mommy'	(Claudia wants her mother to give her a ball)
(5)	*mamma iacca* 'mommy water'	(Claudia wants her mother to give her water)
(6)	*da a nonna bototto* 'give grandma cookie'	(Grandma gives Claudia a cookie)
(7)	*Acesco, dai a palla* 'Francesco give ball'	(Francesco gives Claudia a ball)

Figure 6.1 (from Antinucci and Parisi 1975, pp. 190–1)

child right through this period. Second, although they are not explicit about this, there is nothing to suggest that there will be any *systematic* change in the lexicon throughout this period. That the child lexicalises *da* in (1) is, from the point of view of the model, completely accidental – she could equally well have lexicalised *mamma*. Third, since transformations appear to play no part in the structures Antinucci and Parisi are concerned with, there is no change in this component of the grammar in the six-month period.[8] Thus, there are no changes at all in the child's semantically based grammar in six months! But this strikes one as immediately counter-intuitive; the child's output does change, so how do the authors account for this?

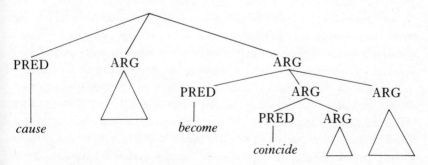

Figure 6.2 (from Antinucci and Parisi 1975, p. 191)

Antinucci and Parisi propose that there is a constraint on the number of lexicalisations a child can perform in one utterance. This number increases from one (in (1) and (2) of Figure 6.1) to three (in (6) and (7)). The overall theory, then, requires this additional component of constraints. And this is not all.

In order to represent the difference between Claudia saying *mamma da* as her mother gives her something and her saying the same thing when she wants her mother to give her something, Antinucci and Parisi propose that the child's semantic representations should also include a performative structure. Accordingly, the first interpretation of *mamma da* is assigned the representation of Figure 6.3(a) and the second, that of Figure 6.3(b).[9] These structures too are assumed to be available to the child right from the beginning of syntactic development, so again, there is no hint of grammatical development in the relevant period. Does this lack of development also characterise later stages? Antinucci and Parisi claim that it does not and propose three additional structural processes which only appear later. These are adverbials, noun modifiers and embedded sentences. What is intended to distinguish the structures underlying these constructions from those of earlier periods is that they each involve sentential structures as arguments of predications. So, it is clear that we do have a developmental theory of a sort with changes taking place, not only in the constraints on lexicalisation, but also in the well-formedness conditions on semantic structures.

General objections to Antinucci and Parisi's ideas can be found in Schlesinger (1974) and Greenfield and Smith (1976). It seems to me that most of these objections, concerning the justification of the elaborate structures we have seen and a failure to distinguish cognitive from semantic representations, are well directed and I will not rehearse them here. Instead I shall restrict myself to some more specific points.

The general theory to which Antinucci and Parisi wish to refer their grammatical proposals is some version of generative semantics – which version is never made clear and see n. 8. However, in publications with which I am familiar, there is no attempt to specify a set of well-formedness conditions on semantic structures, nor is there any suggestion as to how lexical insertion works. What we are offered is structures, of the sort exemplified in Figures 6.2 and 6.3 and, without some more formal justification of these structures, it is difficult to see them as anything more than a pseudo-formalism for representing the authors' intuitions about what children mean. Certainly, the respectability which references to

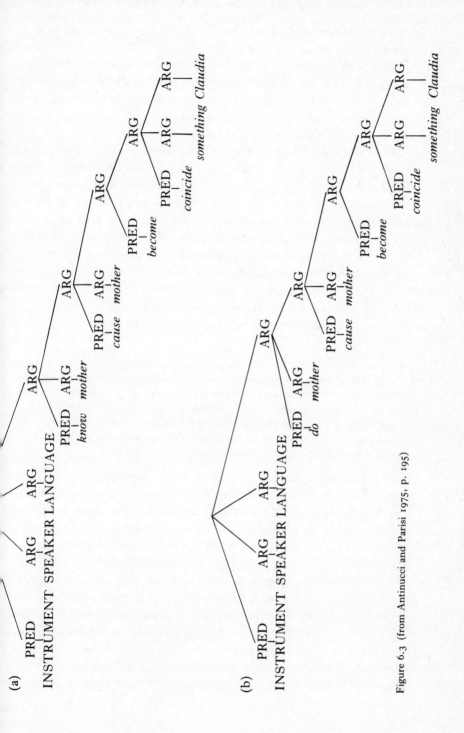

Figure 6.3 (from Antinucci and Parisi 1975. p. 195)

predicate–argument structures might be thought to give rise to is not earned and what is alarming is that there is nothing in Antinucci and Parisi's work to suggest that they are aware that such respectability *has* to be earned. That the parent theories from which the authors are drawing their stock of predicates are often no better in this regard should not be seen as providing an excuse. Let us assume, however, for the sake of argument, that Condition II is satisfied.

For Condition III, within the initial six-month period, we have already confronted the rather odd situation of no development in the most relevant parts of the theory. The only development seems to involve a relaxation on the constraint on lexicalisation and I see this as a relatively minor and uninteresting aspect of the overall proposal. Looking to later development, however, we find an increase in the range of structures available to the child and it is, perhaps, possible to view these as additions to an existing stock of structures. Why do these additions appear relatively late?

It is possible to glean two suggestions from Antinucci and Parisi's writings. One is very general and appears to see some necessary priority in what is cognitive over what is peculiarly linguistic. They say (1975, p. 200):

It can be contended that the information corresponding to the predicate-argument tree is, both in form and content, part of the general cognitive information of the speaker, whereas the additional information contained in the semantic representation of sentences is specific to the linguistic or communicative function . . . the articulation of the predicate-argument tree into performative and proposition, nucleus and adverbials, main configuration and associated configurations, would specifically belong to man as language user.

But there is no argument for this contention. Correspondingly, there is no reason to accept it. A more detailed explanation may be approached along the lines already alluded to above. Recall that the claim is that the late-developing structures all require sentential arguments. It would appear that the way is open for the construction of a teleological argument: the child must first construct simple sentences before he can employ such sentences in more elaborate logical structures. But, unfortunately, this leads Antinucci and Parisi to a totally *ad hoc* restriction, as the structures they offer in Figure 6.3 already involve sentential embedding as the final argument of INSTRUMENT. There is, therefore, no formal explanation within the theory for why performatives appear before, e.g. adverbials. Nor is the general contention of the passage cited above any use in this respect, as both performative–proposition and adverb–nucleus are seen as

distinctions only relevant in the language-specific part of the
Insofar as Antinucci and Parisi offer a developmental theory at a
not satisfy Condition IV.

One is left with a feeling of deep dissatisfaction in connection v
particular proposal. The specification of an inventory of semantic r⸺᷍᷍ᴜᴏns
is blatantly modest but the construction of logical structures underlying
early child speech has an aura of grandness about it. That Antinucci and
Parisi do little more than offer the beginnings of a semantic inventory and
that they make a considerably worse job of justifying it than most of their
contemporaries, while at the same time manipulating logical symbols, can
only contribute to mystification.

6.3 Semantic relations in one-word utterances

The best-known theory of recent years which ascribes rich semantic
interpretations to one-word utterances is that of Greenfield and Smith
(1976).[11] They are at pains to point out that the relations they posit for
such utterances are not initially found in sentence-like structures. They
say (p. 63): 'at the outset of language development the base structure is
not composed of words but consists of a structured perception of real (or
imagined) entities and relations'. Even more clearly, Greenfield (1978a),
in her reply to Dore (1975), takes him to task for aligning Greenfield and
Smith with the holophrase camp, saying (p. 347):

Our view is that at the single-word stage the child may construct complex
messages, not because the word is a sentence, but because the child combines the
single word with nonverbal elements such as gesture, action, object and intonation. These combinations can, in our view, occur because the single word is from
the beginning inserted in a cognitive–perceptual–action framework.

The advantages of this approach are that, according to Greenfield and
Smith (pp. 16–17): 'a semantic approach to language which derives
grammar from relations among perceived aspects of the real world opens
the way to a theoretical treatment of one-word speech as *structurally
continuous* with later grammatical development' (my emphasis – RMA),
and from this it is apparent that, just as one-word utterances are seen as
originating in a non-sentential base, so too for later developing structured
utterances. In this respect, Greenfield and Smith share Schlesinger's
emphasis, and it is not clear that they would wish to see the child as
developing anything like a traditional syntactic competence.[12]

For their study of the one-word utterances of two children, Greenfield and Smith draw up a list of twelve semantic relations. These are seen as being (p. 50): 'roughly those of Fillmore (1968)' and are listed with minimal exemplification below:

(1) *(Pure) Performative* – utterances that occur as part of the child's action (e.g. *bye bye* as the child waves).

(2) *Volition* – a particular kind of performative with the basic function of obtaining some desired response (e.g. *mama* to request something and not necessarily addressed to mother, *no* to reject something).

(3) *Performative object* – divided into
(a) *Indicative object* – refers to the object of some indicative act (e.g. *doggie* as the child points at dog)
and
(b) *Volitional object* – refers to the object of a demand (e.g. *banana* when reaching for a banana) and includes vocatives.

(4) *Agent* – refers to a person decisively connected with an action or change of state. Animacy is criterial for assigning expressions to this category in the study.

(5) *Action or State of an Agent* – refers to an action or state which *requires* an agent (e.g. *eat* or *down* as child climbs).

(6) *Action or State of an Object* – refers to an action or state which does not require an agent (e.g. *on* to record playing, *down* as ball is dropped).

(7) *Object* – refers to an object decisively involved in an action or change of state and which is affected by that action or change of state (e.g. *ball* as ball is thrown).

(8) *Dative* – refers to the animate being who is the recipient or experiencer of an action or state (e.g. *daddy* as ball is given to daddy).

(9) *Object associated with another Object or Location* – refers to an object which is often not present in connection with an object or location that *is* present (e.g. child says *poo* when indicating clean bottom).

(10) *Animate being associated with an Object or Location* – as 9 except restricted to animates (e.g. instances which are interpreted as expressing possessors).

(11) *Location* – refers to location of state or action (e.g. *chair* as child places toy on chair).

(12) *Modification of event* – involves a word that modifies an entire event (e.g. *again* when the child wants an event repeated).

Table 6.1. *Rank orderings for the acquisition of twelve semantic relations by two children (adapted from Greenfield and Smith 1976, pp. 69–70)*

Category	Order of appearance for Nicky	Order of appearance for Matthew
Performative	1	1
Performative object	2	2
Volition	3	3
Agent	4	6
Action or state of Agent	5	7
Object	6	5
Action or state of Object	7	8
Dative	8	4
Object associated with another object or location	9	9
Animate being associated with object or location	10	11
Location	11	10
Modification of event	12	12

Greenfield and Smith provide detailed discussion of each of their procedures for assigning utterances to one or the other of these categories. It is not my purpose to review these arguments here.

The first appearance of each of the twelve categories is noted and, on this basis, a developmental order is postulated for each child. This ordering is summarised in Table 6.1. The rank order correlation between these two orderings is highly significant and if the categories are grouped as indicated by the horizontal lines in Table 6.1, it is perfect. This generalised ordering can be summarised as:

(1) performative categories
(2) categories involving a relation between an action and a single entity
(3) categories involving a relation between two entities
(4) categories involving a modification of events.[13]

There is, then, little doubt that here we are dealing with a substantial developmental theory, based either on the orderings of the two children or on the ordering which abstracts away from differences between them, and, in this respect, Greenfield and Smith's proposal compares favourably with what we have come across earlier in this chapter.

Whether this theory satisfies Condition II depends largely on how seriously we take the reference to Fillmore (1968). It is evident that not all the category labels are taken from Fillmore's proposals and it is probably more appropriate to say that Greenfield and Smith have induced their categories from their data while keeping Fillmore's case-categories in mind. They do discuss the problem of deciding on what distinctions to draw in a set of semantic categories and enumerate a number of criteria relevant to this question (operational distinguishability, productivity and independence of specific vocabulary). However, they do not recognise the necessity for a general theory which supplies 'theoretically distinguishable' semantic functions against a background of which these criteria can operate. One is left with the impression that what is 'theoretically distinguishable' is at the whim of the investigator.

Regardless of our feelings on Condition II, Condition III is satisfied in an additive fashion. As the child matures through the one-word stage, more categories are added to his existing stock and there is no suggestion that earlier categories disappear.

Condition IV is treated seriously by Greenfield and Smith and they search for a reductive explanation for their order of development. Before examining this in detail, however, I would like to briefly mention the possibility of a teleological explanation for the early appearance of Indicative objects (they preceded Volitional objects for both children). The function of utterances involving Indicative objects is to draw the addressee's attention to the object indicated and it is possible to view this as a logical prerequisite for most of the other categories in Greenfield and Smith's list. To give just one example, it is not possible to successfully 'say' that an agent is initiating an action unless one knows that one's addressee can identify the agent. It is possible to ensure that he can by drawing his attention to the object performing the agent function, and, in this sense, the manipulation of attention in the Indicative object category could be seen as logically prior to talking about agents. This argument will appear again in Chapter 7, where it will receive a much more detailed treatment.

Greenfield and Smith's reductive explanation is in two stages. The first of these is rather similar to the argument from Brown, examined in 6.1, and is merely intended to establish the *availability* of the relevant cognitive notions at a stage before the child begins to encode them linguistically (recall that this was as far as Brown could go because he did not specify an order of development within his operations of reference and minimal two-term semantic relations). Basic to their scheme of semantic categories, they claim, is the distinction between *entity* and *relation*. Regarding the availability of this distinction, they say (p. 62): 'there is abundant evidence that such categories have reality for the child even at the very beginnings of life', and they go on to cite studies of perceptual and cognitive development which substantiate this claim.

More specifically, Greenfield and Smith need evidence on the availability of notions akin to Fillmore's case categories, in particular, in their scheme, Agent, Object, Location and Action. This they find in Bower's (1966) work on the perception of the animate–inanimate distinction (see also now, Trevarthen 1974, Trevarthen and Hubley 1978) and his claim that infants distinguish objects from locations half-way through their first year. Finally, we are told that early infant behaviour is clearly consistent with a distinction between noticing something and wanting something being available to the child. Thus, the prerequisites for the distinction between Indicative and Volitional is also present.

This looks like a decent attempt at the first stage of reductive explanation. There are, of course, gaps in their set of categories which the above brief discussion does not account for (e.g. categories 8, 9, 10 and 12) but, by the normal standards operating in this area, their reasoning is impressive.

Turning to the second stage of their argument, accepting Slobin's (1973) remarks on the interaction of cognitive and linguistic complexity (see Chapter 8), they say 'In one-word speech, however, formal complexity is, of course, constant. We would expect, therefore, that semantic development of one-word utterances should occur in the same sequence as the requisite nonverbal cognitive development, but would lag behind it.'[14] Here we have a particularly strong form of cognitive reduction, referred to in Chapter 8 as involving *order-isomorphism*. What it leads us to expect is that, if we take the orderings in Table 6.1 or the ordering common to both of these, we should be able to identify a similar ordering in the non-linguistic cognitive domain. Let us examine the extent to which Greenfield and Smith are successful in this search.

They cite six arguments which address the ordering question directly, along with some general remarks about cross-modal integration. I shall not be concerned with this latter here. The six arguments are shown in Table 6.2. Of the arguments, (a) and (f) establish nothing for the orderings in Table 6.1, although they may be relevant to more detailed aspects of development within the categories, (c) argues for the relatively late

Table 6.2

Linguistic development in one-word stage	Cognitive development preceding related linguistic development
(a) Child encodes change of state before he encodes process. Note that this is a development which takes place *within* two of Greenfield and Smith's categories: Action or State of an Agent and Action or State of an Object.	Evidence from infant perception suggests that infants take account of visual change of state before they infer an underlying process.
(b) One-place predicates appear before two-place predicates (i.e. single entity categories before double entity categories).	Infants act on objects before they are capable of placing them in locations.
(c) The ability to use words for objects which are not *directly* related to the child's actions is relatively late to appear – Greenfield and Smith cite an example of naming an intended recipient when reaching for an object, a complex means–end relation.	Piaget has shown that children treat a barrier as an end in itself before being able to treat it as a means to a distinct end.
(d) From 'embedding' an entity and its name in a pointing gesture the child progresses to embedding a relation in this gesture by pointing at an object and naming an associated object. Generally, such embeddings get more complex through the one-word stage.	Embeddings of action-schemas inside one another become more complex throughout the sensori-motor period.
(e) Early performatives and indications refer to the immediate situation. Volitional objects refer to a potential situation.	Intentionality develops towards increasingly remote goals in infancy.
(f) Encoding of past events follows encoding of present events (note, again, that this is a development taking place *within* categories).	Representational skills are first exercised on present events and only later on past events.

appearance of Dative but not for any detailed ordering (and, of course, the fact that Dative appears early for Matthew makes this claim uncomfortable), (e) supports the facts of development within the Performative object category, and both (b) and (d) support the priority of the second group of categories in Table 6.1 over the third group (i.e. categories involving a relation between an action and a single entity precede categories involving a relation between two entities). Greenfield and Smith also believe that (d) can be used to explain the late appearance of Modification of an event, as this involves the most complex embedding of all.

The result of all this appears to be a fairly convincing reduction for the ordering which is common to the two children in the study, although the correspondences between linguistic development and cognitive development, which Greenfield and Smith point out above, are not always transparent. The extent to which they have achieved more than their contemporaries in this regard will be evident in Chapter 8.

Overall, I find the theories examined in this chapter less than satisfactory, and I suspect that the major reason for this is the lack of any generally accepted analysis of adult language which acknowledges similar terms of reference. Because of this we have no constraint on where the child is going and the way is open for the postulation of intuitively acceptable, but poorly justified, inventories of semantic relations. Until this issue is taken more seriously it is difficult to see much conclusive analysis arising from this enterprise.

7 *The development of speech-acts*

In the previous chapter we have already come across the view that some notion of 'performative' is important in understanding early language development. It will be recalled that Antinucci and Parisi included performative representations in their semantic structures (6.2) and that Greenfield and Smith had certain classes of performatives appearing early in the one-word stage (6.3).

In this chapter we shall take as given that the adult is capable of performing a range of communicative acts using language, and enquire into the ontogenesis of these acts. There are at least two related questions that might be raised in this connection. The first simply seeks to identify the earliest occurrences of particular acts and looks for an order of development within the total set, going on to enquire into the explanation for any discovered order. The second looks at the relationship between the child's developing abilities to perform speech-acts and his syntactic development – what we might see as the development of the system for encoding particular functional or communicative categories. I shall focus on the first question here, as I believe that the issues involved are relatively straightforward. The second question will receive some abbreviated attention as I proceed, but I am of the opinion that virtually everything remains to be demonstrated as far as finding a communicative basis for syntax is concerned and that most proponents of this view have grossly underestimated the complexity of the structures which need to be accounted for.[1] It is a common move to take the fact, if it is a fact, that the functions which language serves appear to be continuous from a non-structured holophrastic period to a structured syntactic period as demonstrative of the correctness of the position. Clearly, it is not. It is perfectly consistent to recognise continuity of function without insisting that functions play any explanatory role in the genesis of structures which eventually come to serve them; consistent, but not necessarily correct, and it seems to me that stronger arguments than have been put forward so far will be necessary before this issue can be resolved.

7.1 Three inventories of functional categories

In this section I wish to introduce three independent approaches to the earliest functional notions that can be identified in the child's communicative system. Strictly speaking, they are not comparable, having distinct goals and using different theoretical vocabularies. However, they do each pay attention to roughly the same period of development, spanning the beginning of recognisable speech, and they each see their categories as having validity for both pre-linguistic (but consistently used) vocalisations and the earliest conventional words. In addition, examination of the significance of particular theoretical terms reveals a good deal of similarity between the three studies in question, as well as some glaring inconsistencies. It will be useful to point these out and, if possible, resolve the latter. In the next section I shall consider the status of these proposals as theories of communicative development.

Dore (1974, 1975) argues for the value of the notion of 'primitive speech-act' in understanding early communicative development. Beginning from the work of Searle (1969), Dore makes the reasonable claim that a child eventually acquires a repertoire of speech-acts and that, therefore (1974, p. 344) 'it is appropriate to ask how he acquires this repertoire'.

The adult notion of 'speech-act' is not the appropriate tool for studying the beginnings of language, Dore claims. The reason for this is that the typical speech-act, within the Searlian framework, has, as subcomponents, acts of referring and acts of predicating. These involve at least two linguistic forms, but the child at the threshold of language does not produce utterances more than one word in length and, therefore, we cannot identify acts of referring and predicating in the same child utterance. To solve this problem Dore coins the idea of *primitive speech-act* which he introduces in the following terms (1974, p. 345):

A primitive speech-act . . . is defined as an utterance, consisting formally of a single word or a single prosodic pattern, which [here the text has 'with' – RMA] functions to convey the child's intention before he acquires sentences. The single word is either a *rudimentary referring expression* such as the names of people, objects or events, or a specifically expressive word like 'hi', 'by-bye', or 'nighty-night'. The utterance of a prosodic pattern counts as a PSA if (1) it contains a consistent prosodic feature produced without the segmental phonemes of a word, and (2) it communicates the child's intention. Prosodic patterns, with or without lexical content, convey the primitive force of the PSA.

Dore then proposes four observational criteria which are to be taken into account in deciding the identity of PSA's. These are: (1) the child's utterances; (2) his non-linguistic behaviour, e.g. gestures and facial

Table 7.1 (*From Dore 1974, p. 346*)

Primitive speech-act	Child's utterance	Child's non-linguistic behaviour	Adult's response	Relevant contextual features
Labelling	Word	Attends to object or event; does not address adult; does not await response	Most often none; occasional repetition of child's utterance	Salient features focused on by child; no change in situation
Repeating	Word or prosodic pattern	Attends to adult utterance before his utterance; may not address adult; does not await response	Most often none; occasional repetition of child's utterance	Utterance focused on; no change in situation
Answering	Word	Attends to adult utterance before his utterance; addresses adult	Awaits child response; after child utterance most often acknowledges response; may then perform action	Utterance focused on; no change in situation unless child's response prompts adult reaction
Requesting (action)	Word or marked prosodic pattern	Attends to object or event; addresses adult; awaits response; most often performs signalling gesture	Performs action	Salient feature focused on by child and adult; change in condition of object or child
Requesting (answer)	Word	Addresses adult; awaits response; may make gesture regarding object	Utters a response	No change in situation
Calling	Word (with marked prosodic contour)	Addresses adult by uttering adult's name loudly; awaits response	Responds by attending to child or answering child	Before child's utterance adult is some distance away; adult's orientation typically changes
Greeting	Word	Attends to adult or object	Returns a greeting utterance	Speech event is initiated or terminated

Table 7.1 *contd.*

Protesting	Word or marked prosodic contour	Attends to adult; addresses adult; resists or denies adult's action	Adult initiates speech event by performing an action the child does not like	Adult's action is completed or child prevents action
Practicing	Word or prosodic pattern	Attends to object or event; does not address adult; nor await response	No response	No apparent aspect of context is relevant to utterance

expressions; (3) the adult's responses both verbal and non-verbal and; (4) the relevant, salient aspects of the context of utterance, such as objects attended to, location of objects and people. Applying these criteria to data he collected from two children yielded nine PSA's, which Dore justifies in terms of his observational criteria as in Table 7.1. One important point to note in connection with this tabulation is that Dore's definition of PSA apparently forces him to recognise a number of categories which are not readily assimilable to theoretical work on speech-acts. In Table 7.1 there are three categories which seem to be independent of the child's *communicative* intentions. Searle's analysis of speech-acts does, indeed, refer to intentions, following, e.g., Grice (1957), Strawson (1964), but the intention is specialised for Searle in every case, making crucial reference to an addressee. It is an intention to communicate and not simply an intention. Griffiths (1979) makes an identical point when he notes that Dore fails to distinguish between communicative acts and informative acts (see Lyons 1977b) where only the former notion assumes an audience-directed intention on the part of the performer of the act. Thus, the constituency of the set of PSA's is not on the firmest foundation and Dore admits another possible source of indeterminacy when he says (1974, p. 347): 'The set is not meant to be exhaustive – a study of other children might well yield PSA types which our children did not perform. Also, in a finer analysis, one might wish to distinguish between, say, different kinds of labelling (for example, labelling an action vs. labelling an object) in which case a different set of PSA's would emerge.' These considerations will loom large in the next section.

Carter's meticulously detailed work on the transition from pre-linguistic to linguistic communication also employs a functional framework (Carter 1975, 1978a, 1978b). Beginning from a slightly earlier stage of develop-

Table 7.2 (*adapted from Carter 1978b, p. 312*)

Schema	Gesture	Sound	Goal
Request object	Reach to object	[m] – initial	Get receiver's help in obtaining object
Attention to object	Point, hold out	Alveolar ([l] or [d]) initial	Draw receiver's attention to object
Attention to self	Sound of vocalisation	Phonetic variants of "David", "Mummy"	Draw receiver's attention to self
Request transfer	Reach to person	[h] – initial (constricted and minimally aspirated)	Obtain object from, or give to, receiver
Dislike	Prolonged, falling intonation	Nasalised, especially [n] – initial	Get receiver's attention in changing situation
Disappearance	Waving hands, slapping	[b] – initial	Get receiver's help in removing object
Rejection	Negative headshake	[ʔʌ̃ʔʌ̃]	Same as for dislike
Pleasure-surprise-recognition	Smile	Flowing or breathy [h] sounds especially *oh, ah, hi, ha*	Express pleasure

ment than Dore's study and using only one child, it postulates a set of eight communicative *sensori-motor schemata* which are defined in terms of occurrence (and often co-occurrence) of consistent phonetic and gestural phenomena, along with inferred communicative intent. Carter's particular aim has been to trace the development of these early phonetic forms into conventionalised forms in English, a process which is accompanied by the gradual erosion of the importance of gesture. What justifies seeing this as a developmental process is the continuity of function served by the varying phonetic forms and, hence, it is clear that it is not inappropriate to compare Carter's categories with Dore's; they are intended to apply to the period studied by the latter. The eight schemata

Table 7.3

Function	Definition
Instrumental	satisfies the child's material needs – the 'I want' function
Regulatory	controls the behaviour of others – the 'do as I tell you' function
Interactional	used to interact with others around him – the 'me and you' function
Personal	used to express the child's own uniqueness – the 'here I come' function
Heuristic	used to explore the child's environment – the 'tell me why' function
Imaginative	creates an environment of the child's own – the 'let's pretend' function

along with their defining characteristics appear in Table 7.2. Note immediately that there is no equivocation here on the communicative status of the categories. This will be the source of some of the discrepancies between Dore's and Carter's inventories.

Finally, Halliday (1975) represents an ambitious attempt to build a model of language development on a foundation consisting of a functional semantic. The model is concerned, on the one hand, with the development of functionally defined semantic notions and, on the other, with the development of a level of lexicogrammar, consisting of realisation rules mapping functional meanings onto forms. Here we are concerned with the former of these, since it is this which is most readily related to Dore's and Carter's work.

Halliday studied one child and divided the course of development into three phases. In Phase I the child's system[2] owes no direct allegiance to the adult system, although plausible adult models are suggested for some of the child's forms. This locates the beginnings of Halliday's study at a point consistent with the work of Dore and Carter. At this stage the system comprises, as well as a small set of functional meanings and a small set of forms, a simple one–one mapping between them, so that each form serves exactly one meaning and each meaning is realised by exactly one form. Halliday sometimes refers to this system as a 'Protolanguage'. Phase II is transitional, with the child making generalisations within the set of meanings which move him towards the abstract notion of function which Halliday perceives in the adult system. Also at this stage he begins to learn lexicogrammar, which can be seen as a complication of the mapping

Table 7.4. *Comparison of three inventories of functional categories*

Dore	Carter	Halliday
Request (action)	{ Request object { Request transfer	Instrumental
Protesting	{ Dislike { Rejection	Regulatory
Calling	Attention to self	Interactional
Greeting	Pleasure-Surprise- Recognition Attention to Object	Personal
Requesting (answer)		Heuristic
Answering		Informative
Labelling		
Repeating		
Practicing		
	Disappearance	
		Imaginative

between meaning and form, making available the possibility of more than one meaning being served by one form. Finally, Phase II is characterised by the child's learning of dialogue which makes it possible for him to indulge in a new function, that of imparting information. I shall return to this in the next section. By the end of Phase II the child has left behind the protolanguage and is ready to embark on the task of learning the language he hears around him, a task which he begins to pursue in Phase III.

Phase I sees the appearance of all but one of Halliday's functions, the Informative function, and so it is this phase we are principally concerned with in the present context. The six functions are summarised in Table 7.3. These six are joined, in Phase II, by the Informative function which serves to communicate information to another who does not already possess it – the 'I've got something to tell you' function.

One striking thing about Table 7.3 is that the language Halliday uses is from a different tradition to that appearing in Tables 7.1 and 7.2. Nevertheless, I now wish to present an informal comparison of the three inventories we have met which, I believe, does no great injustice to any of the authors concerned. This informal comparison appears as Table 7.4, and gives rise to a number of comments:

(a) None of Dore's non-communicative functions is recognised by either Carter or Halliday.

(b) Neither of Dore's categories involving answers are recognised by

Carter. For Halliday, one may correspond to his Heuristic function, but I find Halliday's discussion of this function less than clear. The other corresponds (partially) to the Informative function, but, as we have seen, Halliday claims that this only develops late (cf. 7.4 below).

(c) Carter's Attention to Object schema is not recognised by Dore. Griffiths (1979) suggests that many of Halliday's examples of the Personal function are of this type. On this basis, I propose some correspondence here and feel that Dore's total omission of this category is particularly serious (see 7.4 for extended discussion).

(d) Halliday recognises one function, the Imaginative, which appears to play no role in either Dore's or Carter's systems.

(e) Apart from (a)–(d) there appears to be a fairly solid core of agreement as to the early appearing functions. Differences within this core depend upon whether investigators make distinctions *within* categories or not. Thus, it appears that forms of greeting, vocatives and various species of requests are early to develop. In 7.4 I shall argue that there are good reasons for why this is the case and that, along with attention to object, we can hazard a developmental order within this functional core. However, the immediate task is to turn to the explanatory status of the theories at hand.

7.2 Inventories as theories

Neither Dore nor Carter speculates about development *within* their inventories of functions. For Carter there is a great deal of differentiation within a particular category as the child develops, but this raises many issues which are not relevant here and I shall say no more about it. Clearly, it makes sense to assume that what we are offered in Tables 7.1 and 7.2 are *stages* in functional development. This much is true to the extent that some time before the time represented in these tables, the children involved have no semantic functions available, and, some time after this, they have a rather larger set approximating to that which characterises adult communicative competence. Focusing on Dore's inventory, then, and referring to it as S_C and to the putative set of adult functional meanings as S_A, we at least have a sequence of the form (S_C, S_A) which we can investigate in terms of the conditions of Chapter 1.

Condition II requires that the inventories of speech-acts in the sequence be constructed in accordance with some general theory. But we have already seen that there are problems here, if we wish to make contact with, say, Searle (1969) (p. 149 above). Dore (1975, p. 32) is also fairly keen to deny any close affinity with speech-act theory when he says: 'A PSA is not merely an elliptical adult speech act, but a qualitatively different entity which possesses only some features similar to full speech acts.' However, at the same time, he insists that 'the components of PSA's eventually develop into the propositions and illocutionary forces of conventional speech acts' (*ibid.*). There is some tension here and Dore would appear to be committed to a discontinuity in development between S_C and S_A, but, before examining this in detail, there are some additional remarks to consider.

One obvious way to interpret the requirement of Condition II would involve the specification of a finite set of possible speech-acts from which, at each stage in his development, the child is using a subset. The difficulties in specifying such a set were first made clear by Austin (1962), who claimed to have identified several hundred verbs having a performative use; each of these could be seen as entailing the existence of a distinct speech-act. As different languages and different cultures are considered, such a list would need to be extended and it seems unlikely that a once-and-for-all exhaustive list could be produced. It might, nevertheless, be possible to develop a theory of speech-act types, suggesting general properties which characterise large classes of speech-acts and which will be independent of cultural differences. Searle (1975a, 1975b) can be seen as making preliminary suggestions along these lines, but nothing similar is considered by Dore. We have seen that he considers his set of PSA's as somewhat indeterminate and certainly not exhaustive. A tighter coding procedure with regard to the four observational criteria or, possibly, the employment of different criteria could lead to different inventories and no guide-lines are provided for choosing between such alternatives. In short, Dore's PSA's are simple inductions, only relying on general theory to the extent that they acknowledge a debt to the child's intentions.[3]

Before returning to Dore's own presentation of what happens after S_C, I would like to consider Condition III in a way which he does not. It seems fair to say that, with the exception of the non-communicative acts, all of Dore's categories in S_C would survive into S_A (perhaps having undergone the sort of modification Dore has in mind but this is not my concern here). In addition, a large number of speech-acts, not included in S_C, appear in S_A, e.g. promising, urging, advising, and so we might conclude that there is a simple additive relationship between S_C and S_A. This would amount to satisfaction of Condition III.

Still within this set of assumptions, it is worth pointing out that reference to languages of the world might reveal some language-internal justification for (S_C, S_A) (see Chapter 1). Although, as pointed out above, there is almost certainly a good deal of variation in the world's languages as far as their total inventories of speech-acts are concerned, it seems equally likely that there is a functional core, consisting of a set of speech-acts which can be performed in any language (cf. Jakobson's minimal consonantal and vocalic systems described in Chapter 2). In particular, it is difficult to imagine a language which does not enable its speakers to assert, to question and to command, whereas it does not stretch credibility to consider a language in which it is impossible to sentence, to find (guilty or not guilty), etc.[4] One immediate prediction following from such a state of affairs would be that the functional core will be learned first and we might even hope to discover principles akin to the Laws of Solidarity outside the functional core. Unfortunately, from Dore's point of view, all of this is speculation. The nearest he comes to even raising such possibilities is when he reproduces some claims of Slobin (1971, p. 302) that 'everywhere language consists of utterances performing a universal set of communicative functions (such as asserting, denying, requesting, ordering and so forth)', but it should be clear by now that much more than this is needed if we are to find convincing language-internal support.

Nothing in Dore's work suggests that a reductive explanation of (S_C, S_A) is a possibility. Indeed, there is some indication that, at least in one regard, such a move would be ill-advised. It might, for example, be maintained that the set of PSA's can be mapped onto pre-linguistic intentions, a theory of which would provide the reducing theory in the explanation. But, against this, Dore argues (1975, p. 37) that: 'Certainly, some forms of communicative intentions exist before language emerges, but linguistically expressed intentions are not isomorphic with pre-linguistic intentions and the former need not be derived from the latter. (It is difficult to imagine, for example, what would count as a pre-linguistic 'asserting' of a proposition.)' Thus, even if we had an explicit developmental theory of pre-linguistic communication to put alongside an explicit theory of the development of speech-acts, there would be at least one substantive theoretical term in the latter ('assertion') with no equivalent in the former.[5]

Hopes for providing a teleological explanation for the sequence are remote, as Dore's PSA's are unanalysed units with no logical relationships holding between them (cf. in this connection 7.4). There is no reason to suspect an environmental explanation and so Condition IV is not satisfied on this construal of Dore's proposals. These are not his suggestions, however, so let us now return to his own views on how things proceed after S_C. Although, these views are quite different from those just discussed, I do not believe that they are inconsistent with them. The two sets of opinions could easily complement each other.

Recall that Dore does not view PSA's as abbreviated speech-acts. How then do they develop into speech-acts? Dore (1975) discusses this question in the context of speculation on the development of syntax and offers Figure 7.1 as a 'formalisation' of the PSA.[6] It is not clear what significance

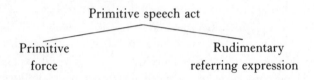

Figure 7.1. (from Dore 1975, p. 34)

we should attach to the use of 'formalisation' in this context (see below). Dore next notes that Figure 7.1 'is clearly inadequate as a representation of the child's *knowledge* after the one-word stage' (1975, p. 34 – my emphasis – RMA), and proposes Figure 7.2 as the next step. On the interpretation of this, he says: 'In this figure a predicating expression is introduced and it combines with a referring expression to form a rudimentary proposition. The force component begins to be expressed by elementary kinds of illocutionary force indicators' (*ibid.*). It is not clear to me, from Dore's discussion, whether at this stage the child controls word-order as a grammatical device, but this is what appears to motivate the development to Figure 7.3 where, for the first time, a sentence node appears, the idea being that it is only at this stage that the child begins to use conventional grammatical means for encoding his propositions. How do Figures 7.1–7.3 fare as a developmental theory? I confess to being puzzled by this, but a later paper (Dore 1978) throws some light on the issue. There he suggests that there are three different sorts of prerequisites for the language acquisition process to proceed appropriately: communicative or pragmatic prerequisites which he views as the precursors of illocutionary force, cognitive prerequisites which provide concepts for lexicalisation, and purely linguistic prerequisites which lead to particular concepts being lexicalised and which also organise syntactic structures. It is Dore's contention, and I believe he makes this point tellingly (see 7.3 for more discussion), that syntactic development cannot be explained in terms of either of the first two sets of prerequisites.

The three sorts of prerequisite come together in facilitating the development of the unit of communication which is for Dore, following Searle, the speech-act. In the light of this it is possible to see that Figures 7.1–7.3 are charting development within *two* of these input modes. The

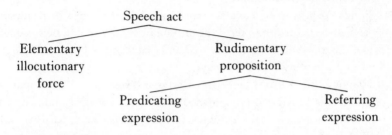

Figure 7.2 (adapted from Dore 1975, p. 35)

left-hand side of each figure represents the child's increasingly sophisticated intentions, while the right-hand side represents his developing linguistic capacities – Dore (1978) draws attention to what he calls the Designation Hypothesis and the Predication Hypothesis as purely linguistic constructs which are necessary for the development of reference, predication and, subsequently, syntax. If this interpretation is correct, there are a number of remarks which are worth making.

(a) To use a standard linguistic formalism and to talk about 'formalisation' in this context is extremely misleading. Dore has said nothing about *how* the various inputs are combined into a unitary speech-act.

(b) The move from 'Primitive force' to 'Elementary illocutionary force'

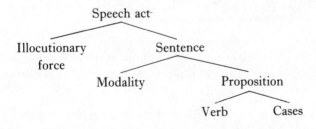

Figure 7.3 (adapted from Dore 1975, p. 35)

to 'Illocutionary force' is mysterious. Dore does not define these, with the exception of the first. Differences between them can hardly correspond to differences in grammaticalisation possibilities as these are dealt with on the right-hand side of the figures. What are the differences between them, and is there a cogent developmental hypothesis underlying the terminology?

(c) There is a similar proliferation of undefined terminology on the right-hand side of the figures.

Points such as these have convinced me that it is not worth pursuing Dore's analysis further in terms of my conditions. It should be reasonably evident that it would not do very well and that we would have to indulge in a lot of guess-work along the way.

Halliday differs from Dore and Carter in presenting a developmental order for his functional categories. Phase I (see above) is studied at six points and, for each of these points, Halliday works out an analysis of the child's functional semantic system. For my purposes, I wish to focus just on the major functions introduced in 7.1. For these functions, taking account of the fact that the Informative function does not appear until Phase II, we have the development schematised in Figure 7.4.

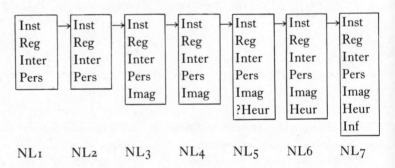

Figure 7.4. Inst = Instrumental, Reg = Regulatory, Inter = Interactional, Pers = Personal, Imag = Imaginative, Heur = Heuristic, Inf = Informative. Numbering of stages follows Halliday's own except for NL7

For Condition II, Halliday, to his credit, provides some discussion. On the one hand, with respect to the form of his theoretical vocabulary, he has this to say:

In general we cannot represent the content of the child's system at this stage in terms of the words and structures of the adult language. We cannot match the child's meanings with the elements of the adult semantic system, which are again too specific. What is needed . . . is a kind of postural notation for the content. What does this mean in fact? It means some form of functional representation of meaning. The content in other words, has to be specified in relation to the functions of language.

Why a functional representation should be more 'postural' (= less specific) than a non-functional representation is not something Halliday elaborates on, but, more importantly from my point of view, he directly addresses the question of constraining the set of functions countenanced by the theory, i.e. he tries to delimit a general theory of functions. For understanding Phase I, he sees the necessary functions as having three sources (p. 15):

The question then is: what are the functions that we can recognise as determining the child's semantic system at this stage, and how do we arrive at them? Here we must try to keep things in proportion shunting between sensible observations on the one hand and imaginative but at the same time goal-directed theory on the other.

Thus, the first source is observation, the standard inductive procedure we have already met in Dore's work. Whatever set of functions emerges from this activity can be used in conjunction with theoretical considerations to arrive at a final set. For Halliday, these theoretical considerations involve two sources: theories of language structure which assign a central role to function and theories of social structure which see language as central. For the former, Halliday turns, not surprisingly, to his own work (Halliday 1967, 1970) and, for the latter, to the work of Bernstein (1971) on 'critical socialising contexts'. Halliday's linguistics supplies three functions: ideational, interpersonal and textual; Bernstein provides another four: regulative, instructional, imaginative or innovative, and interpersonal. These seven functions, along with whatever functions are the product of our observations, are then submitted to some sort of selection procedure which results in the seven used in Table 7.4.

But this procedure is uncomfortable. What appears to be going on can be represented as in Figure 7.5. Here we are told nothing about the membership of X, nothing about how we identify functions across disciplines and nothing about the procedure of selection. It is remarkable that Halliday makes such a bad job of justifying his choice of functions, given his realisation that a mere inventory of functions not related to any general theory would be unsatisfactory. It follows then that Condition II is not satisified in any convincing way.[7]

Condition III, given the unstructured nature of the sets of functions, can apply and, as there is no development in the set of functions from NL1 to NL2, from NL3 to NL4 and from NL5 to NL6, while there is straightforward addition between NL2 and NL3, NL4 and NL5 and NL6 and NL7, it is satisfied.

Consider now the transitions from NL2 to NL3 and from NL4 to NL5 from the point of view of Condition IV. Halliday is not uninterested in order of development and says (p. 37): 'The hypothesis was that these functions would appear, approximately in the order listed [in Table 7.3], and in any case with the "informative" significantly last.' But, as we have

Functions

			Selection	
X	+ Ideational	+ Regulative	→	Instrumental
	Interpersonal	Instructional		Regulatory
	Textual	Imaginative		Interactional
		Interpersonal		Personal
				Heuristic
				Imaginative
				Informative

Source

Observation	Halliday's	Bernstein's
	Linguistics	Sociology

Figure 7.5

already seen, this hypothesis is not confirmed. There is, apparently, no order of development within the first four functions and the Imaginative function appears before the Heuristic function. Had the functions emerged in the predicted order it is not clear what principles Halliday would have invoked as explanatory; the obvious generalisation, using Halliday's terminology, is that the pragmatic functions would have appeared first with the mathetic functions developing later, but, in itself, this is merely to set up superordinate categories and not to approach explanatory adequacy. Condition IV is not satisfied by the transitions from NL2 to NL3 and from NL4 to NL5.

There is more to say in connection with the transition from NL6 to NL7. Here Halliday's prediction that the Informative function will appear last is correct and, to explain this, he introduces the idea that, of the seven functions, the Informative is the only one which depends crucially on language for its fulfilment. He says (p. 31):

> The use of language to inform is a very late stage in the linguistic development of the child, because it is a function which depends on the recognition that there are functions of language which are solely defined by language itself. All the other functions in the list are extrinsic to language. They are served by and realised through language, but they are not defined by language. They represent the use of language in contexts which exist independently of the linguistic system. But the informative function has no existence independent of language itself. It is an intrinsic function that the child cannot begin to master until he has grasped the principle of dialogue, which means until he has grasped the fundamental nature of the communication process.

This passage seems to move Halliday in the direction of a reductive explanation for the late appearance of the Informative function, where the reducing theory is a theory of social context in which the other functions are defined, but I have three difficulties to raise for this suggestion.

(a) Halliday nowhere produces any independent description of the child's developing awareness of the social contexts which could be used as a basis on which to define his language functions, i.e. I suspect there is no appropriate reducing theory.

(b) If Halliday is correct and the Informative function is defined only by reference to language itself, then it clearly must follow *some* language and, if language is construed functionally, it must follow *some* function or functions. But this does not show that it must follow all other functions in the sequence, i.e. Halliday's argument is logically unsound.

(c) There is a crucial reference to 'dialogue' in the passage cited above. If dialogue is the *sine qua non* for the emergence of the Informative function and if an explanation can be produced demonstrating why dialogue follows the six functions preceding the Informative, we would have another path towards explanation. But the nearest Halliday gets to defining dialogue is when he says (p. 30): 'Dialogue is, for [the child], a very new concept. Dialogue involves the adoption of roles which are social roles of a new and special kind, namely those which are defined by language itself.' Unfortunately, this fails to distinguish dialogue from the Informative function. There is little illumination in being told that the Informative function is to be understood by reference to dialogue which is explicated in terms of new social roles where these latter are characterised by instances of the Informative function. The circle is complete and the transition from NL6 to NL7 seems to go the way of the earlier transitions without some independent characterisation of the 'new' social roles which make the development of dialogue possible.

7.3 Perlocutions, illocutions and locutions

Austin (1962), in his general discussion of speech-acts, following his abandonment of the constative–performative distinction, distinguished three types of act: locutionary acts which were acts *of* saying (and included such standard semantic functions as referring, predicating, etc.), illocutionary acts which were conventional acts performed *in* saying (such as promising, ordering, advising, etc.) and perlocutionary acts, associated with effects, which were acts performed *by* saying (such as persuading, worrying, convincing, etc.). Many problems were raised when the distinctions between these categories were pursued in detail. In particular, the differing roles of conventionality and intentionality in distinguishing the latter two categories has led to much (inconclusive) discussion (see particularly Strawson 1964). However, Bates, Camaioni and Volterra (1975) (see also Bates 1976) take the categories as unproblematic and offer a thesis on their ontogenesis.

Within the class of illocutionary acts, Bates *et al.* focus on two, those of ordering and stating and, in connection with these, they define notions of 'protoimperative' and 'protodeclarative'. The former is manifested by the child intentionally using an addressee as an agent to achieve some end and the latter by the child attempting to direct the adult's attention to some object or event. The protoimperative is seen as the source of the mature imperative mode and the protodeclarative provides the basis for the development of statements. Bates *et al.*'s reasons for adopting this stance on declaratives are not convincing, owing a certain allegiance to the highly suspect approach to syntax and semantics found in the work of Antinucci and Parisi (cf. 6.2), but I am not at pains to quibble with their definitions here: manipulating an addressee's attention makes perfect sense, even if seeing this as a primitive species of declarative does not. The attractive symmetry which Bates *et al.* perceive in their definitions is that the protoimperative uses an adult as a way to an object, whereas the protodeclarative uses an object as a way to an adult.[8] For perlocutionary acts and locutionary acts, the authors do not speculate on particular members of these sets.

Bates *et al.* suggest that it is possible to identify three phases in early communicative development. The first, lasting up to about 10 months in the children they studied, they call the Perlocutionary Phase, and it is characterised by the lack of *intentional* communication on the part of the child. During this phase the adult responds to the child's signals (smiles, cries, etc.), but apparently, there is no requirement to credit the child with knowledge of these effects, i.e. with that knowledge which would be vital in the ascription of communicative intentionality to the child. The major evidence offered for this conclusion is that the child makes no effort to invoke help from an adult, e.g. by establishing eye-contact, when frustrated by a particular task: the child does not see the adult as a target for communication. The Illocutionary Phase is the next development and here the child is endowed with communicative intentions. Cognitively, he will now use novel means to establish his goals and this includes the development of the protoimperative and the protodeclarative. Eye-contact with the adult when frustrated indicates that the child is becoming aware of the role of the adult as agent and, at about the same time as the systematic use of eye-contact emerges, the child begins to show objects to adults. Finally, the child enters the Locutionary Phase, when he begins to use conventional linguistic signals with propositional value. The transition into this stage appears to follow a variable period in the Illocutionary Phase and is not smooth. It is not easy to identify the earliest instances of propositional speech and Bates *et al.* discuss the problems they met here at some length.

All of this looks pretty straightforward and it would appear that Bates *et al.* are proposing a developmental theory of communicative acts, with the type of perlocutionary acts preceding the type of illocutionary acts and both of these preceding the type of locutionary acts. Furthermore, the earlier-developing types persist into later stages and so we have a three-stage theory as in Figure 7.6.

Let me say immediately that there is, to my mind, nothing objectionable about Bates *et al.*'s description of the facts of development. In addition, a cursory inspection of Figure 7.6 reveals that their theory is cumulative through the three stages and so we can look with optimism towards satisfaction of Condition III. Furthermore, the paper contains an interesting attempt to satisfy Condition IV, with respect both to the entry into the Illocutionary Phase and to the transition from the Illocutionary to the Locutionary Phase.[9] The former, particularly with reference to the protoimperative and the protodeclarative, is seen as dependent on the child's being able to use novel means to attain familiar goals, an achievement which is definitive of Stage 5 in the Piagetian sensori-motor period. If the protoimperative and protodeclarative involve, in their cognitive representations, some novel means–goal structure, which seems entirely reasonable, it will not be possible for them to appear before Stage 5, and Bates *et al.* cite typical Stage 5 behaviour appearing in the Illocutionary Phase. The transition from Illocutionary to Locutionary Phase is similarly related to Piaget's theory of cognitive development. For Bates *et al.* the Locutionary Phase is characterised by the appearance of genuine reference, i.e. a generalised use of referring expressions which is not tied to any particular object nor to the child's interaction with instances of a category. This is seen as requiring the general representational capacities which only appear in Stage 6 of the sensori-motor period.

Perlocutionary acts	$\rightarrow$ Perlocutionary acts $\oplus$ Illocutionary acts	$\rightarrow$ Perlocutionary acts $\oplus$ Illocutionary acts $\oplus$ Locutionary acts
t_1	t_2	t_3

Figure 7.6

Thus, genuine reference and locutionary acts would be impossible before Stage 6 and a cognitive reduction for the Bates *et al.* theory looks a promising possibility.

My worries arise from a different direction and concern the use of speech-act terminology in this context. The authors might be thought to be satisfying Condition II by reference to Austin (1962) or Searle (1969), but we can rapidly see that this is not so. Consider first perlocutionary acts.

For Austin, and Searle, following him, such acts are *definitionally* connected with a conventional use of language. Searle (1969, p. 28) says: 'Correlated with the notion of illocutionary acts is the notion of the consequences or *effects* such acts have on the actions, thoughts or beliefs, etc. of hearers' (emphasis in original). Bates *et al.* are correct in observing that adults are affected by aspects (vocal and non-vocal) of small children's behaviour. But these effects are *not* consequences of such children's illocutionary acts, because, by Bates *et al.*'s own claim, no such acts are performed in the Perlocutionary Phase. Therefore, children at this stage do not perform perlocutionary acts in the sense discussed by speech-act theorists. What of illocutionary acts?

Searle follows and modifies Grice in his attempt to explicate meaning. As is well known, Grice's views on meaning are notoriously complex and employ the crucial notion of 'reflexive intention'. Nor is it the case that workers in the Gricean tradition have seen ways to simplify Grice's own formulations of what it means for a speaker to mean something on an occasion. In the face of increasingly obscure counter-examples, the embedding of intentions within intentions has continued apace (see, for example, Strawson 1964, Grice 1968, Schiffer 1972). Some have been led to conclude that, if it really is that complex, there is going to be no way into the system for the language learner (see, e.g., Davidson 1974), but there is no hint that Bates *et al.* are of this persuasion. Therefore, we must ask whether they wish to ascribe a complex set of intentions to the one-year-old child. What this would mean, roughly, in the case of the protoimperative, and restricting ourselves to just part of Searle's analysis, is that the child is credited with the following three intentions:

(i_1) to produce in his addressee the knowledge that his utterance counts as a request (command) that the addressee perform a particular action;

(i_2) that the knowledge in (i_1) be produced by means of the addressee's recognition of (i_1);

(i_3) that (i_1) be recognised by virtue of the addressee's knowledge of the (conventional) meaning of the speaker's utterance.

Suffice it to say that, to my knowledge, there is no evidence to suggest that children of this age control such complex intentions. Dore (1978) makes essentially the same point when, commenting on Bates *et al.*'s use of speech-act terminology, he says (p. 91):

the metaphor . . . may be misleading. It implies that [in the Illocutionary Phase] the communicative acts children perform non-verbally are essentially illocutionary acts like 'requesting', and that the later use of propositions is merely a verbal substitute for the prior behaviour. Yet, when one considers the various accounts of the nature of genuine requests . . . the analogy breaks down.

Dore believes that Bates *et al.* describe the development of pre-linguistic communication, not the development of speech-acts, and it should be obvious from the above that I totally concur with this judgement. There is no danger in this strategy so long as we do not take the speech-act terminology seriously. But, of course, as soon as we cease to do that, the general considerations which give Bates *et al*'s work its plausibility and respectability are no longer available.

7.4 A logical explanation for functional development

The positions we have discussed so far in this chapter have each treated particular speech-acts or particular functional meanings as logically primitive. However, in a recent paper (Atkinson 1979), I have suggested that for two such functions there are reasons for postulating a logical relationship between them and, on this basis, for being able to predict their order of development.

A number of authors (Griffiths 1974, 1979; Lyons 1975, 1977a; Keenan 1974, 1975; Keenan and Schieffelin 1976; Ochs, Schieffelin and Platt 1979; Carter 1978b) have pointed out the importance of routines, verbal and non-verbal, for manipulating the attention of an addressee (for some observations on the development of this ability from well before the start of language development, see Bruner 1975b, Bruner and Scaife 1975). Lyons discusses this topic in terms of his notion of quasi-reference and in Atkinson (1979) I argue that the ability to refer to objects or sets of objects 'presupposes', in a large number of cases, a previous act of attention-drawing.

Briefly, linguistic reference to a particular entity assumes that the addressee can identify the entity under the description supplied by the expression used by the speaker.[10] The child, at the beginning of language development, usually refers to objects using simple expressions such as demonstratives, proper names or common names (often, in the acquisition of English, with a schwa vowel in article position (Dore, Franklin, Miller and Ramer 1976). Of course, he cannot expect to succeed in referring to an object using such limited linguistic devices, unless he performs some additional act to somehow reduce the possible range of referents. This act may be an act of pointing, which is interpreted as directing the addressee's attention along a line of regard which includes only one entity fitting the simple description used by the child. Alternatively, the child may resort to linguistic means to direct his addressee's attention and a considerable portion of the argument in Atkinson (1979) is devoted to producing evidence for this possibility. Certain forms such as *see, look, there, here* and *this* (in the speech of one child studied in the project reported in Griffiths, Atkinson and Huxley 1974) were most naturally interpreted as attention-manipulators and this was seen as the beginnings of an explanation for why we find such forms being used so commonly early in language acquisition (see also Gopnik 1978, Carter 1978b). Taking the argument somewhat further, I proposed that some uses of nominals were best interpreted as having the same function, i.e. that some uses of, e.g. *doggie* should be viewed not as holophrastic encodings of something like 'That's a doggie' but as attempts to get the addressee to attend to a particular dog, often, but not always, with the intention of going on to produce a statement about it.

This possibility was then exploited to explain certain aspects of such recalcitrant phenomena as replacement sequences (Braine 1971, Bowerman 1973) and, more generally, repetition. As an additional speculation, I hazarded that instances of apparent questions on the part of the child could be similarly interpreted as attention-drawers and related this to the observation, fairly commonly made, that children often ask a question only to immediately answer it themselves (see Griffiths 1978, 1979 and Ochs, Schieffelin and Platt 1979 for further discussion).[11]

In Atkinson and Griffiths (1973) it is argued, within a quasi-logical framework the details of which are of no concern here, that an appropriacy condition on being able to refer to an entity by *the* + X, where X is a common noun, is that the entity should be the unique object *in the addressee's attention* such that he believes it to be an X. Lifting this condition into the context of language development is straightforward.

If we consider the speech-act of making a statement (or, for that matter, asking a question or issuing a directive), this involves, among other things in the framework of Searle (1969), propositional acts of referring and predicating. It follows that it is a necessary condition on the successful performance of an act of stating that acts of referring and predicating are also successfully performed. But the act of referring itself has, as a necessary condition on its performance, the fact that the addressee's attention is appropriately directed. This can be achieved by non-verbal pointing or, it has been argued, verbal means. It follows then that, while we cannot conclude that verbal acts of attention-drawing are a necessary condition for referring (as the same effect can be achieved non-verbally), we might expect such acts to appear in the repertoire of the child before he produces statements. Atkinson (1979) can thus be seen as amounting to a developmental theory of inventories of speech-acts (or, perhaps, given the reservations of the previous section, communicative acts), with just two stages (S_1, S_2), such that S_1 has one member, the act of attention-drawing, and S_2 supplements this with stating.

In terms of my conditions, the treatment of this proposal is fairly obvious. For Condition II, no one, to my knowledge, working within a speech-act framework has discussed the act of manipulating an addressee's attention, but, as already indicated, it has been considered within rather different sets of assumptions by Atkinson and Griffiths (1973) and Lyons (1975). It certainly appears that a case can be made for the primary function of English sentences of the form *There's* . . . and *Here's* . . . being that of attention-directing.[12] On this basis, we might conclude that a full inventory of speech-acts would include such a function. One further point worth making is that the reference to appropriacy conditions above makes contact with the Austin-Searle tradition, which could be seen as advantageous when comparing this proposal with those already considered in this chapter.

Condition III is satisfied and, as I have tried to argue above, we appear to have at least the outline of a teleological explanation for the order of development I am claiming. If stating really does presuppose attention-drawing, then attention-drawing must precede stating developmentally. The question that now arises is whether we can extend this rather spare theory to accommodate more communicative functions.

Griffiths (1974) having described some of the above ideas, says (p. 8): 'I shall also try to show that drawing attention to something can be decomposed into first getting someone's attention and then, having got it, putting something into it. The act also appears to presuppose one having noticed the something oneself.' The obvious linguistic candidate for securing the attention of someone is a vocative utterance. There are also non-linguistic devices having the same function such as waving, and it is easy to see that an argument analogous to the above can be constructed. Just as the addressee's attention to a restricted set of objects is a necessary condition on a speaker successfully referring, so having an addressee attending to oneself (presumably, part of the definition of being an addressee) is a necessary condition on directing the addressee's attention in a particular direction. Griffiths finds instances of utterances in his data which appear to exclusively serve the 'attend to speaker' function before he finds instances of utterances which can be plausibly interpreted as directing the addressee's attention.

Although Griffiths does not develop his proposals along these lines, it should be evident that there is a three-stage theory implicit in his approach. Furthermore, it is a theory which will satisfy Condition III and, for each transition of which, Condition IV will be satisfied teleologically. If attention-direction presupposes attention-getting, then attention-getting must precede attention-directing.

Griffiths also raises the question of what, following Dore (7.1), we can call Noticing, in the passage cited above. He rightly points out that the speaker noticing an entity is a pre-condition on his directing his addressee's attention towards it, although not, of course, on his directing attention to himself with a vocative. To assimilate this to the ordering we have so far would be straightforward but the problem is that we would, thereby, be blurring the distinction between communicative acts and informative acts (cf. the levelling of this charge against Dore in 7.1 and, implicitly, against Bates *et al.* in 7.3). I shall not, therefore, pursue this possibility here.

Finally, Griffiths (1979) has remarked on the appearance of requests before statements in development and, while I do not feel that we have a simple teleological explanation for this of the sort considered in this section, I believe that there are one or two observations which are worth taking into account.

Griffiths' own plausible account exploits the possibility that a request might be appropriately conveyed by a communication of the appropriate illocutionary force supplemented by non-linguistic gestures. If I can linguistically signal that I want something, then, within the immediate spatio-temporal context, I can usually make it clear what I want. However, the same is not true for statements. As Griffiths puts it (p. 112): 'whereas one may easily use non-linguistic means to elaborate "I request to you" into a worthwhile communication, the same is not true in respect of statements. Read out accurately the phonetic sequence which corresponds to "I state to you" in some land whose tongue you do not know and your audience will wait for linguistic goods you cannot deliver.' How does this fit in with the species of explanation we are examining?

Griffiths is not claiming any logical relationship between stating and requesting and so we do not have a teleological explanation like those already considered. However, he is suggesting that an *analysis* of what is involved in requesting and stating, coupled with a hypothesis concerning restrictions on the child's utterances reveals that, whereas requesting is compatible with the hypothesised restrictions, stating is not – the restriction is that early utterances have force but lack content. Relative to this

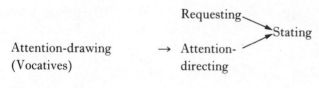

Figure 7.7

hypothesis, then, we have a teleological explanation; the hypothesis itself, however, remains untouched by this and, ideally, requires explanation.

Overall, then, the picture of the development of speech-acts which emerges can be summarised in terms of the partial ordering of Figure 7.7.[13] Naturally, I find the arguments for this particular ordering quite persuasive. Irrespective of that, however, I believe that the most important difference between the analyses in this section and those appearing earlier in the chapter concerns the attention paid to the analysis of what is involved in particular acts. It is only from this perspective that we can move beyond the production of inventories and begin to seriously examine developmental questions.

8 Cognitive reductions

In Chapter 1 I introduced the idea of a reductive explanation for some aspects of language development and have used that concept in an informal way in intervening chapters. The time has now come to submit one particular species of this type of explanation to a more detailed examination. This species is that in which a theory of the child's general cognitive development is cast in the role of the reducing theory.

Initially, it is important to be clear that the employment of a reductive explanation only makes sense if we assume that language development and general cognitive development provide distinct and distinguishable domains of enquiry. To make this assumption entails that the theories we construct in these domains will be of distinct character and the question of whether one can reduce the other will be significant. Not to make the assumption essentially commits the theorist to a definitional position whereby any sort of linguistic structure is regarded as a type of general cognitive structure, and the explanatory status of cognitive development in the study of language simply does not arise. There is little point in arguing that the assumption is a necessary one to adopt from the point of view of empirical research; clearly it is not. However, given the current state of theoretical discussion, it seems to me that rejecting the assumption rules out of court a number of interesting questions.

As a particular example, consider the formal nature of the rules (of various types) used in a transformational grammar and discussed, to some extent, in Chapter 5. Assume that it makes sense to credit the child with such a grammar at some stage in his syntactic development. Then, when presented with the question as to whether the rules of the grammar could be related to the child's general cognitive development, a proponent of the definitional position has to respond that the answer is positive, but uninteresting; and exactly the same response would be forthcoming no matter what the domain of linguistic enquiry. But, with the grammar example still in mind, consider the following question: is it the case that the formal structure of the rule-types used in a sample grammar are found in other *non-linguistic* cognitive domains? For transformational rules it could be claimed, and has been, somewhat tentatively, by Chomsky (1968), that the formal properties which characterise them are not found in any other domain of human or animal cognition.[1] Such a claim is refuted by indicating a domain in which a similar formal device is necessary to explain the organism's behaviour, knowledge, etc. (cf. the work of Clowes 1969 on visual perception which could be seen as an investigation of this problem among other things). The claim and its possible refutation are surely clear and interesting, and I intend, in what follows to regard as a non-cognitive linguistic construct any such construct which is not identifiable in a cognitive domain other than language. This is not to claim that such constructs exist and, indeed, it is the burden of this chapter to investigate opinions on this matter, but it is to claim that, understood in these terms, issues concerning the relationship between language development and cognitive development cannot be reduced to vacuity definitionally.

In general, then, I shall be taking as the theory which is to be reduced one which is presented in terms of linguistic constructs. Ideally, it will concur with the principles of some general theory in the relevant domain (i.e. satisfy Condition II), but I shall not pursue this requirement in detail in the present context.

8.1 A spectrum of positions

Earlier discussion has enumerated a number of legitimate domains of enquiry in the study of language development. Recognition of this multiplicity immediately indicates that we should be suspicious of the suggestion that *language development* can be explained by reference to cognitive development. What could such a suggestion amount to?

The strongest position that it would be possible to adopt would insist that *all* aspects of language development require a grounding in non-linguistic cognition, if we are to seek explanation and understanding. Whether anyone has subscribed to this extreme position is not a matter to be settled here – its initial plausibility might appear questionable if only from the point of phonological development (but see Schwartz and Folger 1977) – but it is apparent that alternatives exist which still offer a central role to cognition in explaining language development.

Referring to a set of domains of linguistic investigation, each of which we regard as reasonably delimited, as D_1, D_2, . . ., D_n, we can suppose that theories[2] have been constructed in each of these domains and that these theories have, not necessarily disjoint, sets of formal properties, P_1, P_2, . . ., P_n.[3] Thus P_i is the set of formal properties associated with theories in D_i ($1 \leqslant i \leqslant n$). Then it may be the case that some or all of the properties in P_i ($1 \leqslant i \leqslant n$) can be identified with properties associated with theories in domains of non-linguistic cognition, and this may be the case in a number of ways, each leading to slightly different formulations of the relationship between linguistic and cognitive development. For example, we might find that *all* the members of a particular set of properties, say P_j, could be identified in theories of the non-linguistic cognitive domain D^*. In such a case we would be in a position to investigate the explanatory value of our theory of development in D^* for our understanding of development in the linguistic domain D_j. A positive outcome to such an investigation would lead to the conclusion that linguistic development in D_j could be explained by reference to cognitive development in D^*. Alternatively, we might find that only a subset of P_j can be identified in theories for D^* (and, for simplicity, that the other members of P_j are not found in theories for any other domain of non-linguistic cognition). In this case too we would proceed to investigate the explanatory value of development in D^* for our understanding of development in D_j, but now a positive outcome would lead to the conclusion that the relevant linguistic development is only *partially* explained by reference to D^*; we are left with a residue of properties in our theories of D_j which have not been identified in any non-linguistic domain, and, at this stage of our enquiry, we would be forced to conclude that they constitute autonomous aspects of language development.

Remarks along similar lines can be found in Chomsky's recent speculations, although within a different framework and in a different context (see Chomsky 1974, 1976, 1980). In these publications Chomsky discusses the 'thesis of independence of grammar' and the 'thesis of autonomy of formal grammar'. The first of these is concerned with the possibility of there being an interaction of such a kind between the speaker's knowledge of his language and his system of 'common-sense understanding' that the latter may serve as an explanatory basis for the former, and the second with there being a similar interaction between the speaker's knowledge of linguistic form and his semantic knowledge. It is in connection with the latter that Chomsky makes his clearest statement when he says (1974, pp. 15–16):

Suppose that among the primitive notions of linguistic theory we can distinguish some that are 'semantic' and others that are 'formal'. Thus we might take such notions as 'synonymous', 'significant', 'denotes', 'satisfies', 'refers to concrete objects', to be core notions of semantics, let us say, primitive in our linguistic theory; while the primitives of phonetic theory . . . may be taken to be formal notions. Given a bifurcation of the primitive notions into 'formal' and 'semantic' we can ask, for each defined concept, whether terms of one or the other category appear in its definition. There are then purely formal concepts. We may refer to the theory concerning just these as 'the theory of linguistic form'. We might discover that this theory – which excludes the core notions of semantics – is virtually null, or quite uninteresting. Or, at the other extreme, we might find that it includes an interesting concept of 'grammar' and 'structure', perhaps all linguistic levels apart from semantic representation.

The latter possibility is referred to by Chomsky as the 'absolute autonomy thesis' and is contrasted with the 'parameterized autonomy thesis' which represents something between the two extremes introduced in the cited passage.

Clearly, a similar distinction can be made for the interaction between systems of linguistic knowledge and systems of 'common-sense under-standing', and it seems to me that it is not implausible to regard my discussion of the possible relationships between linguistic and cognitive development as entailing a similar spectrum of positions. Thus, consider again the possibility of theories in the linguistic domain D_j involving a set of formal properties P_j. It may be the case that none of these properties can be identified in any non-linguistic cognitive domain, and, in this situation, we could talk of the absolute autonomy of development in D_j with respect to cognitive development. Alternatively, we may discover a subset of P_j being identified in theories of D^* in which case we could talk of the parameterised autonomy of development in D_j with respect to cognitive development. Finally, it might be that the full set of properties P_j could be identified in theories of D^*; then we could speak of the absolute dependence of development in D_j on cognitive development.[4]

Taking the discussion one step further, we can now consider the full set of domains $D_1, D_2, \ldots, D_n$, and again, a set of possibilities emerges. It may be that development in each of the domains is absolutely dependent on cognitive development, that development in each of them is dependent on cognitive development but that, in some (or all) cases, this dependence is only partial, that development in some of them is totally dependent while development in others is totally independent of cognitive develop-ment, and so on. Only for the first possibility would we be justified in asserting that language development depends on cognitive development without qualification.[5]

8.2 The reduction condition in cognitive reductions

The situation we are to consider is one in which we have a sequence of theories $(L_1, L_2, \ldots, L_n)$ in some domain of language development D along with a sequence of theories $(C_1, C_2, \ldots, C_m)$ constituting an adequate theory of cognitive development.[6] Furthermore, we know the temporal ordering across the two sequences, i.e. we can collapse the two sequences to give one composite sequence.[7]

Having obtained a collapsed sequence of this sort, what can we demand of it if we are to claim that the theory of cognitive development contributes to explaining the linguistic development in which we are interested?

Already discussed in Chapter 1 is the requirement that there must be some significant relationship between the theoretical terms and formal operations (defining the syntax) of the two sequences of theories. Some of the linguistic theories we have considered have very poorly developed formal structures, but, while we can hope that such a situation will change, this fact is immaterial to the analytic task at hand. Repeating the claims of Chapter 1, we can say that, for the cognitive theory to be explanatory in the relevant domain of linguistic development, it must be the case that:

(1) the theoretical terms of the linguistic theory can be translated into theoretical terms of the cognitive theory;

(2) the formal operations of the linguistic theory must be identifiable in the cognitive theory.

So, as an example, we can imagine a developmental theory of syntax which consists of a sequence of grammars using a set of grammatical categories and a set of rule-types. If there is to be the required sort of relationship between this theory and a theory of cognitive development, then it must be the case that:

(i) Each of the grammatical categories can be translated into some theoretical term of the cognitive theory (e.g. NP is translated as 'Entity' and VP is translated as 'Action', where 'Entity' and 'Action' are theoretical terms in our cognitive theory).

(ii) Formal properties corresponding to rule-types must be identifiable in the cognitive theory (e.g. if the linguistic theory includes phrase-structure rules, then formal operations building hierarchical structures must appear in the cognitive theory; if the linguistic theory includes transformational rules, then the cognitive theory must embrace processes which are structure-dependent in the familiar sense).

Similarly, if our linguistic investigation is concerned with the development of the lexicon and leads to a sequence of theories employing binary features, then, in order for a cognitive theory to provide the beginnings of an explanation, it must be the case that:

(i)   For each of the features used in the linguistic theory, there is a translation into some theoretical term of the cognitive theory (e.g. ± object translates as 'Entity' and ± animate translates as 'Animacy', where 'Entity' and 'Animacy' are theoretical terms in our cognitive theory).

(ii)   Each formal property in the theory of lexical development (perhaps, binary categorisation and set formation in this case) can be identified in the cognitive theory.

Clearly, while this much is necessary if the theories are to be related in the required way, it is not sufficient – no account is taken of the ordering relations in the collapsed sequence.

On the basis of the discussion in Chapter 1, it is apparent that we need a third condition:

(3)   The translations of theoretical terms and corresponding formal properties required by satisfaction of (1) and (2) above must appear in the sequence of cognitive theories before they are required by a linguistic theory.

To illustrate, we can again use syntactic development, conceived of in terms of transformational grammars. Assume that we have the collapsed sequence (C_1, L_1, C_2, L_2), where L_1 and L_2 are grammars and C_1 and C_2 are theories of non-linguistic cognition. Assume further that L_1 is a phrase-structure grammar and that L_2 contains transformational rules. Finally, assume that C_1 contains operations which construct hierarchical structures and that C_2 contains structure-dependent operations. Then, restricting our attention to formal properties, (3) is satisfied and the view that cognitive development explains syntactic development is consistent with such a sequence. If, under the same assumptions, we had obtained the sequence (C_1, L_2, C_2, L_1), (3) would not be satisfied and the hypothesis that cognitive development explains syntactic development would be refuted.[8]

It appears that these three conditions, while being the obviously necessary ones to impose on cognitive reductions, do not conjointly guarantee the sufficiency of such an explanation. They demonstrate, if satisfied, the *existence* of relevant cognitive structures and the fact that these structures *precede* the associated linguistic structures. However, they can be satisfied and allow variant orders in the appearance of related cognitive and linguistic constructs, and it will be useful to conclude this section by formulating two additional conditions which move in the direction of establishing the sufficiency of cognitive development for language development. These conditions, though important, will not play a major role in my subsequent discussion of particular arguments.

Consider first a collapsed sequence satisfying (1)–(3) above. Satisfaction of (1) and (2) ensures the existence of a mapping F from the theoretical terms and formal operations of the linguistic sequence to those of the cognitive sequence such that, for theoretical terms, F is the translation mapping required by satisfaction of (1) and, for formal operations, it is the identity mapping. The sets of terms and operations in both sequences of theories – $(L_1, L_2, \ldots, L_n)$ and $(C_1, C_2, \ldots, C_m)$ – can be seen as partially ordered by the total orderings on the theories (cf. n. 6) and we can enquire whether F preserves the partial ordering of the linguistic terms and operations in the cognitive terms and operations, i.e. we can consider whether $X_i \leqslant X_j$ entails $F(X_i) \preccurlyeq F(X_j)$ where '$\leqslant$' is the partial ordering induced on the linguistic terms and operations by the total ordering on the set of linguistic theories, '$\preccurlyeq$' is the corresponding partial ordering for the cognitive terms and operations, and X_i and X_j are terms or operations from the linguistic sequence.[9] If this is so for all terms and operations in the linguistic sequence, we shall say that the two sequences are *order-isomorphic*.

As a further possibility, consider the collapsed sequence $(C_1, L_1, C_2, L_2, \ldots, C_n, L_n)$ where each C_i is a subsequence (possibly containing only one member) of cognitive theories and each L_i is a subsequence (possibly containing only one member) of linguistic theories. If the sequence satisfies the following condition we shall say that it is *intermeshed*:

($\forall$ i, j, X)((X is a term or operation in L_j and (i < j → X is not a term or operation in L_i)) → (F(X) is a term or operation in C_j and (i < j → F(X) is not a term or operation in C_i)))

In other words, if the sequence is intermeshed, each innovation in the developing linguistic system is *immediately* (this, of course, being relative to sampling intervals) preceded by the corresponding innovation in the cognitive system.

As a concrete example, consider again the collapsed sequence (C_1, L_1, C_2, L_2), where (L_1, L_2) is a developmental theory of syntax with L_1 a phrase-structure grammar and L_2 a grammar including transformational rules. If C_1 is a cognitive theory including operations for forming hierarchical structures and C_2 contains, in addition, structure-dependent operations, then the innovation between L_1 and L_2 is exactly paralleled by the innovation between C_1 and C_2 and the sequence is intermeshed.

To see a simple example in which theories are not intermeshed, we can consider the collapsed sequence (C_1, L_1, C_2, L_2) where (L_1, L_2) is as above except that the structure-dependent rules in L_2 are restricted to those involving the elementary operation of adjunction. Assume that C_1 contains operations for forming hierarchical structures and structure-dependent operations restricted to adjunction and that C_2 contains everything in C_1 plus deletion operations. The innovative aspects of L_2 over L_1 include the introduction of adjunction rules, and, as is necessary to satisfy (2), the operation corresponding to adjunction can be identified in (C_1, C_2). However, what is innovative in the transition from L_1 to L_2 cannot be identified with what is innovative in the transition from C_1 to C_2, as this latter involves the introduction of deletion operations which are unknown to both L_1 and L_2. In this case, therefore, the sequence is not intermeshed, although the possibility remains open that, with more stages sampled, we would have a case of order-isomorphism.

In fact it is easy to see that two theories being intermeshed is a special case of their being order-isomorphic, and, if theories of cognitive development and language development can be related in this way, we would be strongly tempted to see the former as approaching sufficiency in explaining the latter.

Equipped, then, with a set of five conditions on cognitive reductions, I shall now consider a number of arguments from the literature in which authors have been at pains to emphasise the explanatory role of cognition in language development.

8.3 Semantic arguments

In this section I shall focus attention on a set of arguments that have sought to establish that the *content* of what children say at certain periods of their linguistic development can be explained by reference to their non-linguistic cognitive abilities. This is to be contrasted with the following two sections where *structure* and *strategy* will hold the stage. These distinctions are not always clearly made, but, as I shall argue, there are important differences in what we can ask of a cognitive reduction in these different areas.[10]

Earlier parts of this book have introduced the sort of argument we are interested in here. In particular, Nelson's work on the FCH (Chapter 3), Brown's views on the semantics of early two-word utterances and those of Greenfield and Smith on the properties of one-word utterances (Chapter 6) could be readily assimilated to the structure of this section. However, I shall not re-introduce the work of these theorists here – enough has already been said to indicate the major strengths and weaknesses of their proposals, and the interested reader can easily construct a fuller treatment using the concepts of this chapter. Rather, I shall introduce some different ideas, paying particular attention to arguments advanced by McNamara (1972), Cromer (1974, 1976b), Antinucci and Miller (1976) and Sinclair-de-Zwart (1969).

Before beginning it is necessary to clear up a general point. Discussions of semantic development are inevitably going to credit the child with a set of meanings, however these are construed. Now it seems clear that if the child controls a meaning, then he must also control a 'concept' corresponding to that meaning. The alternative that the child may control the meaning without the associated 'concept' is not readily intelligible, unless we are to view meanings as socially defined over a communicating dyad rather than existing as part of *the child's* linguistic system. The proposals I am concerned with do not adopt this latter stance. Again, the suggestion that one cannot distinguish meanings from 'concepts', while having some plausibility (but see Bowerman 1974 for interesting discussion), here has the effect of subsuming linguistic development under cognitive development definitionally. Such a strategy, as pointed out above, leads to there being nothing to discuss.

If we accept the above and, furthermore, take theories of cognitive development as primarily concerned with the development of concepts, the first condition of 8.2 will always be vacuously satisfied so long as we restrict ourselves to semantic development, i.e. there will be a concept corresponding to each meaning with which we credit the child. Similarly, for the third condition, the emergence of the relevant meaning will be at worst simultaneous with that of the associated concept and typically will follow it. It seems, then, that any discussion in this area, to avoid trivialising the issues, must focus on at least one of the following:

(1)   the *existence* of an appropriate cognitive theory – it does not follow from the necessity of concepts preceding associated meanings that we are in possession of a cognitive theory ascribing the right concepts to the child at the right time;

(2)   *formal* aspects of semantic development (e.g. modes of combination of semantic primitives to form complex semantic representations);

(3)   satisfaction of order-isomorphism or intermeshing from 8.2.

McNamara (1972) made a big impression in the field of child language, and is often cited as one of the seminal papers on the topic of this chapter. Yet, on close inspection, its relevant content is remarkably slight, despite the author's summary which says (p. 11): 'All that is needed for my position is that the development of those basic cognitive structures to which I referred should precede the development of the corresponding linguistic structures.' Such a statement would appear to indicate that McNamara has explicitly discussed some of the conditions on reduction, but this is mere fancy.

The body of his paper is devoted to a plausible argument that the child, in learning some aspects of syntax, must have access to semantic information, using it to provide a way in to what is otherwise an apparently impossible task. But this is quite consistent with the view that the formal syntactic operations, conceived of as a formalisation of knowledge or as a set of procedures for converting meanings into forms, are independent of semantics and that, correspondingly, syntactic development is autonomous of cognitive development (at this point in his argument, McNamara appears happy to identify semantic and cognitive development). To show otherwise it is necessary to consider the properties of particular syntactic theories and attempt to satisfy the reduction clauses. Nowhere does McNamara undertake this task.

If McNamara's argument does not offer insights into syntactic development, what does it concern? He discusses vocabulary development and raises the two following points, among others:

(1)   Names for entities are learned before names for certain attributes.

(2)   Names for varying attributes are learned before names for permanent attributes.

As far as the first of these is concerned, he says (p. 4): 'It is obvious that an infant has the capacity to distinguish from the rest of the physical environment an object which his mother draws to his attention and names. It seems clear too that in such circumstances he adopts the strategy of taking the word he hears as a name for the object as a whole rather than as a subset of its properties, or for its position, or weight, or worth, or anything else.' The most plausible interpretation for this credits the child with a cognitive category, say 'Entity', at a stage at which he does not possess a distinct cognitive category, say 'Attribute', and, while this is not an unattractive suggestion, possibly providing a basis for the child learning the syntactic distinction between Nouns and Adjectives, one looks in vain for a clear statement of the cognitive theory which would make it more than plausible.[11]

An exactly parallel argument can be constructed for McNamara's second point, in connection with which he says (*ibid.*): 'If there is a differential set in small children to attend to varying states and activities rather than unvarying attributes, we need look no further for an explanation for the order in which the corresponding terms are learned.' Here we are faced with the suggestion that the child controls a cognitive category 'Varying attribute' before he controls categories 'Unvarying attribute' or 'State', a suggestion which, while plausible, requires to be backed up by some firm cognitive evidence before we can subscribe to it wholeheartedly.[12]

Cromer (1974, 1976b) offers a battery of arguments in favour of what he calls the Cognition Hypothesis.[13] Some of the data he cites in this connection have already been discussed and here I shall restrict myself principally to his treatment of his own earlier work (Cromer 1968). Although Cromer sees his arguments as having relevance for *grammatical* development, I believe that in a number of cases this is misguided, hence their inclusion in this section. The reasons for this should become clear as we proceed.

Cromer's earlier work was concerned with the development of the linguistic expression of various temporal concepts, and the first argument he offers from this area is to do with the order of events in time (see also Ferreiro and Sinclair 1971). The sentences in which he is interested contain two verbs, each of which has a distinct temporal reference. So we can compare, for example, *Can I put (future) it on his chest so it be (later future) a button*, in which the linear order of the sentence preserves the temporal order of the events referred to by the verbs, with *D'you know (present) the lights went (past) off*, which reverses this order. With this distinction in mind, Cromer says (1974, pp. 218–19):

At the earliest stages almost all utterances with relations between two points in time preserved the occurring order of events, and it was not until after four years in Adam and four years two months in Sarah that the children began to reverse these relations occasionally . . . the ability to reverse the order of events in time did not arise with new linguistic forms such as the acquisition of particular conjunctions . . . Most of the reversals use linguistic forms which were available to the child at an earlier age.

What can we make of this in terms of our present framework?

There appear to be at least two interpretations and the first of these requires a number of dubious assumptions. Recalling that Cromer claims to be discussing cognitive effects on grammar, we could assume:

(1)   There are grammatical devices which are instrumental in reversing the order of mention away from the order in which events occurred.

(2)   There is a cognitive theory employing a theoretical term somehow corresponding to this notion of reversibility.

(3)   We have evidence for the child going through a stage where he controls the cognitive item before he acquires the grammatical devices of (1).

Now (1) is highly questionable. English grammar has no brief for taking account of the actual order in which events occurred and so a device which is sensitive to this order can hardly be a part of English grammar. With this first assumption gone it makes little sense to pursue the rest, although the Piagetian notion of 'reversibility' might be useful in elucidating (2) and (3).

More profitable is a second interpretation which notes that there is a stage at which the child possesses all the necessary formal devices to compose utterances manifesting reversal. At this stage, however, the child does not use such sentences. Therefore, in order to explain the time-lag between the child's acquisition of the relevant formal apparatus and his using it to express reversals, we postulate an intervening cognitive stage where the child learns something about reversibility. Talking in terms of sequences, this becomes an argument for a collapsed sequence $(L_1 \, C, \, L_2)$, but the question of the identity of the L's immediately arises. They can hardly be grammars as Cromer admits that there is no significant grammatical difference in the forms available to the child at the two stages. Conceivably, they could be semantic theories, although what the details of such theories would be is difficult to discern. We are left, then, with theories which cannot be comfortably assigned to any linguistic domain, and, when we couple this with the fact that no independent evidence is adduced for the existence of C – it is merely convenient for explaining the lag in linguistic expression – we are forced to conclude that the proposal does not add to our understanding.

A similar conclusion can be reached in connection with Cromer's treatment of the development of hypotheticals. Again, we see the child equipped with all the formal devices for constructing hypothetical utterances but not doing so, and, to explain this, we propose a cognitive advance making the notion of 'hypotheticalness' available to the child. This argument is less worrying than the previous one to the extent that it is clear that what distinguishes the two linguistic stages in question (those at which the child does not and does produce hypothetical utterances) is an advance in the set of *meanings* the child can express. But now our first and third conditions from 8.2 are immediately satisfied; the child cannot express the meaning of 'possibility' or the meaning of 'hypotheticalness' until he has acquired the related concepts. The only substantive question concerns the status of the intervening cognitive advance and, in particular, its place in a theory of cognitive development. Unfortunately, as in the previous argument, no independent evidence is cited for its existence.

A third argument centres on the notion of 'relevance' and its connection with the use of the Perfect in English. Taking it for granted that some such notion is involved in the appropriate use of this aspect (see, for example, Palmer 1965) and without committing ourselves on the exact nature of this involvement, we can consider Cromer's argument in some detail.

The important observations are that the Perfect was very uncommon in the speech of the children studied, only appearing marginally productive at $4\frac{1}{2}$ years. Nevertheless, the children possessed all the syntactic apparatus necessary for the production of Perfects at a much earlier age, i.e. they used *have* as an auxiliary, they used some participle forms and, by their use of *be-ing* in Progressives, they indicated that they controlled a version of Affix-hopping. Just as in the case of hypotheticals, the gap between the acquisition of the formal devices and their use in the production of Perfect sentences is explained by postulating a cognitive stage C at which some concept of relevance emerges, i.e. again we have a collapsed sequence (L_1, C, L_2). It is apparent in this case too that the L's must be construed as theories of the sets of meanings the child is capable of expressing linguistically,[14] and they will differ in that L_2 will contain some *semantic* embodiment of relevance whilst this is not so for L_1. Thus far, the argument is identical to the previous one, but Cromer is on slightly stronger ground here regarding the postulated intervening cognitive stage. This is because he can refer to the children's use of certain forms, before they used Perfects, which seemed to involve some notion of relevance. For example, Adam produced utterances such as *Hey, what else you bring the pyjamas for, How come you didn't bring your car today?* and *This one is the mostest tight you ever saw* all of which Cromer sees as requiring this concept. To the extent that this evidence is convincing, the cognitive stage C has that much more plausibility. It would, nevertheless, be reassuring to have independent non-linguistic evidence for C and assimilation of C into a theory of cognitive development.

The final temporal category discussed by Cromer is 'timelessness'. He remarks on the relatively late appearance of timeless habituals or generics and notes the puzzling aspect of this, given their simple syntactic expression. The logic of the argument is identical to that just considered and there is no point in going into detail. It is worth mentioning that the argument is weaker than the previous one and similar to that concerning hypotheticals in that there is no independent evidence for the intervening cognitive stage at which the child acquires a concept of timelessness.

Taken together, it is probably true that these four arguments point to a significant cognitive change in the child's categories of time and related notions round about 4 years. But, until they are integrated into a wider framework they will remain suggestive and not satisfy our desire for explanation.[15]

An analysis of Antinucci and Miller (1976) also deals with temporal reference and will provide some perspective for the discussion of Cromer's views. They begin their paper with a statement of intent (p. 168): 'In what follows, we will try to argue that a correct understanding of the child's first past-tense forms and their gradual development cannot be attained unless we place them in relation to their cognitive prerequisites. We will see that the meaning the child encodes in his past forms is strictly based on his construction of the cognitive dimension of time.' Already we see a familiar fallacy: how else could it be other than that the child's intention to communicate particular meanings follows on his conceptualisation of notions related to those meanings? We may have to look hard for substantive points.

Of the two common Italian past-tense forms, the *imperfetto* and the *passato prossimo*, the latter appears from the beginning of data collection (children in the study were aged 1;6 to 2;5) except that the auxiliary (corresponding to *have* or *be*) is not present and the participle forms of transitive verbs were marked for agreement in number and gender with their direct objects – this latter situation only obtains in Italian when the object is a pronoun. Antinucci and Miller suggest that this indicates that the children are focusing on the *result* of the event described by the verb, treating the participle as an adjective, and attempt to support this suggestion by means of a semantic analysis of the verbs used by children in their past-tense forms. This analysis recognises three reasonably self-explanatory classes: STATE verbs, CHANGE OF STATE verbs and ACTIVITY verbs and leads to the generalisation that only CHANGE OF STATE verbs are used in the past, although the other two categories do appear in present-tense forms.

The moves to explain these facts in terms of cognitive development now follow. The only past tense forms used by children are those referring to events which resulted in changes in a state of affairs. *John broke the doll* is related to the state of affairs represented by *The doll is broken* which is usually taken to obtain at the time of the past-tense utterance.[16] *John ran down the street*, using an ACTIVITY verb, is not, or, at least, not as intimately, related to some existing state of affairs, e.g. that which would be referred to by *John is down the street*. For CHANGE OF STATE verbs (p. 183): 'the past event (process) and the present moment (end-state) are related not simply by an abstract temporal relation but by a more concrete effectual relation. This concrete link is exactly what enables the child to represent the past event once he has access to the present end-state.' Thus we have an intuitive sense in which past reference involving CHANGE OF STATE verbs might be regarded as more simple than past reference involving the other verbal categories, and the relationship of this intuitive analysis to cognitive development is developed in the following way (p. 185):

As Piaget has emphasised the construction of the temporal dimension has its roots in the practical co-ordination of sensori-motor schemata, in which the first is preparatory to the second or the second is the result of the first. Therefore, it seems reasonable that the child is first able to represent and encode past events only in those situations in which this concrete, practical co-ordination is present. This offers the child a support which leads him from the present, observable state of an object to the representation of the preceding event involving the object.[17]

What we appear to have is a claim that when the domain of investigation is the 'semantics of pastness', there is a stage, before the stage where *past* means 'before the time of utterance' at which it has a more restricted meaning. Compare, in this connection, Antinucci and Miller's statement (p. 183) that: 'The meaning of the child's past tense is at this point rather limited. He is able to encode a past event, but only if it results in a present state. Looking at this fact from a linguistic point of view, we could say that the past "tense" has more of an aspectual than a temporal value.' Exactly how we should gloss this more restricted 'aspectual' value is far from obvious but let us refer to it as X. Then the claim embodied in the passage cited above which refers to Piaget seems to be that there is a collapsed sequence (C, L), where C is the cognitive theory referred to in the passage and L is a linguistic theory including a semantics for past-tense forms with *past* meaning X. It seems to me that such a sequence fails to satisfy the conditions on cognitive reductions as there is no transparent translation from the theoretical term X of the linguistic theory into a theoretical term of C. Certainly 'concreteness' can be seen as a concept characteristic of both theories but this is merely an intuitive observation and can hardly warrant being called an explanation. Taking this one step further, we might expect that, if the child's first references to past events are somehow rooted in the co-ordination of his own action schemata, then those references will be to changes of state which he himself has initiated. But a quick survey of the data presented by Antinucci and Miller gives no indication that this is so – we find such examples as *E arrivato il cane* ('The dog arrived') and *Che ha mangiato tutti i pulcini* ('That ate all the chicks'). It could be, of course, that at an earlier stage there was a consistent bias towards encoding of past events only involving the child's own initiated changes of state. Equally, it may be that the suggestion under consideration is an illegitimate extension of the authors' position. It is, however, a fairly concrete and tangible interpretation and the sort of thing which is necessary if the proposal is to be rescued from destructive vagueness.

A second problem discussed in the same paper is the subsequent emergence of reference to past events encoded by STATE verbs and ACTIVITY verbs. When this sort of reference appears, the child uses the imperfect tense and not the past form involving a participle. An examination of the contexts in which these early uses of the imperfect appeared indicated that nearly all of them occurred in 'stories' (p. 186): 'The examples of story-telling share an interesting characteristic. The child is not narrating a past event, and in most cases is not even narrating a story that someone previously told him. The child is inventing a story at the moment . . . These examples show that the first uses of the imperfect do not mark a past event at all.' The attempt to relate this fact to cognitive development is straightforward (pp. 186–7):

Our claim with respect to the child's linguistic development is that the first instances of the imperfect form mark linguistically the cognitive distinction of pretend world vs. real world. The ability to make this distinction, as Piaget shows, is more complex, and later to develop than the ability to take account of physical transformation (which, we have argued, is the basis for the use of the participial form). This may explain why the imperfect forms appear later.

Here the argument seems clear. There is a cognitive theory C which includes the theoretical terms REAL and NON-REAL and a linguistic theory L which contains the theoretical terms *present* and *past*. In addition, we have a sequence (C, L), and the reduction of the linguistic development to cognitive development is achieved via this sequence and the translations:

present → REAL
past   → NON-REAL[18]

With this account, the earlier treatment of the participial past becomes somewhat more convincing, as we can now contemplate a sequence (C_1, C_2, L_1, L_2) where C_1 is a cognitive theory containing a translation of X from L_1 and C_2 contains the theoretical terms REAL and NON-REAL as translations of *present* and *past*.[19] This sequence, apart from the difficulties in translation from L_1 to C_1, appears to satisfy the conditions on reduction and, insofar as its structure is specified, to manifest order-isomorphism.

An argument of a quite different sort emerges from the work of Sinclair-de-Zwart (1969). This has been seen by some as supporting the Cognition Hypothesis (Cromer 1974). Others, most notably, Schlesinger (1977) and Karmiloff-Smith (1979) have been more circumspect, although for reasons different to those advanced here. It is not clear that Sinclair-de-Zwart herself would wish to interpret her work as supporting the sort of position under analysis in this chapter.

In this study a group of children were tested on a standard Piagetian conservation task and, on the basis of the results, divided into conservers, non-conservers and those at an intermediate stage. Each of these groups was then tested on a set of verbal tasks involving vocabulary considered relevant to the cognitive processes underlying the ability to conserve. This vocabulary includes comparatives, differentiated terms (e.g. the use of dimension-specific adjectives like *thick* and *thin* as opposed to non-specific adjectives like *big* and *small*) and structures involving conjunctions of properties such as *longer and narrower* and *shorter but fatter*. These tests investigated both comprehension and production and the outcome was that there was no significant difference between the groups of children on comprehension tasks. On the production tasks, however, the conservers were much more ready to use the vocabulary and constructions mentioned above than were the non-conservers. Now, as Cromer points out, this fact in itself does no more than establish a correlation between certain cognitive abilities and related linguistic skills;[20] the next part of the experiment investigated the causal relationship between the two sets of skills by attempting to teach the non-conservers to use the vocabulary and structures relevant for conservation. The vital conclusion of the experiment is that, of those children who did successfully begin to use the vocabulary and structures, only 10% advanced on the conservation task. Similar conclusions have been reached by Holland and Palermo (1975), so what is their significance for the relationship between cognitive and linguistic development?

It is immediately evident that such studies show that the relevant linguistic development is not a *sufficient* condition for the related cognitive development (assuming that we are satisfied with 'relevant' and 'related' here), and this could be seen as a refutation of a strong form of linguistic determinism. But such a refutation is not an argument for the Cognition Hypothesis. Sinclair-de-Zwart has not demonstrated that a sequence of the form (L, C) does not obtain, where L is a semantic theory for the stage of linguistic development at which the child produces and comprehends the vocabulary and structures considered most relevant for conservation and C is the cognitive theory corresponding to operational thinking. She has demonstrated that C does not follow immediately on L and this would seem to suggest a degree of autonomy for cognitive development.

Now, if she has not demonstrated that (L, C) *does not* obtain, she has certainly not demonstrated that (C, L) *does* obtain. Obviously, if it did it would provide support for the Cognition Hypothesis and for the reduction of the acquisition of comparatives, differentiated vocabulary, etc. to prior cognitive development. Note, however, that things are even worse for such a proposed reduction because what Sinclair-de-Zwart appears to have done is teach some children enough to credit them with L while admitting that they do not control C. For these children, the only conclusion we can draw is that any attempted reduction is impossible.

8.4 Syntactic arguments

In the previous section we have seen that arguments using semantic development have to struggle for significance in the terms of this chapter. However, there is every reason to believe that this will not be so for arguments whose point of departure is syntactic development. While formal properties must assume some cognitive organisation, it is far from obvious that this will extend beyond the linguistic domain, and we can anticipate that satisfaction of the relevant clauses in 8.2 will be non-trivial. Proposals aimed at explaining syntactic development in this manner are rather thin on the ground and I shall confine myself to a discussion of a set of arguments advanced by Sinclair (1971) and to a series of studies performed by Greenfield and her associates (Greenfield, Nelson and Saltzman 1972, Goodson and Greenfield 1975, Greenfield and Schneider 1977, Greenfield 1978c). Arguments concerned to establish the autonomy of syntactic development will be considered in 8.6 below.

Sinclair (1971) takes as given that children acquire syntactic systems having the general characteristics outlined in Chomsky (1965). She notes several formal properties of such grammars: concatenation, categorisation in the formation of syntactic categories, functional notions such as 'subject-of' and 'direct object-of', and recursiveness. For each of these she points to an aspect of sensori-motor development which, she claims, can be seen as accounting for it, Thus, concatenation is related to the child's ability to order things temporally and spatially, categorisation to classification by sets of action schemas, functional notions to the ability to relate objects and actions, and recursion to the ability to embed one schema inside another. We can consider each of these claims in more detail.

For the relationship between the child's ability to order things and the presence of a concatenation operation in the syntactic theory the case seems reasonable; an analogue of this formal operation must reside in a cognitive system which makes possible the sort of ordering phenomenon to which Sinclair refers. It follows, therefore, that the second condition of 8.2 is satisfied with respect to concatenation. For such properties the satisfaction of the first condition does not arise, and, if we go along with Piaget's and Sinclair's views on the achievements of the sensori-motor period, then the relevant formal property turns up in cognitive development before it does so in linguistic development. Consequently, our third condition is satisfied.

Consider Sinclair's second claim concerning the relationship between the child's ability to classify in action and the presence, in the developing syntactic system, of categories, particularly NP and VP. These latter are, of course, theoretical terms in the linguistic theory we are adopting and so it is satisfaction of the first rather than the second condition of 8.2 to which we must look. In order to achieve this, it is necessary to specify a translation of NP and VP into theoretical terms of the cognitive theory, but it is far from clear that we are provided with such a translation by Sinclair's exposition. What might be thought to be necessary is the provision of a cognitive basis for the notional categories of 'thingness' and, perhaps, 'doing', traditionally seen as forming the central part of definitions of nominal and verbal categories. But, while classification in action can lead the child to form categories, it is not apparent that they are at the level of generality required here. Rather, we end up with particular categories of objects (which fit into a certain schema) and categories of action (which apply to particular objects), but it is difficult to see how the further level of abstraction, necessary to arrive at 'thingness' and 'doing', is achieved. Cromer (1974), in a discussion of Sinclair's paper, is perhaps aware of this deficiency when he chooses to back up her analysis with a statement made by Lyons (1966), the essential part of which is (p. 131): 'By the time the child arrives at the age of eighteen months or so, he is already in possession of the ability to distinguish "things" and "properties" in the "situations" in which he is learning and uses language.' Here Lyons is more directly concerned with the issue at hand than is Sinclair, but he provides no independent cognitive evidence on the ontogenesis of 'thingness', etc. and so his remarks too remain programmatic. Thus, it seems that the necessary condition is not satisfied convincingly by Sinclair's argument and, under these circumstances, the satisfaction of our third condition does not arise.

The argument dealing with functional notions is weak. The grammatical relations 'subject-of' and 'object-of' depend, for their definitions, on both formal and substantive aspects of linguistic theory. The formal aspects include concatenation and dominance, while the substantive aspects involve reference to such categories as NP, VP and S. Relevant to this, we are offered the child's ability to relate objects and actions, which clearly presupposes 'thingness' and 'doing', but we cannot get much further than this. In particular, there is nothing in the ability to relate actions and objects corresponding to the category S; nor can we see any source for the formal property of dominance in this ability. As it stands, Sinclair's suggestion lacks rigour and precision, forcing on us the conclusion that neither the first nor second condition on reductions is satisfied by this part of the argument.

Finally, consider recursiveness. The claim is that the formal property of recursion, which is necessary in the assumed linguistic theory, can be identified in our cognitive theory with the child's ability to embed one action schema inside another. It is important to note, however, that this sort of embedding, in itself, does not qualify as recursion, unless it is related to a theory which makes precise the idea of a process or rule applying to its own output. In syntactic theory this is achieved by invoking a recursive rule or recursive sequence of rules, the output of which can be input to the rule (or sequence of rules) again. So, there must be a level of abstraction in the cognitive theory at which it makes sense to talk about embedding an object of a certain kind in *itself*. Talk of embedding one action schema inside *another* does not necessarily satisfy this requirement. I assume that no major modification in the cognitive theory would be required by making its recursiveness explicit and, if this were followed through, I believe that satisfaction of our second condition would follow. The third condition on reductions is then also satisfied by way of the observation that recursion is identifiable in cognitive development before it appears in linguistic development. Figure 8.1 summarises the above

	Condition 1	Condition 2	Condition 3
Concatenation	NR	+	+
NP and VP	—	NR	DNA
Functional relations	—	—	DNA
Recursion	NR	+	+

'+' = 'satisfies', '−' = 'fails to satisfy', 'NR' = 'not relevant', 'DNA' = 'does not apply

Figure 8.1

discussion. This is not a startlingly impressive result and we are led to conclude that Sinclair's attempt to reduce grammatical development to cognitive development falls short of its target in important respects.[21]

Greenfield, Nelson and Saltzman (1972) attempt to establish parallels between a certain kind of non-linguistic cognitive behaviour and formal aspects of grammatical structure. They say (p. 291):

Systematic observation of American children from 11 to 36 months of age playing with seriated nesting cups tested the existence of a developmental sequence of rule-bound, that is, consistent strategies for combining the cups. A related objective was to investigate the question of formal homology between strategies for cup construction and certain grammatical constructions.

Briefly, their procedure was to present the child subject with a set of nesting beakers in one of two configurations, manipulating the initial conditions by, for example, handing the child the smallest cup. The effects of the different configurations and initial conditions are not relevant to the discussion which follows. Three identifiable strategies used by the children in playing with the beakers were isolated. Strategy 1, or the Pairing Method, involved placing one cup in or on another cup; this strategy yields one or more *pairs* of cups. Strategy 2, or the Pot Method, involves placing two or more cups independently in or on a third cup, resulting in a structure of *three* or more cups which, when ordered by size, is referred to as a 'pile'. The cup which receives two or more cups remains stationary throughout the operation and is the 'pot'. For Strategy 3, or the Subassembly Method, the child moves previously constructed units into or onto other cups or structures. It differs from the Pot Method in that for the latter no structure is moved as a unit.

Most children in the study had a dominant strategy and the authors conclude (pp. 297–8):

The consistency with which a single strategy is employed by a given child demonstrates that these strategies function as internal 'rules' governing the child's play over a range of concrete situations . . . the term 'rule' seems preferable to the term 'habit' because the dominant strategy manifests itself in the child's very first approach to the task in 56 out of 64 cases.

Furthermore, the children's dominant strategy appeared to depend on age, with the youngest children preferring Strategy 1, those of intermediate age, Strategy 2, and the oldest children, Strategy 3.

Turning to the relationship between this developmental sequence and the development of linguistic abilities, Greenfield *et al.* suggest that one cup acting on another amounts to a relation of actor–action–acted-upon and that this relation corresponds to the sentence-structure subject–verb–object (SVO). For the Pairing Method the child only produces instances of one cup acting on another, but for the Pot Method there is a complex sequence of behaviour in which each of the two (or more) cups is an actor entering into an action with the same acted-upon. A sentence adequately describing this sequence would be a conjunction: *cup a enters cup b and cup c enters cup b*. In the case of the Subassembly Method the cup which is acted-upon in one part of the sequence becomes actor in the second part and this is seen as requiring a description along the lines of *cup a enters cup b which enters cup c*.

What do these suggestions amount to? If we are interested in the development of a set of sentence-types, then it may be that we can translate the theoretical terms that we use in describing this set of sentence-types into terms which are used in a theory of the child's developing strategies for manipulating cups, thus satisfying the first condition of 8.2. More fully, we have the three sentence-types which we may refer to as Simple, Conjunction and Relative. These may be described, using terminology which Greenfield *et al.* put forward as:

Simple: Subject–Verb–Object
Conjunction: Subject-Verb–Object–*and*–Subject–Verb–Object
Relative: Subject–Verb–Object → Subject–Verb–Object

Of the theoretical terms here, Subject translates into Agent, Verb translates into Action and Object translates into Acted-upon (assuming that Agent, Action and Acted-upon are used in the theory of cup-manipulation), and we now meet the additional argument (p. 304):

We have seen that the cup strategies develop in . . . sequence, but do the corresponding sentence-types follow the same developmental order? Certainly simple sentences appear first. One source of evidence on the relative ordering of the other two types of grammatical construction is provided by data from two of the children participating in Brown's longitudinal study of speech development. The conjunction of two sentences by *and* was frequent in the corpus of both children before relative clauses were a regular feature of their speech.

Therefore, we have a claim that the three relevant linguistic stages, marked by the introduction of a new sentence-type from the above set are order-isomorphic with three non-linguistic stages. The argument appears to be one of the stronger ones we have considered in this chapter.[22] Nevertheless, there are some crucial weaknesses in it.

First, Greenfield *et al.* suggest that, rather than seeing the cup-manipulating ability as *causing* the emergence of grammatical structures in the order in which they appear, it would be more realistic to consider 'a single competence underlying certain forms of action and grammar' (p. 308),[23] and this possibility leads them to claim that 'evidence as to the universality of the action forms is desirable' (*ibid.*). Preliminary work on Tzotzil speakers is reported which provides supporting evidence for this suggestion, but to appreciate the problem which now arises it is necessary to take account of the fact that the sentence-types under consideration not only employ theoretical terms but also have formal properties. Consequently, as well as asking for satisfaction of the first condition in 8.2, we can also look for satisfaction of the second. What are the formal properties in question?

If the theoretical terms, subject, verb and object, are being used in anything like their standard sense, a measure of hierarchical structure is immediately entailed in the sentence-types. Traditionally, in the structure of the simple sentence-type, the verb and the object would be taken as comprising a higher-order unit, the verb phrase. But there is no suggestion by Greenfield *et al.* that, in the action sequences with the cups, the Action and the Acted-upon have some sort of integrity not possessed by, say, the Actor and the Action. Indeed, it is difficult to imagine what such a suggestion could be based on. The relative sentence-type involves an embedded structure and so we might look for evidence that in the corresponding action sequence one action is somehow subordinate to the other. No such evidence is offered and it rapidly becomes apparent that there is essentially only linear structure involved in the action sequences with which the child manipulates the cups. Thus, hierarchisation and its particular case, subordination, are not available in these action sequences.[24]

This might be taken as merely demonstrating that the reduction is partial (cf. discussion in 8.1), but, even within the limits imposed by linear structure, it is possible to raise some serious problems. Recall that action sequences are claimed to be universal. In connection with the correspondences between action sequences and linguistic structures, Greenfield *et al.* say (p. 304): 'A convention governing the paallels between language and action . . . is that *grammatical relations must appear in the same temporal order as the corresponding action relations.*' (my emphasis – RMA). It follows that, whatever the language being learned by the child, his simple sentences should manifest SVO word-order (or, at any rate, agent–action–acted-upon, taking account of the case-grammar approach of Greenfield's later work). Unfortunately, there are now numerous recorded instances of children using a dominant word-order distinct from SVO.[25] To mention just two examples, Gvozdev's Zhenya used SOV before switching to the most common word order of SVO in Russian and Seppo, one of the children studied by Bowerman (1973), used SOV more frequently than the dominant SVO when acquiring Finnish. For these two children, then, the parallel between the structure of action sequences and grammatical structures breaks down.

Obviously, the temporal sequencing of events in cup-manipulation is inflexible; if you are going to put cup *a* inside cup *b* you have to pick up cup *a*, move it and place it in cup *b*; there is no way in which you can move it first! The same inflexibility does not characterise children's initial word-order.

In summary, it seems to me that, so long as one attends to very simplistic ideas about sentence structure, the analysis of Greenfield *et al.* is plausible. However, syntactic structure is not simply linear and, as soon as we begin to take account of constituency relations, even in simple sentences, it proves impossible to identify any correlate for them in action sequences. Even as far as linear structure is concerned, there remains the important problem of flexible word-orders.

The arguments considered in this section are interesting principally in the extent to which they reveal the vast gap between contemporary views on syntactic structure and the elementary aspects of this structure which have been tentatively explored in terms of cognitive development. The successes have not been spectacular, and certainly anyone wishing to tackle the problem should not underestimate the task. This is not to decry the achievements of Sinclair and Greenfield and her associates – they have taken important first steps – but it is to plead for caution in interpreting the extent of success.

8.5 'Strategic' arguments

In two important papers, Bever (1970) and Slobin (1973) introduced and attempted to systematise a set of observations on language development by reference to 'strategies' of one sort or another, and, since then, this notion has played an increasingly important role in language acquisition research (cf. discussion in Chapter 4 and, for a recent review, Cromer 1976a). For Bever, strategies were seen as principally important in the perception of sentences and formed part of a mapping from 'external' to 'internal' forms.[26] His attention to the development of such strategies was limited and I shall not pursue his ideas here. Slobin's speculations, however, were presented in a developmental context, and, for him, the notion of 'strategy' seems somewhat wider than for Bever, accommodating Bever-like processes but also including what we might regard as 'heuristics for language learning'. These are intended to govern the course of a child's learning rather than the form of his perceptions as he learns.

The beginning of Slobin's paper can be seen as adopting a definitional stance on the relationship between linguistic and cognitive development. He says (pp. 175–6):

> Every normal human child constructs for himself the grammar of his native language. It is the task of developmental psycholinguistics to describe and attempt to explain the intricate phenomena which lie beneath this simple statement. These underlying phenomena are essentially cognitive. In order for the child to construct a grammar: (1) he must be able to cognize the physical and social events which are encoded in language, and (2) he must be able to process, organize and store linguistic information. That is, the cognitive prerequisites for the development of grammar relate to both the *meanings* and the *forms* of utterances.

As suggested in 8.1, taken at face value this view seems to remove an interesting set of questions from the arena of discussion. We can agree with Slobin that the phenomena are 'essentially cognitive' but still ask whether we can identify appropriately related phenomena in non-linguistic domains of cognition. As we shall see, Slobin himself is not consistently a definitionalist.

Before introducing strategies, his argument is launched by asking whether it is possible to 'trace out a universal course of linguistic development on the basis of what we know about the universal course of cognitive development' (p. 180), and he offers the following summary of data in support of a positive answer to the question:

> The earliest grammatical markers to appear in child speech seem to express the most basic notions available to the child mind. For example, in languages which provide a vocative inflection, this is typically one of the earliest grammatical markers to emerge in child speech . . . One of the earliest semantic relations to be formally marked in child speech is that of verb-object. In order languages like English, this relation is marked early by consistent word-order. In languages which provide an inflection for marking the object of action (accusative) this is typically an extremely early inflection to emerge – often the first. In Luo the first inflections are subject and object affixes on verbs . . . In every language for which relevant data are available, there is an early form of negation in which a negative particle is affixed to a simple sentence. In languages as diverse as English, Arabic, Czech, Latvian, Japanese and Samoan, early yes-no questions are formed by rising intonation (*ibid.*).

All of this is well backed up by research findings, but what exactly does it show? It would appear to demand that there is an ordering of 'concepts' in some cognitive theory such that each of the linguistic phenomena mentioned in the above passage corresponds to a concept relatively early in the ordering. But, to my knowledge, no cognitive theory with properties amenable to treatment in these terms exists, nor is it *a priori* clear why 'vocative', 'verb-object' and 'negation' (among others, presumably) should comprise the 'most basic notions available to the child mind'.[27]

The more substantial parts of Slobin's argument develop from his discussion of the work of Mikeš and Vlahović on children being brought up bilingually in Hungarian and Serbo-Croatian, focusing on their acquisition of the locative systems in the two languages (see Mikeš 1967). The two systems are acquired at different rates and this cannot be explained by reference to the *content* of locative utterances in the two languages since this content is assumed to be the same whichever language is being spoken. However, the grammar of Serbo-Croatian locatives is considerably more complex than that of Hungarian locatives, and the organisation of these two systems is seen by Slobin as a cognitive task (adopting the definitional stance again), although, as I shall argue in 8.6, it is perhaps more rewarding to view this as an empirical question, awaiting further research in linguistic and other cognitive domains. Of more immediate interest is the fact that differential complexity of grammar is not the only variable which Slobin identifies in his attempt to account for the differences in acquisition. He points out that the Hungarian locative is consistently expressed by noun *suffixes* and a considerable amount of evidence is amassed to indicate the facilitatory effect, in acquisition, of coding locative notions by suffixes (rather than by prefixes or prepositions).[28] A more extensive survey of the acquisition of suffixes in general leads Slobin to postulate an 'operating principle' which biases the child to pay attention to the ends of words, and it is the status of this principle which deserves fairly detailed discussion.

First, it appears that the domain of enquiry from which the principle emerges is something like 'strategies and heuristics for facilitating the learning of language' rather than 'strategies and heuristics for the perception of particular utterances', i.e. such a strategy has, as its rationale, a theory of the language being acquired and not an understanding of utterance-tokens. This interpretation seems to be confirmed by Slobin's reference (p. 187) to the 'information-processing devices used and developed by children to understand speech and *to construct grammars*' (my emphasis – RMA). Presumably, as the child develops, the set of operating principles he has available changes. In this light they are, perhaps, best seen as part of a mechanism which determines his *representation* of linguistic input (see Chapter 10 for some discussion).

Slobin is again happy to suggest that such principles as that introduced above are cognitive, and we can ask whether any close relative of a bias to attend to the ends of words can be seen at work in non-linguistic cognitive domains. Obviously, as it is formulated, the principle under discussion is a purely linguistic device, referring as it does to 'the ends of words'; but it is, perhaps, possible to see it as emerging from a general cognitive principle which we might formulate as follows:

> In any temporally ordered sequence of events pay attention to the most recent ones.[29]

Of course, there is a good deal of vagueness in such a principle – does paying attention to most recently occurring events entail ignoring earlier events or simply paying less attention to them, etc.? Nor is it obvious to me that there is any support for this principle from the field of cognitive development, but such issues do not concern me here. The important point, from my perspective, is that the formulation of a general cognitive principle is raised in an intelligible form. Slobin does not raise the question, and, in apparently *assuming* that the principle is cognitive, buries the interesting issue.

A section of Slobin's paper entitled 'Constraints on linguistic perform-ance' is introduced with (p. 195): 'By and large, the language processing variables to be discussed below are determined by the fact that human language is produced and received in rapid temporal sequence . . . The sorts of processing variables considered here are therefore closely linked to general perceptual and performance-programming principles.' This makes the domain of enquiry sound very much like that examined by Bever, but Slobin goes on (*ibid.*): 'The constraints on linguistic performance are both short-term and long-term. The short-term have to do with the ongoing use of speech, and the long-term with the storage and organisation of the linguistic system.' The second category here sounds more like what we have already been considering – heuristics which the child brings to language learning – than like heuristics for sentence perception. The extent to which this distinction remains clear in Slobin's presentation is something to which I shall return briefly below. For short-term con-straints, he makes his position clear, saying (p. 196): 'the short-term limitations under which children operate . . . are universal human limitations on sentence processing, and they are based on general percep-tual and information-processing principles', and, from this general stand-point, another operating principle is introduced which suggests that the child is constrained to pay attention to the order of words and morphemes.

We might ask first whether this is a short-term strategy or a long-term heuristic vital to the child's eventual grasp of the language? Slobin's discussion does not provide an answer, but the answer required appears to be 'both', i.e. it will clearly facilitate the child's learning of (most, perhaps, all) languages if he assumes that the order of the morphemes in the utterances he hears is significant, and it will facilitate his comprehension of utterance-tokens too.

However the principle should be taken, can we make sense of the claim that it is based on 'general perceptual and information-processing principles'? Again, as it stands, it is restricted in its application to linguistic materials, mentioning such linguistic constructs as 'word' and 'morpheme'. Perhaps it is possible to see it as an instance of a general principle along the lines of:

> Pay attention to the order of events or to the order of items which are presented serially and regard it as significant.

If a serious argument were to be proposed on this sort of basis, we would need to see this general strategy being accommodated in a theory of cognitive development and appearing there before there was evidence that children were using the strategy in linguistic tasks. While such a possibility does not strike me as implausible, it is evident that much more discussion would be necessary before the matter could be regarded as closed.

Slobin continues to introduce and discuss several further operating principles in his paper. However, there would be little to be gained by submitting each of these to the analysis I have proposed for the two above. Suffice it to say that the considerations I have raised in these analyses are relevant to the further principles, almost without exception (for more detailed discussion, see Atkinson 1978).

In summary of Slobin's position, it seems to me reasonable to make the following points:

(1)   He appears, at times, to take a definitional, and, therefore (for me), uninteresting stance on the relationship between linguistic and cognitive development.

(2)   At other times, he indicates that aspects of grammar can be seen as autonomous of cognitive development.

(3)   Regarding content of linguistic utterances, he appears to fall into the trap of believing that there is a substantive issue concerning the *existence* of appropriately related concepts (cf. 8.3). The issue only

becomes substantive when we are in possession of a cognitive theory of the required type. For the phenomena Slobin cites, such theories are conspicuously absent.

(4)   For grammars, Slobin attempts no formal statement of the properties which appear to give rise to complexity and does not contemplate the possibility of identifying such properties in non-linguistic cognitive domains, i.e. the interesting questions are simply not raised.

(5)   There are some problems concerning the status of operating principles: are they heuristics for language learning or for sentence perception or both? Slobin is sometimes not clear on this issue, perhaps not seeing the distinction as an important one which needs to be drawn.

(6)   For the relationship between his operating principles and general cognitive strategies, Slobin fails to provide any account to substantiate the view that the former are 'essentially cognitive'. This could be because he sees the relationship as self-evident, but I believe that there are cases where this is not so. Where it is possible to speculate intelligently about the identity of general cognitive strategies, it seems that Slobin might be correct, but the matter deserves much more detailed investigation than has been offered here.

(7)   No ordering relationships are established between the operating principles and their cognitive analogues when these latter exist.

8.6 Arguments for the autonomy of linguistic development

In 8.3 I discussed some of Cromer's arguments for the dependence of language development on cognition. In the same paper he cites Brown's views on the relationship between the semantics of Stage I speech and sensori-motor intelligence (cf. Chapter 6), saying (p. 236): 'the possession of sensori-motor intelligence would still not explain the *expression* of that intelligence in language. That early grammar expresses the meanings which sensori-motor intelligence makes possible does not in itself solve the mystery of how these meanings are conveyed by a grammar.' This is true and raises a clear issue. If we have a theory of the meanings available to the Stage I child and we also have a theory which provides representations of the form of Stage I speech, then we ought to be able to work out a mapping between the two. However we conceive of this mapping, one would assume that it will use theoretical terms and have formal properties. Consequently, we should be able to examine non-linguistic cognitive domains searching for translations of these terms and identical formal properties.

The programme I have just outlined seems to me to be sensible and to ensure that open questions remain open for as long as possible. I also believe that we have only taken the most tentative steps with regard to this programme and that there is virtually nothing substantive that we can offer by way of results at the moment. On the one hand, the theory relating the child's meanings to his forms awaits precise formulation and, on the other, our knowledge of the formal properties and relations with which it is necessary to credit the child in order to explain his developing abilities in other cognitive domains is rudimentary. In particular, it seems unnecessarily restrictive to consider only the Piagetian model of cognitive development as a source for relevant properties at the expense of, say, theories of visual or auditory perception.

According to the most straightforward interpretation of Cromer (1974, 1976b), he disagrees with the above and assumes an answer to the question of the independence of the child's developing system of expression. However, he does this without even raising the issue of what other domains of the child's behaviour and knowledge should be considered relevant. The fact that some researchers are of the opinion that non-human organisms also possess the set of meanings associated with sensori-motor intelligence has no bearing on this argument. Brown and Cromer point out that, although the chimpanzee Washoe shows evidence to suggest that she manipulates these meanings (Gardner and Gardner 1969, 1975), she does not appear to control a system for their consistent expression (see Seidenberg and Petitto 1979 for particularly clear arguments to this point as well as many other interesting remarks on Washoe's achievements). But this does not necessarily demonstrate the language-specificity of the properties of such a system. Just as Washoe lacks a grammar with its associated properties, so also she may lack the cognitive system X which has these (or a subset of these) properties. The human child could control both a grammar and the system X and the fact that X is a non-linguistic system indicates that the development of grammar need not be autonomous of development in another cognitive domain.[30] Therefore, *nothing* can be concluded from the case of Washoe on these issues. Of course, the system X is hypothetical and, perhaps, the best course is to assume the autonomy of the system of expression until evidence to the contrary is forthcoming – this seems to be the strategy Chomsky has adopted throughout his writings.[31]

Cromer considers a number of additional arguments for the independent development of grammar. The first concerns negation and the central fact on which it hangs is that, given Bloom's (1968) three-way distinction of Non-existence, Rejection and Denial, the syntactic expression of each of these categories changes, becoming more complex, as the child develops. Cromer says (p. 239): 'If to express the meaning of non-existence, the child comes to use more and more complex techniques over time, these new structures cannot be being acquired due to advances in "meaning".' But the assumption here that there is no change in meaning is to take the status of Non-existence, Rejection and Denial as semantic categories too seriously. To see this, compare a selection of one child's utterances, categorised by Bloom as expressing Non-existence, with a selection of his utterances expressing the 'same' semantic category from a later stage.

> Stage II: *no more juice, no more noise, no more*
> Stage V: *no more ball, no more bridge, oh no fire engine, you no bring*
>   *choo choo train, I no reach it, I didn't do it, I didn't crying*

In the second list there are some sentences which are identical in structure to those in the first list, but, of course, they are not relevant to an evaluation of Cromer's claim. Of the other sentences on the second list, how is it possible to say that, as far as their negativity is concerned, they do not differ in meaning from the sentences on the first list? It is not, and this amounts to a criticism of Bloom's semantic categories which are no more than broad notional sets, and fairly misleading ones at that. It is not the case, contrary to Cromer's assertion, that there is a clear syntactic development in the expression of a single unchanging semantic category.

But suppose for a moment that he were correct. Nothing would follow from this until the 'new' formal principles (and, perhaps, theoretical terms) involved in the more complex system of expression are spelled out in detail. Then we would be in a position to investigate whether these formal principles are already in use in some non-linguistic cognitive domain. As things stand, Cromer's assertion has no more support than any of the conceivable alternatives.

A similar argument draws on the work of Bellugi on the development of the child's abilities to refer to himself (see Bellugi-Klima 1969, Bellugi 1971). The relevant development can be summarised as follows:

> Stage I.   Child refers to self with own name.
> Stage II.   Child refers to self with *I* or *I* + own name in sentence-
>   initial position and uses *me* in any other position.

Stage III. Child refers to self with *I* in 'nominative' positions and *me*
in 'accusative' positions.

Regarding this sequence, Cromer says (p. 242): 'the developments are not
solely based on meaning or reference. Throughout, the meaning remained
the same – reference to self.' But this is fallacious. Certainly when the
child says, e.g. *That what I do* he is referring to himself and using *I* to do
so. However, this is not to say that *I*, in the child's semantic system, has
the same meaning as the child's own name at that stage (or at an earlier
stage). This is to confuse meaning with reference and, indeed, an identical
argument could be constructed for adult usage with absurd consequences.

Putting this aside, assume that, for the forms 'own name', *I* and *me*, it
makes sense to talk about their meaning being some constant 'reference to
self'. Then we can suggest that the child must operate with 'rules' at the
three stages in question and we might represent these rules in the
following way:

Stage I: 'reference to self' → 'own name'
Stage II: If 'reference to self' is sentence-initial, then
            'reference to self' → *I* or *I* + 'own name'
            Otherwise
            'reference to self' → *me*
Stage III: If 'reference to self' is nominative, then
            'reference to self' → *I*
            If 'reference to self' is accusative, then
            'reference to self' → *me*

These 'rules' are not intended to be taken very seriously but they do begin
to make apparent the child's development in formal terms. So, it is clear
that the Stage I rule is context-free while the Stage II and III rules are
context-sensitive (only an impressionistic comparison with rewrite systems is intended by the use of these terms). Further, the context of the
Stage II rule is provided by the linear structure of the sentence, whereas
the Stage III rule appears to have to make reference to hierarchical
structure (assuming that nominative/accusative can be identified with
subject/direct-object). From this we might conclude that the Stage II rule
has something in common with context-sensitive rewrite rules and that the
Stage III rule is reminiscent of a transformational rule. All of this could be
quite accidental and is anyway incidental to the main point which is that
the rules we formulate should have identifiable properties for which we
can search in non-linguistic cognitive domains. Nothing is gained by
prejudging the outcome of such activities.

The final set of arguments presented by Cromer is also used by Slobin and concerns the relatively late appearance in some languages of the appropriate linguistic encodings for particular semantic contents, when this is compared with the appearance of encodings of the same content in other languages. For example, although it has often been reported that children acquiring English ask their first yes/no questions using rising intonation, Finnish children do not ask yes/no questions when they are at an otherwise comparable stage of development (see Bowerman 1973 for details). The explanation offered for this is that Finnish lacks a simple intonational device for forming yes/no questions (but see Sauvageot 1948), having resort to a relatively complex operation involving a moved question particle. Note that, in this case, since it is claimed that Finnish children do not ask yes/no questions at all, there is no evidence to support the view that they control the relevant meaning. This puts the claim that the late development of yes/no questions in Finnish is due to the complexity of the mapping from meaning to form on somewhat weaker ground than in other examples.

A second argument concerns the acquisition of plurals in Arabic which Omar (1973) claims are not acquired fully by the age of fifteen. This is put down to the severe irregularities which are encountered in the system.

Finally, the best-known example comes from Slobin's interpretation of Mikeš's work (see 8.5 for a brief description). In each of these three cases Cromer claims that there is something *peculiarly linguistic* about the development. Unfortunately, again, it seems clear that he is prejudging the issue in a clumsy fashion. So long as we only recognise the semantic system as capable of interacting with the cognitive system he would seem to be correct by definition. But no plausible reason is advanced for restricting the enquiry in this way and it is much more interesting not to do so. For the case of the Finnish yes/no question, it would be necessary, before the relevant issues can be precisely formulated, to have a detailed statement as to exactly what formal properties are central to this area of Finnish grammar. Given such a statement, we would be in a position to investigate other cognitive domains looking for just these properties. If we can identify them in such a domain and if, furthermore, it transpires that they are manifest in that domain before they appear in the child's linguistic structures, then we would have the beginnings of a reduction.

Cromer concludes (p. 245): 'We can see then, that cognitive development and linguistic development do not necessarily proceed together . . . cognition can make certain understandings available, but there may be linguistic constraints.' In my view he has offered no convincing arguments to this conclusion.

The authors considered in this chapter succeed to varying degrees in their attempts to relate linguistic and cognitive development. However, the overall impression is that so far there has been a remarkable lack of awareness of the complexities involved in approaching this relationship. The next chapter will consider whether the same claim is justified in the case of workers who have chosen a 'social' theory as their reducer.

9 *Social reductions*

The general approach I have examined in the previous chapter has been criticised on the grounds that it fails to take account of the child's developing knowledge of persons and social relationships except insofar as these can be construed as part of his physical environment. The Piagetian perspective adopted by most of the authors seeking cognitive reductions has itself come under attack precisely for this failure (see, for example, Trevarthen and Hubley 1978). Yet, as Shields (1978) has pointed out, when we turn to the work of psychologists who do regard persons and person-based relationships as having special significance in the child's developing conceptual system, we also find a reluctance to view the child as a 'model-builder' or 'theory-constructor'. As Shields puts it (p. 530):

the student of emotional and social development is doing the same kind of job that the student of cognitive development is doing, he is developing classifications, measuring constants, creating conceptual systems and theories about personal and interpersonal behaviour. He does not usually, however, regard his subject as engaged in the same activity at all. While the researcher is developing concepts about affiliation, his subject is affiliating, while the researcher is evolving categorical systems for observing interactions, his subject is interacting. The developmental psychologist does not appear to think that any of this behaviour does or could result from his subjects doing what he himself is doing; that is, forming a reasoned model of the social and personal world, using inference and deduction, deriving logical models from his own and other people's social actions and elaborating hypotheses, expectations and rules.

To the extent that this is correct we might anticipate problems in examining social reductions, as I would like to insist that something analogous to the conditions on cognitive reductions, formulated in 8.2 above, are vital to evaluating such proposals. But, of course, those conditions assume that the theorist has available a theory of linguistic structure (in the appropriate domain) and a theory of cognitive structure *of the same type*. This type-identity is necessary if we are to have any hope of identifying formal properties across the two theories. It will follow, therefore, that unless we have a developmental theory of the child's social knowledge (or behaviour) consisting of an axiomatisation of structural possibilities, we shall be unable to pursue the conditions on reduction meaningfully.

We have already seen (7.2) one attempt to examine communicative development in terms of social structure, viz. Halliday (1975). Beyond saying that Halliday avoids the problem raised in the previous paragraph by restricting himself to a taxonomy of communicative functions and not getting involved with the finer details of syntactic or semantic structure, I shall refrain from further discussion here. The course that such further discussion would take is reasonably obvious. One influential figure who has so far escaped attention in this book is Bruner. He has attempted to produce a theory of linguistic development which looks to pre-linguistic social interaction between a mother and her child for its explanatory constructs; this attempt will be examined in 9.1. Section 9.2 will look briefly at recent efforts to trace the genesis of the symbolic function (and, in some cases, syntax) back through gesture and ultimately to non-communicative action taking place in an interactional context.

9.1 Language structure and interactional structure

The exact subject-matter of Bruner (1975a) is not easy to assess. Although the title of the paper is 'The ontogenesis of speech acts', there is little in it of direct relevance to this topic, except, perhaps, for a general emphasis on language use and some rather confusing discussion of the standard philosophical literature. Some of what Bruner says points to an interest in perlocutionary force and its relationship (if there is one) to the intentions of the speaker, but it is difficult to glean anything systematic on this issue from the discussion. It is most appropriate to see the real content of the work as falling outside the domain of speech-acts, unless, of course, we inflate this latter notion enormously.

What the arguments of the paper boil down to are that there are interesting correspondences between the structure of pre-linguistic communicative acts and the linguistic structures which the child subsequently acquires. There appear to be three aspects of linguistic structure (broadly interpreted) approached by Bruner. The first is to do with sequencing in conversation and the breaking down of conversations into units; as such, it has nothing to do with sentential structure (although, see below). The second is concerned with case relationships and their realisation in linguistic structures. And the third, perhaps most closely related to the title of the paper, discusses subject–predicate structures in language and their relationship to topic–comment structures. I shall consider each of these in turn.

The relevant data on the imposition of unitising structure on conversations is provided by the study of interactions between mother and child. The claim is advanced that many of these interactions, before the child has any language, are broken down by the mother into 'segments' (p. 12):

> In the case of intention-oriented interactions, the principal form of signalling is MARKING THE SEGMENTS OF ACTION. Most usually it begins by the use of terminal marking, the use of what might be called a COMPLETIVE. The child takes a mouthful of newly introduced food from a spoon; the mother exclaims, *Good boy!* with distinctive intonation. Or he offers back an object handed to him, and the mother exclaims *There!* Or he removes a ring from a peg-and-ring toy, and the mother cries *Aboom!* It may well be that completion marking of this kind serves as an initial step in primitive semantic segmentation, the forming of units.

The suggestion seems to be that the child's primitive model of interaction does not recognise 'turns' – in some way the child regards the interaction as continuous. For the adult, however, this continuous activity is broken down into units, each corresponding to a 'turn' in the interaction, and the child is 'taught' this structuring by the mother's use of completives (there is no suggestion that this is the only device the mother has available for signalling the end of a 'turn'). Once this amount of structuring is achieved, Bruner claims that the child is in a position to individualise items in the interaction sequence, to repeat items, to vary items, to substitute items for others, etc. (p. 13); 'Segments of action are, in effect, positions occupied in a sequence by varying or substitutable acts. It is in this sense that we conceive of them as representing privileges of occurrence for classes of acts and, consequently, a particularly important form of psycholinguistic learning.' What is the relevance of this to psycholinguistic learning?

There seem to me to be two interpretations available for Bruner's argument. The first takes the position of completives at the end of acts as important and has it that the argument is of no relevance for our understanding of sentence structure. Completives typically terminate an action which would subsequently be encoded by a whole sentence and they do not terminate 'pieces' of action which could be related to sentence-internal units. Therefore, their importance for language learning must lie at some level of structure above the sentence. Now, undoubtedly, there are principles governing the construction of well-formed conversations, although these have not been clearly articulated; it appears that this is the most likely domain for identifying structures which are isomorphic to Bruner's action sequences. But, even in this domain, remarkably little is shown by this argument.[1] In conversation we have the phenomenon of a question followed by an answer or some response to indicate that an answer is not forthcoming – this represents a special pair of 'turns' in the conversational sequence. Bruner has not indicated any sequences in pre-linguistic interaction which could be interpreted in a parallel fashion. Further, we have the notion of a speaker meaning something distinct from the literal meaning of his words, this speaker's meaning being determined from literal meaning by poorly understood principles which almost certainly make reference to the conversation in which the relevant utterance is embedded (see Grice 1968, 1975, Searle 1975c for the beginnings of a theory in this area). Where are the correlates of this complex facet of conversation in non-verbal interaction?[2] In short, for this interpretation, it seems that Bruner has succeeded in identifying only the crudest and least interesting aspects of conversational structure in non-verbal interaction. This, coupled with the fact that the structural properties under analysis are at a level above the sentence, makes Bruner's suggestion that this argument can be viewed as part of a thrust against Chomsky's variety of linguistic nativism very implausible.

The second interpretation is more abstract and requires the child to view completives as general segmentation devices, creating for him the notion that linear sequences can be segmented (at a number of levels) and that substitutions can be performed in such sequences on a segment-for-segment basis. Put like this there are obvious resemblances between the interpretation and the traditional procedures of segmentation and classification advocated by North American linguists between the 1930s and 1950s (see Harris 1951 for the most highly developed statement of this approach to linguistic description). Against this interpretation, however, it must be noted that Bruner offers no textual reference to express this affiliation and that, even if it is correct, it fails to make much impact on Chomskyan nativism, as the latter does not gain whatever plausibility it has from the existence of classificatory devices in natural languages; Chomsky could happily admit that such devices could be learned on the basis of exposure to linguistic or non-linguistic data and still offer facts about language structure which could not be similarly accommodated.

Moving on to the second set of arguments, these are of more obvious relevance to the development of sentence structure. The first observation is in support of the general proposition that (p. 6): 'The facts of language acquisition could not be as they are unless fundamental concepts about action and attention are available to children at the beginning of learning.' This observation follows from a collation of the evidence, much of which has already been mentioned in this book, from Bowerman, Brown and Schlesinger on the semantic characteristics of the child's earliest one- and two-morpheme utterances. Summarising this evidence, Bruner says (p. 7): 'These various sets of data suggest that the child in using language initially, is very much oriented towards pursuing (or commenting upon) action being undertaken jointly by himself and another.' As a general description this is unexceptionable, but examination of later stages in the argument reveals that Bruner probably intends something more than description.

Recall that the mother's completives are claimed to impose a structure on a sequence of actions. Going inside each unit in such a sequence, Bruner claims that mothers, from an initial stage where the child focuses his attention on the agent of actions, go through a process of (p. 13) 'dramatizing or idealising the act itself with some kind of serial marking'. This is described in terms of the mother making sounds to accompany the action, the end result being a distinction between the Agent and the Action within a single act in the sequence. Further speculation shows how this can be elaborated to allow reference to a Recipient and, presumably, a Patient, although there is no discussion of this latter category. It is necessary, then, to assume for the argument which follows, that the output of this structuring of actions is action units, each of which can be seen as having a structure of the form:

Agent–Action–Patient–Recipient

and this corresponds, in linear order, with the most normal word-order in an English sentence encoding each of these notions, a correspondence which Bruner grasps and uses when he says (p. 17): 'The argument has been that the structures of action and attention provide bench-marks for interpreting the order-rules in initial grammar: that a concept of agent–action–object–recipient at the pre-linguistic level aids the child in grasping the linguistic meaning of appropriately ordered utterances involving such case categories as agentive, action, object, indirect object and so forth.'

This is a poor argument at two levels. The first is concerned with facts to do with word-order in individual languages. Not all languages have Agent–Action–Patient–Recipient as their canonical word-order and, therefore, the action sequences described by Bruner could not have a facilitating effect on the acquisition of such languages. Important in this regard is the finding that children do not universally adopt SVO as their first dominant word-order and do not necessarily follow the dominant order in the adult language (for detailed treatment, see Bowerman 1973 and for discussion in a different context, 8.4 above). The only way to save the hypothesis at this level would be to suggest that the strategies mothers and children employ in breaking down action sequences differ according to the language being acquired, but I have seen no evidence cited in support of this suggestion and, indeed, it seems highly implausible.

At the second level, let us assume, for the sake of argument, that the first objection can be answered and that, for all languages, relationships can be observed between canonical word-order and segmentation of action sequences. Still some serious issues would remain unresolved. For example, no progress will have been made on the question of how non-canonical word-orders are learned and it will also remain to explain the source of the formal relatedness between sentences with different structures. In short, I believe that Bruner seriously underestimates the structural complexity of human languages and that, even if his attempt to reduce certain superficial facts to a non-linguistic domain worked, it would only produce a chink in the armour of the Chomskyan position on innateness.[3]

The third set of arguments concerns the relationship between aspects of attention and the topic–comment and subject–predicate organisation of linguistic utterances. The hypothesis being explored is that (p. 4): 'early language, to be acquired, must reflect the nature of the cognitive processes whose output it encodes. One instance has to do with the isomorphism between a central linguistic form, predication, and the nature of human attention-processing.' Further (*ibid.*):

Concerning predication, I refer to the topic-comment structure of utterances, reflected formally in such devices as subject-predicate in grammar or as function and arguments in logical analysis. Topic-comment structure reflects an underlying feature of attention . . . and its realisation in language by the use of subject-predicate rules is sufficiently akin to this characteristic of attention to make these rules easily accessible to a language learner.[4]

The sort of evidence cited in favour of these claims comes from work on visual attention which Bruner describes, following Neisser, as (p. 4): 'positing wholes (topics) to which parts or features or properties may be related and from which the new wholes may be constructed'. This can, perhaps, best be viewed in a manner analogous to that used above in connection with the breaking down and internal structuring of action units within interactional sequences. Here we could view the child's perception as initially undifferentiated, then broken down into units, each unit being subsequently elaborated as a topic–comment structure. The topic consists of the child hypothesising a particular 'object' of perception and the comment of his filling in details of that object. The claim appears to be that the topic–comment structure emerging from this sort of process is formally analogous to the Topic–Comment distinction which is used in analysing the structure of (some) utterances.

While the proposal as outlined is somewhat vague, it is difficult to see it as amounting to anything very profound. First, although it may make sense to see the Topic–Comment distinction as one of the organising factors of utterances and discourse-structure, it cannot be identified with the subject–predicate distinction, an organising principle in the theory of grammar (for some discussion, see Atkinson 1979). Second, without giving the reader some clearer idea of what the 'subject–predicate rules' are supposed to be, it is impossible to evaluate the substance of Bruner's claim. Third, even if the child can get access to some aspects of grammatical organisation via the structure of attentional routines, again this would only represent the primitive beginnings of the acquisition of language structure. It seems to me to be more productive at the moment to view routines manipulating attention as geared to the establishment of topics in discourse, and I hope to have gone some way towards demonstrating the value of such an approach in 7.4.

Bruner (1975b) contains amplification of some of the points discussed above, but does not succeed in providing enough detailed argumentation to make his positions convincing. Strengthening confidence in my first interpretation of the first set of arguments above, we find (p. 28): 'Let me suggest that the development of the exchange mode marks the beginning of privileges of occurrence in discourse, the emergence of rule-bound exchanges that operate on a wide variety of objects, gestures and calls which, so to speak, become tokens in a standardised transaction.' And, for the second set of issues (p. 29): 'In such exchanges, the child is learning to deal practically with such relational concepts as Agent, Action, Possession, Instrument, Recipient of Action and so forth . . . Is it unreasonable to suppose that mastery of the concept of a reciprocal task may provide the basis for later interpretation of sentences?' The topic–comment organisation of visual processing and pre-linguistic play is explored at some length, again with a view to seeing the germs of predication in it, but what I find an extremely confusing discussion of the properties of predication can only conclude that (p. 35): 'full transition from these early components to full subject–predicate organization in language is as obscure as ever it was'.

Rather more argument is provided on the relationship between the order of events and the order in which the 'components' of these events are encoded in an utterance. Furthermore, the existence of non-canonical word-orders is recognised along with the problems they create. That Bruner is making a strong claim with regard to serial order in events and sentence structure is reflected in his references to the work of Cromer (1968) and Clark (1971) discussed in earlier chapters of this book, and his citing of data from a child Matthew who, at twenty months (p. 39): 'sees an airplane approaching overhead, points and says "Airplane", follows the plane across the sky with his eyes, and comments finally "All-gone", followed a moment later by a connected utterance "airplane allgone". The serial intercalation of comments and context is appropriate, well-timed, and natural. The order of events provides the serial order of the utterances.'[5] Once again, though, we must note the existence of languages which would not be readily learned in terms of such strategies, as well as the existence of non-canonical orders in English. Noting this latter point, Bruner says (p. 40): 'For adult grammar, of course, event order is a weak and rigid rule. Adult grammar obviously is ripe with inversion rules, as in the interrogative and passive.' The mastery of such non-canonical orders cannot be located in the normal order of events and Bruner's solution is to argue for a 'pragmatic approach' to the problem. I find his reasoning on this issue difficult to follow. To locate a source of non-canonical word-order in pre-linguistic interactional behaviour, it would appear necessary to establish at least the following:

(1) There is pre-linguistic interactional behaviour preceding the development of non-canonical word-orders in which order is a vital consideration.

(2) There is a notion of canonical order definable in this non-linguistic domain.

(3) Non-canonical orders can be identified in this domain before non-canonical word-orders appear.

(4) The relationship between sequences manifesting the canonical and non-canonical sequences in the non-linguistic domain should be relatable to the relationship (formal and/or semantic) between canonical and non-canonical word-orders.

Much of this requires further discussion, but one argument offered by Bruner does approach satisfaction of these conditions. He says (p. 42):

There is also order violation in play. Reynolds (1972) uses the expression 'simulative mode' to emphasise the fact that play bears a close resemblance to 'real action', yet departs from it and need not achieve the useful results of real action. Means and ends are uncoupled and conventional or adaptive order loosened. Once conventional or natural order is no longer the sole determinant of the order of acts, new principles of ordering emerge. One such is the principle of emphasis. It is a principle used in adult speech as well. In ordinary adult discourse the order of a sentence is often chosen for emphasis.

There is clearly an attempt here to satisfy (1)–(3) above and to begin the grapple with (4) via the reference to 'emphasis'. Of course, in general, the explanation would not work because there are severe constraints on non-canonical word-orders which, so far as I am aware, have no correlates in play.

The only other suggestion in Bruner (1975b) which is not examined in detail in Bruner (1975a) concerns the relationship between the emergence of a competence to use deictic expressions and the source of this competence in pre-linguistic routines. What the proposal amounts to is that the appropriate use of deictic expressions presupposes, on the part of the speaker, some acquaintance with his addressee's point of view (surely correct) and that various pre-linguistic routines to do with the direction of gaze as well as some early linguistic phenomena such as the use of *here you are* and *thank you* in giving and taking games can be seen as indicating just such an acquaintance. At this level of generality the suggestion is correct but does not have an exciting amount of content; I shall not pursue it.[6]

9.2 Action, gesture and symbol

Several of the papers in Lock (1978) put forward versions of the argument to be considered in this section. This argument is motivated by two principal concerns:

(1)   to get away from the 'cognitivist' view of the child as a problem-solver who is, in some sense, outside the problem he has to solve;

(2)   to establish contact with views on the evolution of language (e.g. Hewes 1973) by attempting to indicate parallels between ontogenesis and phylogenesis. This leads to an emphasis on the origins of gesture.

At the outset let me say that I am not unsympathetic to such motivations, although I am not convinced that (1) leads to any intelligible research programme (see Atkinson 1980 for some justification for this attitude). What is of direct concern to me in the context of this book is to get clear what is achieved by this sort of argument, and, more importantly, to examine what aspects of language structure remain untouched by considerations of this kind. Perhaps the most eloquent statement of the position I am concerned with is made by Clark (1978), and I shall largely confine myself to a discussion of his views – I believe that they are not unrepresentative of many of the other contributors to Lock (1978).

Clark does not hesitate in adopting a bold position (p. 234): 'The development of language can be viewed as a progressive complication of the basic communicative function, and the emergence of certain abilities in conjunction with this.' We might be puzzled by the reference to 'certain abilities', but what is clear from this statement is that a full understanding of the 'basic communicative function' should take us some way towards understanding the development of language. Clark sees two distinct phases in the ontogenesis of this function – his discussion takes place with reference to activities involving the transfer of objects from mother to child and vice versa, and, obviously, the events he describes are not intended to exhaust the phenomena the student of early communication might be interested in.

In the first 'primitive phase' the child, by his actions, communicates something to the adult, but there is no *intention* to communicate on the child's part. For example, he reaches towards an object and the mother moves the object within reach, interpreting the child's action as if it were expressing a desire for the object. However, at this stage, the child himself remains totally unaware of the communicative status of his action, and, indeed, does not even see his action as having any significance outside its role in acquiring the object in question.[7]

This primitive phase is contrasted with a later 'gestural phase', when the child's actions do become intentionally communicative and take on the status of *gestures*. The reaching behaviour which occurred in the primitive phase may persist, but is now likely to be accompanied by the child monitoring the mother's reactions to his activity, thereby making it clear that the action is intended to be noted by her and to prompt a response in her. The action is now genuinely communicative. Clark notes that there might be problems in assigning superficially identical behaviours (reaching in the two phases) to qualitatively distinct categories, but suggests that this is, perhaps, a purely practical problem, the solution of which depends on our observational techniques, rather than on a profound theoretical issue.

Up to this point Clark's description is reasonably convincing and, as a characterisation of two phases of mother–infant interaction, unobjectionable. But it is worth considering how far and in what manner the child has progressed into the language system at the gestural stage. Confronted with these questions, it seems to me that there are two sources of worry in Clark's account, one of which the author himself is clearly aware of.

The transition from the primitive phase to the gestural phase involves a completely novel mode of mental organisation.[8] Thus, while it might be legitimate for Clark to emphasise the continuity of the development between the two phases, justifying this in terms of the identity of the vehicle of communication (the reach), it would be equally legitimate to regard this new mode of organisation as something which cannot readily be accommodated into or reduced to some structure in a theory of social interaction. Clark's own position would, of course, be stronger if he could say something about *how* the new organisation emerges from the old, but on this he repeatedly professes ignorance (p. 250): 'In the gestural phase there is communication at the intramental level. The child becomes aware of what is implicit in the social structures in which he is already immersed. Precisely how the change from primitive structures to gestural structures comes about is, of course, a matter for investigation.'

The second source of worry becomes clear when we look at the small child's gestural abilities. Clearly, these manifest some basic symbolic capacity,[9] but it is generally not the case that those authors who have pleaded for a language-specific learning ability in children, have identified the symbolic function involved in language as a property requiring such an ability. Their speculations have focused, in the main, on more elaborate syntactic details of language structure (cf. similar comments at various points in Chapter 8). It follows, then, that, even if Clark has succeeded in providing an adequate account of the ontogenesis of a primitive symbolic system, this need not have any direct bearing on the logical problem of the acquisition of language, if the latter is viewed as a complex set of structures organised at a number of levels. Furthermore, given the conceptual gap between the two levels of mental organisation implicit in Clark's account, it must remain doubtful that he has succeeded in reducing the development of a symbolic capacity to social parameters.

The above discussion covers the core of Clark's argument, but his paper also includes a brief discussion of the development of communication with arbitrary sound sequences. His reasoning here is very loose and does not justify extensive discussion. However, it is worth pointing out that the two concerns expressed above also apply to the transition from the gestural phase to a 'symbolic phase'. Clark offers us a description of how an arbitrary vocal sequence could develop symbolic significance. He does not tell us how such a sequence becomes a symbol for a *particular category*, i.e. the whole system of semantic categorisation is left out of his account, nor does he have any views on *how* the transition from gestural phase to symbolic phase is achieved (p. 255): 'The last phase is that of communication structures mediated through arbitrary sounds, which structures derive *in some way* from the abilities developed in the gestural phase' (my emphasis–RMA).

Overall, it seems to me that Clark has presented an interesting *description* of early communicative interaction consisting of three phases:

(1)   The mother responds to some of the child's actions *as if* they were communicative.

(2)   The child uses gestures (some of his actions resembling those in (1)) which are genuinely communicative.

(3)   The child uses arbitrary vocal signs communicatively.

Unfortunately, *nothing* of interest is said about the transitions from (1) to (2) and from (2) to (3). There is the hint that different sorts of social structures underlie these communicative differences but no description of such structures which is not specific to communication is offered. The achievements of (2) and (3) do not take us very far into the language system, and everything Clark says is consistent with the symbolic capacity involved in (2) and (3) not having any parallel in the underlying social structures and constituting an autonomous aspect of communicative development. However, even if this were not so, there is so much of language structure left untouched by the argument, that one who wished to subscribe to a version of the autonomy thesis (see Chapter 8) would be unlikely to feel threatened by it.

The one attempt to go beyond the level of the above discussion within this general argument form with which I am familiar is contained in the editor's introduction to Lock (1978). There, having offered an argument very similar to the one presented by Clark for the transition between action and gesture, in connection with the child raising his arms to be picked up, and assuming the child to be equipped with a set of gestures, Lock goes on (pp. 7–8):

If we look at the developmental history of the child's ability to combine gestures, we find three phases. One in which the ability to use single gestures is developed, a second in which single gestures occur in sequences – the child cries . . . and then points or raises his arms, say; and finally a period in which two or more gestures occur together – the child cries and points 'at the same time'. A similar sequence is found in language development: the so-called holophrastic period of one-word-at-a-time; the occurrence of two words in a sequence; and that of true multi-word utterances. This is another hint that the two processes – of language and gesture – are very similar.[10]

Here there seems to be an attempt to establish correspondences between at least one syntactic property – co-occurrence – and a similar property in the gestural system. To the extent that the development of the gestural system can be explained in terms of social development, this would, perhaps, constitute a significant reduction of language development.

However, there are a number of points which make me uneasy with the argument:

(1)   If we accept the correspondences between language and gesture, Lock has *not* provided an explanation for gestural combination in terms of social interaction.

(2)   The correspondence is inappropriate as one of the major characteristics of 'genuine' two-word utterances is the significance of linear order (cf. Chapters 5 and 6). For Lock, combined gestures appear simultaneously, and, somewhat anomalously, the earlier putative stage in gestural development would appear to provide a more appropriate vehicle for syntax.

(3)   Ignoring (1) and (2), there remain many properties of language structure unaccounted for. *Combination* of signs *per se* has not provided the premise for nativist arguments.

(4)   The generality of the correspondence is not well-established. Lock gives an example of the two-word utterance *mummy up* and a two-gesture act of crying and arm-raising, pointing to their similarities. But if we consider the various syntactic/semantic relations which have been put forward as characterising two-word utterances (see Chapters 5 and 6), it seems unlikely that we are going to find gestural correlates for each of them.

In this chapter I have selected what I consider to be the two most interesting arguments for the involvement of social development in language development. There are other such arguments, but many of them are at too general a level for us to get any grip on any particular aspect of language development (see, for example, Shotter 1978 and several papers in Lewis and Rosenblum 1977). I do not believe that this sort of discussion can be profitably conducted outside an explicit framework of assumptions about language structure (unless one is to adopt the stance of producing one's own framework on the basis of social considerations – no author with whom I am familiar except Halliday suggests that this is what they have in mind). When we make such a set of assumptions, the conclusion, as in the previous chapter, appears inevitable: social reductionists have at best scratched the surface of language structure with their efforts. Of course, the assumptions might be completely wrong, but, unless we can replace them with another set of comparable descriptive richness, that is beside the point.

10 *Learnability and mechanisms of learning*

Previous chapters of this book have been concerned with attempting to explicate criteria which could be used in evaluating proposals for explaining the *course* of language development. There is, however, a different major question confronting language acquisition theorists which, it might be argued, is logically prior to that addressed by the body of this book. This question arises from the need to explain the *fact* of language acquisition, i.e., given that we wish to maintain that a certain type of linguistic system (say a grammar) is acquired, we are obliged to consider whether such a system could indeed be acquired on the basis of exposure to data of a specified kind. Clearly, this question can be raised without taking account of the detailed course of development in the domain of study, and it is in the context of work within this sphere that the most extensive discussion of learning mechanisms has taken place.[1] Before considering this, I would like to briefly attempt to establish correspondences and differences between my own work and that in learnability theory in terms of a scheme offered in Pinker (1979).

Pinker suggests that adequate theories of language acquisition ought to meet six conditions. These are:

Learnability: the theory must offer an explanation for the fact of development.

Equipotentiality: the theory must be consistent with the fact that children are capable of learning any natural language as their native language.

Time: the theory must make acquisition possible within the time scale in which it actually occurs.

Input: the theory must allow language acquisition to proceed on the basis of empirically valid assumptions about the nature of the input data.

Cognitive: the theory must be consistent with what we know about the child's general cognitive abilities.

Developmental: the theory must be consistent with what we know about the course of development.

I have focused so far on the last of these conditions, requiring rather more of theories of language acquisition than mere consistency with the data. Thus, my attempts to provide criteria for when we might regard such theories as explanatory involved reference to theory-internal considerations (not obviously related to any of the above), environmental considerations (related to the Input Condition) and reductive considerations (related, in the case of cognitive reductions, to the Cognitive Condition). As Pinker points out, most work in language acquisition has also been concerned with the Developmental Condition, although, as I have argued extensively in previous chapters, there have been few attempts to approach explanation within this emphasis. Recent attempts to elaborate on the Cognitive Condition have been discussed in Chapter 8, and the work of the last decade on the Input Condition will be briefly mentioned below, as this bears crucially on Learnability. It should be clear from this brief discussion that there is no straightforward correspondence between Pinker's conditions and those I have introduced in this book. The two sets of conditions arise from taking different perspectives on the nature of language acquisition research, and, while admitting that learnability considerations are an important omission from my original set of conditions, I would also wish to insist that some of the factors important in learnability are already implicitly recognised in my conditions (Condition V, of course, explicitly, requires a learning mechanism which, as we shall see, is an important component of theories of learnability), and that, in providing a fuller analysis of the notion of a developmental explanation, those conditions can, for the moment, be seen as complementing the work I shall examine in this chapter. That there is some relationship between the concepts of Chapter 1 and work on learnability theory can be seen by introducing the best-known general framework for studying the latter.

Wexler and Culicover (1980), summarising and expanding on Hamburger and Wexler (1975), Wexler, Culicover and Hamburger (1975) and Culicover and Wexler (1977), is an impressive demonstration of the progress that has been made in learnability theory in connection with the acquisition of syntax.[2] Quite simply, what the authors are involved in is a demonstration that a certain class of grammars is learnable (in the sense that the learner can select the 'correct' grammar from the class), given assumptions about the nature of the input data, the mechanism which selects grammars and the notion of 'correctness'. Accordingly, they propose that a theory of grammar acquisition should have four components:

(1)   A class of possible grammars (defining a class of possible languages). Initially one might assume that this class is very large and not subject to any interesting linguistic constraints, but the main thrust of Wexler and Culicover's argument is that such an assumption leads to unlearnability (see below, 10.1). That the class of possible grammars is initially delimited in some way is, of course, compatible with my Condition II which requires the theories in a developmental sequence to be constructed according to a set of general principles.

(2)   A class of possible *inputs*. This represents an assumption about the type and quantity of data that the child has available for the induction of a grammar from the initial set.

(3)   A *learning procedure* which determines how grammars are selected from the given set in the light of incoming data.[3] The claim that any adequate theory must contain such a procedure is equivalent to my Condition V.

(4)   A *criterion* for learning, i.e. we need to have a precise definition of what is meant by the claim that a learner has acquired a grammar.

Within this general framework it has been possible to demonstrate a number of interesting results.

10.1 Results in learnability theory

The earliest work in the field on which everything else builds is due to Gold (1967). He began from the simple assumption that a language is learned on the basis of exposure to a finite number of well-formed sentences in the language. Presentation of positive instances in this fashion is referred to as *text-presentation*, and Gold was able to show, making a number of auxiliary assumptions, that the various classes of languages studied by mathematical linguists (finite state (regular), context-free, context-sensitive, recursive, recursively enumerable) are *not* learnable given this mode of presentation.[4] The only class of languages which is learnable in this way is the class of finite cardinality languages, which, for obvious reasons, has been of little interest to linguists. In fact, it was possible to prove that if the class of languages under investigation included one infinite language bearing a particular relation to the finite languages in the class, then the class of languages is not learnable. The conclusion for finite state and larger classes of languages then follows from the observation that these classes of languages are supersets of unlearnable classes.[5]

The role of the learning procedure in these early demonstrations was not of any positive significance, given the negative nature of the results. It is, however, worth mentioning that the negative results follow even if the learning procedure is enumeration; that is, if the learning procedure has available an enumeration of the relevant class of grammars and selects grammars compatible with the data to which it has been exposed so far in a way determined by the enumeration, there is still no guarantee that the correct grammar will be selected in a finite time. As is well known, there is no procedure more powerful than enumeration, and so the lesson to be learned is that if we find the conclusions of Gold's arguments unpalatable, we shall not be able to defuse them by strengthening the learning procedure.[6]

There are, of course, alternatives to strengthening the learning procedure if we wish to escape from Gold's results. We can contemplate modifications to one or more of the other components in the acquisition model. Constraining the class of possible grammars has already been mentioned in n.5, and is possibly worth pursuing in the current climate without considering concomitant modifications in the model. Indeed, this is the direction in which Wexler and Culicover move, but they see the constraints they impose in this respect as intimately connected with changes in other components. Therefore, I shall not give further consideration here to this strategy. Changing the criterion of learning has also been the subject of some discussion, but this has not led to any insightful developments (see Pinker 1979, pp. 230–1 for summary). We are left with the characterisation of input, and it is in this connection that most progress has been made.

Along with text-presentation, Gold (1967) introduced the idea of *informant-presentation*. For this mode the learner's datum at any point in time is either a positive or negative instance of the target language. Equivalently, at any point in time the learner is provided with information as to whether a sample string is in the language or not. Under this condition and, again, given a number of auxiliary assumptions, Gold was able to demonstrate that, in particular, the class of context-sensitive languages was learnable. If we now assume, as many have, that, restricting attention to weak generative capacity, natural languages are a subset of the context-sensitive languages, we would appear to have a much more promising line of approach to the learnability of natural languages. The crucial question becomes whether the informant-presentation mode is empirically appropriate from the point of view of the child-learner. There is little point here in summarising what is amply documented elsewhere: suffice it to say that the classic study of Brown and Hanlon (1970) produced no evidence for children being provided with negative information about the status of strings in their language.[7] So we find ourselves in a situation where a changed assumption about the nature of the input data would enable us to move in the direction of learnability, but the assumption is not available to us on empirical grounds. Are there other assumptions which might be useful in this respect and which would not involve us in counterfactual claims?

The negative results briefly summarised above have not concerned classes of transformational grammars. However, it is not difficult to show that some classes of transformational grammars are also not learnable from text. In particular, if we consider the class of transformational grammars defined on a context-free base and assume that grammars containing no transformations or, equivalently, only the identity transformation are members of this class, it follows immediately that this class is a superset of the class of context-free grammars. Therefore the languages generated by the class include the set of context-free languages and the unlearnability of the class follows from Gold's results. Even if we assume that the base is extremely restricted (the limiting case of this is to assume the Universal Base Hypothesis which says that *all* languages share a single context-free base), the unlearnability of the class of transformational grammars will follow from Peters and Ritchie's (1973) results, briefly mentioned in Chapter 5. However, consideration of the transformational components of grammars opens up the possibility of considering a different definition of learnability, and it is this alternative that Wexler and Culicover develop.

The basic idea is that a transformational component of a grammar can be seen as a function mapping base-generated structures into surface-structures (or, if we wish to ignore structural information at the surface, into surface strings).[8] We can imagine a learner being presented with instances of the argument and value of a function, his task being that of identifying the function. If, for a particular class of functions, the 'correct' function can be identified in a finite time, then the class is *function-learnable*. It is easy to see that any enumerable class of functions is function-learnable. Presented with a datum (a, f(a)), he takes the first function in the enumeration, say F_1, and checks whether $F_1(a)$ is identical to f(a). If it is, he guesses F_1 and moves on to the next datum. If it is not, he takes the next function in the enumeration, F_2, and checks whether $F_2(a)$ is identical to $f(a)$. Eventually he must find a function in the enumeration which agrees with f on a – this is ensured by the fact that the 'correct' function is in the enumeration and will be selected at some point – and he then goes on to the second datum. It is clear from this that the 'correct' function will be guessed after some finite time and that it will continue to be guessed thenceforth, as it will agree with all subsequently presented data. If now, for the sake of argument, we assume a universal base, it is possible to demonstrate that the class of transformational components defined on this base is enumerable and it follows immediately that this class is function-learnable.

It is useful at this point to make the assumptions of the above paragraph explicit. We are assuming a universal base or, perhaps, a highly restricted base simply to ensure that there are no learnability problems with *that* component of the grammar. We are assuming that the learner is presented with data which consist of a pair, the first member of which is a base structure and the second member of which is a surface string; the base structure is in the domain of the transformational component being learned and the surface string is in its range. Finally, we are assuming that the learning mechanism is enumeration, whereby the learner has available an enumeration of the class of transformational components which he can test in turn against input pairs. Given these assumptions, the class of transformational components on a universal base can be shown to be function-learnable. How happy should we be with the assumptions in the light of the situation a language-learner finds himself in?

The idea of a universal base is not currently a popular one. However, most recent work in transformational grammar has adopted some version of $\overline{X}$ theory (Chomsky 1970, Jackendoff 1977), which can be viewed as imposing severe constraints on the form of the base (see Koster 1979 for discussion in the context of learnability theory). Anyway it is not an assumption that can readily be questioned by looking at the child learner, and so I shall say no more about it here. That the child is presented with surface strings is, of course, no more than the assumption involved in the definition of learnability from text, and is uncontroversial.[9] More significant is the assumption that the child is also presented with base-generated structures and this requires some justification. Wexler and Culicover provide this by assuming (1) that in many cases the child is capable of working out the semantic interpretation of a surface string even when he does not fully comprehend the syntax of the string, and (2) a version of the standard theory according to which semantic interpretation is determined by base structure. They say (p. 82): 'If much semantic information is related to the deep structure of a sentence, and if a child sometimes has available the semantic interpretation of a sentence even when he doesn't understand its syntax, perhaps it is plausible that in some cases the child might be able to compute what the deep structure of a sentence is even when he doesn't understand the syntax of a surface sentence.' The plausibility of this view and the authors' attempts to provide more justification for it will be considered in 10.2.

Finally, the assumption of an enumerative learning mechanism is seen as implausible and this leads to interesting developments. The implausibility arises in connection with the amount of memory for data necessary for it to work. Quite simply, if the child is to use such a mechanism, he must have available, at each point at which he is presented with a new datum, a complete record of the data he has experienced so far. This is because the enumerative procedure requires rejection and hypothesisation of *complete* grammars rather than modification of existing grammars and a new complete grammar will only be acceptable if it is consistent with all the data which have confronted the child. The alternative is to see syntactic development as a gradual modification of existing systems, in which the learning mechanism at any time will have available only the new datum along with the current grammar.[10]

The details of Wexler and Culicover's learning procedure are closely tied up with several assumptions about the form of grammars which would take us too far afield here. Suffice it to say that if the learner is confronted with a datum (a base structure–surface string pair) which can be related by his transformational component, then the transformational component remains unmodified, i.e. there is no learning from positive information. If, on the other hand, the datum cannot be handled by the transformational component, then a modification will take place. This modification will consist of either the rejection or hypothesisation of a single transformational rule, and Wexler and Culicover offer criteria for determining which transformations from the current transformational component are available for rejection and which transformations from the total set of possible transformations are available for hypothesisation. These two sets will be finite and any possible rejection or hypothesisation is equiprobable. This, then, is the first 'interesting' learning procedure we have met. The points to emphasise in connection with it are that it operates on the basis of *one* negative piece of information and that it changes its associated hypothesis by the addition or subtraction of *one whole* rule.[11]

Because this learning procedure is not as powerful as enumeration (the latter *guarantees* that the 'correct' grammar will eventually be selected if it is in the enumeration), it is no longer the case that all transformational components on a universal base can be learned. One of the most interesting aspects of the whole exercise is that of seeing the way in which making assumptions about learning more plausible leads to restrictions on the form of grammars if learnability is to be preserved. Before coming to Wexler and Culicover's major result, it is necessary to introduce one final consideration of this sort. Recall that learning, in the model, only takes place on negative-information trials, i.e. when the learner is presented with a datum which his transformational component cannot handle. Intuitively, then, errors are necessary for the learner to ultimately select the right grammar. Now assume that data are presented to the learner according to some probability distribution. Referring to sentences with no embedding as 0-degree and to sentences with n levels of embedding as n-degree, we can see that for any finite n the probability of occurrence of any sentence of degree less than or equal to n will be bounded away from 0 (there are only a finite number of such sentences), whereas the probability of occurrence of any sentence of degree greater than n will not be bounded away from 0 (there are an infinite number of such sentences). Putting these last two points together, it appears that for us to be in a position to guarantee learning, we have to be able to ensure the possibility of errors on sentences with degree less than some finite n, and this, of course, accords well with the observation that children are not exposed to sentences of arbitrary syntactic complexity.[12]

Accepting this package of assumption, Wexler and Culicover have shown that a class of transformational components satisfying a number of constraints is learnable on the basis of exposure to data of degree less than or equal to 2. What this means is that if a transformational component makes an error on an arbitrary datum, then there is always a datum, the first member of which is a degree-2 (or less) base structure, such that the transformational component makes an error on it, i.e. all errors can be detected from degree-2 (or less) data.[13]

The constraints which Wexler and Culicover find necessary in order to ensure this result are not worth going into in detail here. The most notable of them are the Binary Principle (apparently equivalent to Chomsky's 1973 Subjacency), preventing transformations analysing more than one level down from that reached in the cycle and the Freezing Principle, which prevents transformations from analysing nodes dominated by frozen nodes, the latter being nodes that immediately dominate configurations which could not have arisen as the result of a base rule. Wexler and Culicover present an extensive array of evidence for these constraints being operative in adult transformational components, and see their mode of argumentation, where constraints are first discovered and justified in the context of learnability questions and later seen to be descriptively useful, as particularly attractive.[14]

10.2 Learnability in non-syntactic domains

Not surprisingly, there has been no work of significance in other areas of language acquisition within frameworks which are comparable to that developed by Wexler and Culicover for studying the acquisition of transformational components of grammars. The amount of formal precision in many areas of linguistic study leaves a great deal to be desired, and one of the messages of earlier chapters of this book is that this makes evaluation a difficult and poorly determined exercise. However, even given this lack of formal rigour, it remains difficult to understand the apparent total lack of concern with the specification (even in outline) of learning mechanisms, i.e. with satisfaction of Condition V from Chapter I.

For example, if we consider lexical development along the lines of Chapter 3 and 4, it seems clear that there are intelligible questions to be asked concerning the nature of learning mechanisms in this domain. Accepting, for the sake of argument, that children do learn word-meanings by successively acquiring features of meaning, it is reasonable to propose that there is a determinate procedure which leads them to modify their hypotheses about the meanings of particular words. It seems highly likely that explicitly negative information will have a role to play here, as Brown and Hanlon (1970) claimed that semantic corrections did occur in the speech of mothers. However, I am familiar with no study of the efficacy of negative semantic information in the natural word-learning situation. Of course, on the assumption that the lexicon consists of a finite number of entries, each one coded in terms of a finite number of semantic dimensions selected from a finite set of possible semantic dimensions, enumeration would work as a learning procedure. But, just as in the case of the learning of transformational components, it seems an empirically implausible procedure and the search for alternatives is a reasonable task to undertake.[15]

When we turn to consideration of the development of the semantic structures of sentences, one of Wexler and Culicover's own assumptions becomes crucial. Recall that they take for granted a context-free universal base. This has two positive implications. The first is that the base itself need not be learned and the second, vital for the assumption that the base structure of a surface string can be inferred on the basis of situational information, is that the mapping from semantic representation to base structure becomes learnable. It is clear, then, that there are *two* components of an overall model of language structure presupposed by Wexler and Culicover's arguments: a system of semantic representations and a mapping from this system to base structures. For both of them, we can, in principle, enquire into their learnability properties, and the authors provide some preliminary discussion of the second issue.

The Universal Base Hypothesis is recognised as incorrect on the grounds of word-order differences. Yet it seems that a highly constrained base is necessary in order to ensure the learnability of the mapping from semantic representations to base structures and the subsequent availability of base structures for transformation learning. Wexler and Culicover's solution to this problem is to invoke strong constraints on the base which are not so obviously inconsistent with word-order data. Essentially, the base is seen as a series of rules for ordering constituents, with the relations between the constituents being defined semantically. Thus, the semantic representation for a sentence will specify a set of unordered constituents along with semantic–grammatical relations between them. The constraints on the base are stated as the Invariance Principle which requires the ordering rules to preserve the continuity of semantic constituents. Equivalently (p. 460): 'These ordering rules . . . apply by ordering the immediate constituents introduced by each [semantic] rewriting rule, and they may not reach down to order any other constituents.'[16] This principle is subsequently modified in the light of data from a number of languages, but that is not what concerns me here. I introduce it merely to indicate that there has been some consideration of the problem of the mapping from semantic representations to deep structures.

Turning our attention to the semantic representations themselves, Wexler and Culicover are less convincing. Here they are driven back to universality with its implication that there is no learnability problem. They say (*ibid.*): 'the semantic grammar (the set of rules introducing the unordered constituents) is universal; that is, every language has such a scheme for semantic representation'. Now, such an assumption is an attractive one and has been adopted by a number of workers in child language in the last decade (see Chapter 6 for discussion of this sort of proposal). Unfortunately, in their discussion of one such worker (Schlesinger 1971), Wexler and Culicover make it clear that it is not an assumption they themselves accept. In general, their particularising of the sloppiness in Schlesinger's mode of argument is impeccable, but it is difficult to reconcile the position they adopt above on the universality of semantic representations with their negative remarks on Schlesinger's adoption of a very similar position. It is certainly true that (p. 406): 'We know very little of the calculus of concepts and of how they differ from language to language' and that (*ibid.*): 'a major thread in anthropological thinking has been that different cultures interpret the same objective situation in different ways', but what follows from this is that any assumptions about universals of semantic representation must be treated with extreme caution. Wexler and Culicover are careful to emphasise the preliminary nature of their enquiry and the tone of their presentation contrasts strongly with that of authors like Schlesinger, who often seem to regard the universality of semantic and conceptual structures as something which can be assumed without cost. Of course, if we do not make the assumption about the universal semantic grammar, we have to ask how it is learned, and this approach has led Marshall (1979) to question the significance of much of the work on learnability.

Marshall takes issue not only with the work of Wexler and his associates but also with that of Anderson (1976) and that of Power and Longuet-Higgins (1978). Anderson's system, which has the virtue of existing in the form of a computer program, has been shown to learn significant chunks of English when presented with data consisting of semantic representations and surface sentences. The semantic representations are in a particular format and, Marshall argues, this format too has a syntax. How is this syntax learned? As Marshall puts it (p. 2): 'Given an input-language as rich as this it is not surprising that the program can learn a few extra fancy bits.'[17] Power and Longuet-Higgins also offer a computer program which will learn the grammar of numerals for a number of languages. In order to work, however, this program is supplied with a syntax for parsing numbers. Again, the question to be asked is obvious: how is this syntax learned?

In connection with Wexler and Culicover's own work, it appears that they are sensitive to the sort of problem Marshall raises and make some effort to solve it. It is difficult to see any viable alternative in our present state of ignorance about semantics to focusing attention on syntax and making assumptions about the role of semantics in the overall theory. The important thing to be clear on is the nature of our assumptions and the fact that they are assumptions.

If we consider other areas of language development, there is very little to say. Most of these areas are so poorly understood that to ask questions of the sort being considered here would be quite inappropriate. Again, however, it would be legitimate to offer informal sketches of possible learning mechanisms and the fact that such offerings do not generally exist must count against the adequacy of theoretical proposals. In particular, 'functional' theories of the sort I have considered in Chapter 7 of this book appear to be extremely remote from the type of formulation which would make the considerations of this chapter relevant to their evaluation.[18] Generally this sort of theory lacks any elaborate internal structure, amounting to little more than a taxonomy. Whether the nature of the domains of investigation demands this lack of structure or our theories are simply misconceived at the moment will have to await further research.

10.3 The problem of representation

One aspect of the problem of representation was alluded to in the previous section in connection with Marshall's reservations about the semantic richness required as input by theories of learnability. Two further aspects of the same problem will be briefly mentioned here.

The first of these is discussed by Wexler and Culicover and concerns the amount of preprocessing of the input to the child which is required by their theory. They say (pp. 60–1):

we must note that the concept of information, data, or input has to be taken in a special sense, because, in one sense, the only information is the physical data impinging on the learner's senses. In a broader sense, any conception of information will assume that the learner imposes order on the raw information. Thus, what the theory will consider information will be this preanalyzed information. It may be that part of this preanalysis of information has to be itself learned. If this is the case, then we simply assume that this kind of learning takes place first and in sufficient measure that the level of learning that we investigate can take place.

What this amounts to, in the context of the theory Wexler and Culicover go on to develop, is an assumption that the data presented to the learning mechanism are already in a form where an input sentence has been segmented into its component morphemes and these morphemes have been assigned to the appropriate grammatical classes. Clearly, this assumption begs the question of how the child learns to segment the continuous acoustic signal into component morphemes and how he learns to assign morphemes to grammatical classes. The justification for the assumption is that it is only by making it that progress can be made on the problem of how transformational components are learned. Whether one subscribes to this view or not will, to some extent, depend on the significance one attaches to Wexler and Culicover's learnability results. They obviously see these results as providing sufficient motivation for the assumption, but Marshall is less sure, saying (p. 4): 'Acoustic tokens do not carry their syntactic type labels with them. Grandmother cells and labelled lines may be fine for sensory systems . . . but I have my doubts about the existence of innate noun-detectors.' Marshall, it seems, has not fully understood Wexler and Culicover here, as they are not saying that devices for assigning morphemes to syntactic categories are innate – they explicitly recognise that there may be interesting learnability problems here – but he is surely correct to make explicit the magnitude of the assumption being made.[19]

The second aspect of the problem of representation is, perhaps, more problematic and bears on the question of whether the child is supplied with unlabelled negative instances of the target language (cf. informant presentation and n. 9). At various times the idea has been put forward that children are biased towards particular parts of input utterances. Thus, Slobin (1973) made the suggestion that children paid particular attention to the *ends* of words and (in order for all his arguments to be relevant) the *ends* of sentences (see Chapter 8 for some discussion). Again, Newport, Gleitman and Gleitman (1977) produce evidence to suggest that the child filters the mother's speech in such a way that *utterance-initial* position is salient. Whatever the facts in this matter, and, of course, these two suggestions are not necessarily incompatible, the important point is that if the child is devoting more attention, processing capacity, etc. to certain segments of an utterance, then the chances are that his perception of the rest of the utterance will be downgraded in some way. It seems inevitable in these circumstances that the child will be confronted with ungrammatical data which are not labelled as such.[20] In terms of a traditional psychological distinction it is the *proximal* stimulus which is relevant for the learning procedure and not the *distal* stimulus.

Once this is realised, it becomes apparent that, for all domains of language acquisition, we must pay much more attention to the representation of input by the child if we are to seriously pursue the study of learning mechanisms. This will be no less true in phonology and semantics than it is in syntax (for some remarks in connection with representation in child phonology, see Kornfeld 1971, Kornfeld and Goehl 1974, Waterson 1970, 1971). Without the sort of information emerging from such study, it is not difficult to see that yet another source of indeterminacy rapidly infects argumentation in the field. That this is so is beautifully illustrated by a recent discussion in White (1979).

In connection with an investigation of the Specified Subject Constraint (Chomsky 1973), Matthei (1978) asked a group of children to act out the appropriate tickling for sentences like *The chickens want the pigs to tickle each other*. In this sentence *the pigs* is a specified subject and this blocks the rule relating *each other* to its antecedent, i.e. *each other* cannot have *the chickens* as antecedent. Matthei found that over 60% of his child subjects responded by making the pigs tickle the chickens and vice versa, thereby, apparently, treating *the chickens* as an antecedent for *each other* in violation of the Specified Subject Constraint. This is Matthei's own interpretation of his results but White offers two alternatives. Suppose, she suggests, that the children in the study treated *each other* as an ordinary pronoun, i.e. they had not fully sorted out its syntactic properties. Then, the child might interpret (represent) the sentence in question in a fashion analogous to his representation of *The chickens want the pigs to tickle them* and such a representation would be consistent with the children making the pigs tickle the chickens. Recall, though, that the children also made the chickens tickle the pigs. This suggests that *the chickens* and *the pigs* are both antecedents for *each other* and that the child is some way from comprehension of the relevant sentence structure, treating it instead as something along the lines of *the chickens and the pigs tickled each other*. If such an interpretation is correct, there is no embedding and no specified subject *as far as the child's representation of the stimulus is concerned*. Accordingly, there is no question of violation of the Specified Subject Condition.

It is not my purpose here to arbitrate between these differing interpretations of Matthei's results. The important point is that the possibility of alternative interpretations arises and, in this case, we can locate the genesis of these alternatives in different views on the nature of the child's representation of the experimental stimuli. Furthermore, we have no independent characterisation of this representation and, until we have, the indeterminacy must persist.

10.4 Concluding remarks

I can be brief. A number of issues have arisen in the course of this book which I would like to see as constituting the foci of language acquisition research in the near future:

(1) Workers in the field will have to take the task of specifying general theories much more seriously than has been the case in the past. Failure to do this leads to problems in interpreting the notion of development and an inability to approach the logical problem of acquisition in a particular domain. In the one case where theoretical linguistics provides reasonably precise tools – syntax – child-language theorists have not been very circumspect in applying these tools (Chapter 5). For other domains, most notably semantics, the student of child language is in a difficult position as there is no generally accepted adequate theoretical framework to which he can relate his observations. Whether it is possible to make significant progress in this theoretical vacuum is unclear. I lean towards the position that it is not (Chapters 3, 4, 6 and 7), sharing the tone of Marshall's (1979) remark that (p. 3): 'An accurate summary of the appalling non-formal theorizing in developmental psycholinguistics over the last decade or so would be this: precisely-stated innate syntactic universals have been replaced by vague innate semantic universals into which an unprincipled syntax has been smuggled.'

(2) Attempts to provide reductive explanations for developmental sequences have not been successful when addressing substantive questions. The overwhelming tendency appears to be one in which the complexity of linguistic structure is hopelessly underestimated. Nevertheless, this mode of argumentation is interesting. For it to be possible to more adequately evaluate instances of it, it will be necessary to be more careful about specifying exactly what aspect of linguistic development is being explained and about providing a suitable reducing theory. It seems to me that, at the moment, the dominant cognitive theory (Piaget's) has little to say on these issues, and that no theory of social development even approaches the level of explicitness necessary to give it serious consideration (Chapters 8 and 9).

(3) Learnability questions should be tackled in domains other than syntax. This, however, will depend on progress being made in formulating adequate theories in these domains and will also have to take account of the problem of representation. Unless we are in a position to independently justify input data as *the* data available to the child learner, it is not clear that much progress can be made on these problems. Of course, we

might hope that the sort of formal argumentation offered by Wexler and Culicover will be available in other domains, but without solutions to representation problems the empirical significance of such argumentation will remain unclear (Chapter 10).

(4) Theorists of language development must look more closely at the status of the theories they produce *qua* psychological theories (my Condition I in Chapter 1). This has not been a recurring issue in the book simply because there is so little to say about it in terms of existing proposals. Obviously, however, it is at the foundation of any reflective treatment of the discipline and is deserving of much more attention.

Of these prognoses, it seems to me that (1) and (2) are relatively straightforward. It is not easy to produce adequate theories in any linguistic domain, but at least we have a reasonably developed sense of what constitutes an adequate theory and can hope to be sensitive to progress. Similarly, although I am not in a position to formulate the sort of cognitive or social theory which might be interesting from the point of view of linguistic structure, I have a feeling for the *type* of theory required and see no reason in principle why instances of this type should not appear in the future. (3) and (4), though, do not seem to be readily approachable. The relative paucity of comprehension studies over the last twenty years or so points to the difficulty of studying this process, nor is it clear that in studying it, the investigator is gaining reasonably safe access to representations. The philosophical web surrounding the question of psychological explanation is not likely to become less dense in the near future. Nevertheless, I believe that it is only by workers in the field being continually aware of such issues, that a respectable and cogent field of language acquisition research will emerge. We have fiddled with and patched up poorly formulated proposals for long enough; it is perhaps time to see ourselves as presenters of theories which are going to deal with the facts *and* be intellectually stimulating.

Notes

1 Criteria for adequacy

1. Exceptions can be found dotted around the child language literature and, of course, there are some systematic treatments of the concept of development in the literature on developmental biology (Weiss 1939, Saunders 1970) and developmental psychology (Harris 1957a, Mischel 1971). With minor exceptions the issues raised in these works do not bear on the major arguments of this book.

2. This somewhat dismissive tone should not be taken as implying a dismissive attitude. I believe that the pioneering work of Leopold as well as that of such scholars as Grégoire (1937), Guillaume (1927) and Lewis (1936) produced a great deal of fascinating data and is, in some ways, superior to much of what we have seen in the last 15 years or so. However, the fact remains that it was not theoretically sophisticated and was, in some cases, atheoretical in emphasis. Cf. Leopold's manifesto in the preface to Leopold (1939).

3. The use of 'stage' here is to be interpreted neutrally. It is a necessary concomitant of a developmental study that data will be sampled at a number of points and analysis of the data may yield discontinuous stages which have some explanatory significance or it may not. Nor is this to suggest that a stage theory can only emerge from prior consideration of data by purely observational and inductive methods. For whether stages, as understood in Piagetian theory, have any explanatory status, see the discussion in Brainerd *et al.* (1978, 1979). Parts of this discussion can be seen as sympathetic to points made later in this book.

4. Fodor (1968) says: 'Hence, for an adequate simulation to be an adequate explanation it must be the case *both* that the behaviours available to the machine correspond to the behaviours available to the organism *and* that the processes whereby the machine produces behaviour simulate the processes whereby the organism does' (p. 136). Fodor later points out that the restriction to theories which are simulations is not necessary here.

5. As far as developmental psychology borrowing standards from non-developmental psychology is concerned, Fodor hints that he might not go along entirely with what I am suggesting here. He says: 'I want to emphasise that what I have to say concerns a rather special kind of psychological explanation. The kind in which we account for the behaviour of an organism by reference to its psychological states. This sort of account is perhaps more characteristic of certain branches of learning theory and perception theory

than, say, social or developmental psychology' (1968, pp. vii–viii). While agreeing that developmental theories admit of additional analysis, it seems to me perverse not to regard the methodology of a static experimental psychology as contributing to our understanding of the status of developmental theories.

6. This is not to suggest that practice must always move from the general theory to the particular. Obviously, the construction of theories should continue in parallel at both levels with suggestions and advances at one level having implications for the other level.

7. From now on I shall often suppress reference to mechanisms unless providing statements of conditions.

8. I borrow the term from Flavell (1971) where he introduces it as a 'suitably noncommittal and general term for any sort of cognitive acquisition that a developmental psychologist might define and study. Thus an "item" might be a structure, skill, concept, rule, strategy, operation, belief, attitude, or any other cognitive element, large or small, that he has isolated for consideration' (p. 422).

9. This illustration is artificial in at least two senses. First, to my knowledge, no general set of principles defining systemic grammar is available. It is easy to imagine that this is not the case. Second, no theorist has ever proposed such a bizarre theory nor is it clear, given the rather different aims of systemic grammar and transformational grammar, that they would both recognise the domain D as constituting an appropriate area of study. I merely plead for the reader's tolerance as the example is for purely illustrative purposes.

10. Chomsky (1965) says: 'It is also apparent that evaluation measures of the kinds that have been discussed in the literature on generative grammar cannot be used to compare different theories of grammar; comparison of a grammar from one class of proposed grammars with a grammar from another class *by such a measure*, is utterly without sense' (p. 38).

11. Flavell talks throughout in terms of additional *responses* becoming available to the child at t_2, but, again, it does not appear to be obviously inappropriate to see Addition as a relationship between two theories.

12. Regarding the reliability of this phenomenon, see Brown (1973) and Kuczaj (1977).

13. The notation here is merely intended to reflect the fact that

is, at one level of analysis, a single item. No theoretical significance is attached to it.

14. Flavell is somewhat pessimistic about being able to draw clear boundaries for his categories. As my subsequent suggestions in the text involve collapsing some of his distinctions, this pessimism is, perhaps, not crucial for my purposes. Note also that I am not proposing that Flavell's set of categories is inappropriate to his own purposes.

15. In practice there is no reason to believe that we are going to produce theories which do or do not admit of analysis in terms of additive complexity. What we might expect is that, given a sequence of theories $(T_1, \ldots, T_n)$ a subsequence

$(T_i, \ldots, T_j)$ $(1 \leqslant i < j \leqslant n)$ will be analysable in these terms and that the relationships between T_{i-1} and T_i and between T_j and T_{j+1} will be instances of Substitution. Obviously a more complex formulation of Conditions IIIa and IIIb could be produced to take account of this but I shall not pursue this possibility here.

16. Of course, the traditional concept of simplicity may still be applicable to two or more *developmental* theories which account for the same range of developmental data and which satisfy conditions of the sort I am formulating.

17. For sequences which are related via Substitution early appearing items disappear as development proceeds. We should not, therefore, expect any interesting relationship between order of appearance in development and distribution in the world's languages since a great many of the early appearing items will not show up in the mature system.

18. Flavell says: 'there is considerable certainty (specificity, substantiveness, etc.) about an item-structure explanation. Definite and precise reasons can be given for the developmental priority of X_1, and there is the feeling that these reasons are virtually incontrovertible' (p. 334).

19. Lass (1980) contains discussion of teleological explanations in historical linguistics. The major difference between the historical and ontogenetic contexts is that the former lacks any well-defined end point, whereas the latter (ignoring the small amounts of individual variation) can recognise the adult language-system as the goal of development. For the view that teleological arguments are uncontroversial when applied to ontogenesis, see Grene (1976) and for a survey of the most important historical positions, Woodfield (1976).

20. Inevitably, to indulge in this sort of speculation will leave unanswered the question concerning the explanatory status of the reducing theory. In a discussion of theories of language development this is permissible as all we are concerned with is the fact that the reducing theory is viewed as more general or more basic than the reduced theory. One can, of course, speculate along the lines of further reductions or ultimate maturational bases.

21. It is, perhaps, worth mentioning that Flavell's category of Mediation (see 1.6) might be relevant to the discussion in this section.

22. Note that the three categories of explanation are not always exclusive. So, we could have, for one and the same sequence, a teleological and a reductive explanation. This would require that the same item–structure relations appear in both the reducing and the reduced theories. Similarly, in a particular case, one can imagine being offered both a teleological and an environmental explanation. Here, however, the environmental explanation would be an accidental pseudo-explanation, as manipulation of the environmental variables could not possibly affect the order of development of the relevant items.

2 Jakobson's theory of phonological development

1. Further discussion of theories of phonological development, in particular Smith (1973), is contained in Atkinson (1978). An attempt to apply a set of criteria to theories in this domain, which bears some resemblance to mine, is

Ferguson and Garnica (1975). In my view the results of this attempt are disappointing.

2. The features compact and diffuse can be treated as the two values of one opposition within consonantal systems. The need to recognise two distinct features, each with positive and negative specifications, arises in connection with languages which have three or more phonologically distinct vowel heights.

3. Ferguson (1977) has clearly pointed out the inadequacies of Jakobson's formulation on this matter. Are *all* fricatives acquired later than *all* stops? Or are fricatives acquired after homorganic stops which would allow *some* fricatives to be acquired before *some* stops?

4. Those familiar with phonological theory will immediately recognise a restatement of the motivation for the feature ± syllabic in Chomsky and Halle (1968).

5. The point made in the text about the restricted function of features is again relevant here. At t_2 the acquisition of ± diffuse could make available the distinction between front (+ diffuse) and back (− diffuse) consonants but, apparently, it does not do so. Similarly, ± grave, first manifested in the consonant system, could immediately be applied to vowels giving a distinction between front and back vowels some time before t_3 in Figure 2.2. But, again, this does not happen.

6. Occasionally, Jakobson talks of the child 'substituting' one segment for another, thereby neutralising a contrast which appears in the adult system. If we were to take this sort of talk seriously, we might credit him with the view that the child controls *all* the relevant oppositions at some level but his actual production is constrained by a set of substitution procedures. This would move Jakobson in the direction of Stampe (1969) and Smith (1973), and might also be seen as offering a fuller psychological account on which certain predictions could be based. I shall not pursue this possibility in the text.

7. There may, of course, be intermediate stages in a sequence such as this. Jakobson is not saying that there is a point where stops are acquired followed by the acquisition of fricatives as the *next* significant change in the phonological system.

8. Note that there is no problem here in relating the two claims from language development and the study of the world's languages following from my previous discussion of the difficulties with ± continuant. Both of the claims are formulated in the language of phoneme theory rather than distinctive features; even if we feel that the formulation in terms of the acquisition of ± continuant has to be abandoned, these claims could stand.

9. But, for example, the feature ± strident is not applicable in a distinctive way to vowels: all vowels are redundantly specified as − strident. It is not clear that this sort of interdependence could be used to formulate teleological explanations for later stages of development.

10. To the same point it should be added that Jakobson makes the further observation that ejective and glottalised consonants involving double obstructions are learned relatively late just like nasal vowels.

3 Early lexical development

1. This should not be seen as implying any positive evaluation of Katz's or Bierwisch's approach to semantics. It is merely making clear that those approaches operate under constraints which do not apply to Clark's speculations.

2. Clark (1973) says: 'No theoretical issues will be raised here, although I will use a binary type of notation to represent the child's semantic knowledge about particular sets of words. This notation does not imply any theoretical commitment to binary features and will simply be used for clarity's sake in presenting the data' (p. 74). From the examples discussed in the text, it is clear that the intention expressed in this passage is not adhered to by the author (cf. p. 43 below).

3. One thing which is immediately obvious from Table 3.1 is that there is an intolerable amount of vagueness in the right-hand column, vagueness which is going to be crucial in any study interested in determining the principles which fix the extensions of terms in the child's vocabulary. What this amounts to is one aspect of a general reservation concerning the sources from which Clark drew up her generalisations, particularly with respect to their variant methodologies and differing standards of precision. A second point which emerges and which, in fact, is presupposed in the use of the word 'overextension' is the assumption that the word which is overextended has been used appropriately by the child to begin with. That this is not an obvious consequence of Clark's theory will become apparent presently.

4. At this point it is worth noting the distinction drawn by Lyons (1975, 1977a) between reference and quasi-reference where the former is tied to a concomitant notion of predication, whereas the latter can stand alone and is, to Lyons' way of thinking, indeterminate between reference and predication. Since a great many of the data which can be used in evaluating Clark's proposals come from a stage where it is difficult to distinguish reference and quasi-reference in the speech of the child (Lyons would say there are many instances of quasi-reference), my usage of 'referential' should be seen as neutral with respect to Lyons' distinction. The distinction and its implications will be discussed at greater length in Chapter 7.

5. Clark (1973) says: 'One of the basic assumptions of the theory clearly is that the meanings of words can be broken down into some combination of units of meaning smaller than that represented by the word' (p. 74).

6. Although the child's semantic features are seen as drawn from the set used in describing the adult language, Clark does not make it clear whether this is also true for each form acquired by the child (i.e. does the child, in sampling a set of features and associating them with a particular word, sample a set which is going to stay associated with *that* word for the remainder of his lexical development?). The possibility is raised, but nowhere explored, that the child may abandon features as he develops (see Bloom 1973, Reich 1976 for examples of 'underextension' which clearly violate the subset requirement, if interpreted in a feature framework). The clearest position Clark adopts demands that the loss of features is unlikely, if not impossible.

7. In a sense, this sampling can be seen as imposing a constraint on the data available to the child as a word-learner. As such, it would properly enter into considerations of a mechanism for learning (cf. Condition V in Chapter 1).

8. 'Simultaneously' here hides the problem of the directionality of the relationship between the words and the features which are held to make up their meanings, which is not discussed in Clark's work although it is obviously crucial to a fully explicit theory. Is it the case that the child hypothesises that certain perceptual features are important in determining the applicability of words and then looks around for words to hang on to the distinctions made available by the features; or is it that the child realises that a plurality of words is being used in circumstances where he would use only one and looks around for a basis for distinguishing them? See Bowerman (1976) for discussion of some of the issues involved.

9. Strictly speaking this should be restricted to the child's 'concrete' lexicon at the stage under analysis. This qualification should be taken as read in what follows.

10. Exactly how we are supposed to represent the meaning of *bow-wow* at this stage is not something Clark expands upon. From Table 3.2 it might appear that something like + dogshaped would be in order but this is hardly enlightening. That the child might *not* use an overextended form appropriately before overextending it is easy to see. He may meet an instance of category C being referred to as *a*, sample an accidental perceptual feature F of the instance and assign it to the meaning of *a*. Subsequent instances of F appear in categories other than C and the child labels such instances with *a*. However, he himself has never used *a* appropriately.

11. Obviously, new lexical forms enter the child's repertoire, leading to one sort of additive complexity. In this connection, we should note, however, the phenomenon of 'lexical mortality' which is found in the early stages of language development, particularly with reference to the child's idiosyncratic 'words'. From Clark's discussion, it seems that she does not contemplate changes in the combinatorial possibilities of features in lexical entries. If we were to get a move from pure conjunction to other combinations of features, we could see this as another sort of additive complexity.

12. It is worth noting here that there is a concern for psychological reality in the literature on componential analysis (see, e.g., Romney and d'Andrade 1964) but little attention to components of meaning which can be regarded as *perceptual*. Exceptions are provided by recent work on classifier systems, e.g. Adams and Conklin (1973). In particular cases one can even go so far as to say that lexical items which are used to refer to concrete objects in the adult language *cannot* be analysed semantically in terms of a conjunctive set of perceptual features. In the case of, say, *cow*, the sort of development envisaged by Clark will result in an entry something like:

   $Cow \longleftrightarrow$ + 4-legged, + moo, jSize, etc.

   but, as Putnam (1970, 1975) has pointed out, we cannot consider such a conjunctive set of features as even fixing the extension of *cow*. Three-legged cows, non-mooing cows and midget cows are all cows; they are peculiar cows but not peculiar enough to not be cows.

13. Clark, as has already been indicated, has recourse to the view that *general* features are acquired first but, unfortunately, she gives no indication as to what is to count as a general feature. Griffiths (1976) suggests that Clark intends to equate 'general' with 'occurs in the analysis of many words'. This remains vague and promissory as we lack an analysis of the language being acquired in the appropriate terms. The early appearance of ± moo in Clark's own hypothetical example does not sit very happily with this interpretation.

14. That Clark would rapidly embrace such a sequence is shown by her statement that: 'Since learning to attach meanings to words involves the interpretation and encoding of perceptual data, we might expect to find an *analogous* sequence of development in perception' (1973, p. 101 – my emphasis – RMA).

15 It might be pointed out here that this issue is more controversial than Nelson suggests. She cites Leopold for support but his conclusion to the relevant discussion is hardly encouraging to her view. He says: 'My frantic search for standard bases [for apparently invented forms – RMA] proves that my experience had by that time convinced me that all of Hildegard's words proceeded from standard words. Students who approach the problem with the conviction that children do invent words will undoubtedly take these words as proof of their thesis' (1949, p. 117).

16. The SFH is not, on the face of it, concerned with conceptual development. Nevertheless, it does not seem unfair to suggest that, if Clark were to speculate in this direction, her speculations would have the tone Nelson offers.

17. There are difficulties in discussing Nelson's proposal as abstractionist, since she appears to readily admit disjunctive specifications along some parameters. This hardly affects the logic of the point being pursued.

18. In this connection it must be pointed out that Bowerman (1976, 1978) found that the majority of overextensions she could identify in the speech of her two daughters were based on perceptual properties of objects rather than on function. The extent to which such evidence is damaging to Nelson's hypothesis will become clear in the next section.

19. In addition, as discussed in 3.3, at some point the concept will change its status and manipulate object-identifying attributes. This could be seen as involving a discontinuity, although it is difficult to see Nelson as making a precise claim on this. Interestingly, she is one worker in child language who explicitly adopts a continuity position. 'There is a basic continuity in developmental processes and structures. The same types of structures and processes are utilized throughout development, and changes in them are gradual and continuous' (1973a, p. 2).

20. I am by no means convinced that Nelson has this interpretation in mind, particularly in the light of the discussion in 3.3 where it was suggested that, even in the development of a particular concept, it is possible for non-relational and non-dynamic information to play a criterial role right from the start.

21. Note also that there is no reason to expect internal linguistic evidence to provide any plausibility for the approach in this case. To my knowledge, there

has been no attempt to analyse any part of the vocabulary of any natural language using terms which could be related to those of the FCH.

22. It should be evident now why the evidence of Bowerman (1976, 1978) is not particularly damaging for Nelson's position. She can accommodate any sort of overextension.

23. Nelson (1979) does not provide any new insight into this rather tangled position. It does, however, contain a claim that it is mistaken to take assumptions about the logical structure of theories into a developmental context. The illustration she chooses in this connection is from Barrett (1978) and is not terribly clear to me. Obviously, my notion of a teleological explanation is at variance with this suggestion, but, since Nelson provides no argument and does not refer to any developmental literature, I shall continue to assume that the views I put forward in Chapter 1 on this issue are worth pursuing.

24. More recent work with related goals is Bartlett (1978), Dougherty (1978).

25. This book created a great deal of critical discussion in the anthropological and linguistics literature. Doubts have been raised concerning both the substance of Berlin and Kay's findings and the methodology they adopted in producing them. See, for example, Hickerson (1971), Durbin (1972), Collier (1973). Collier *et al.* (1976) takes account of some of the methodological problems and substantially supports the original conclusions, while Kay (1975) attempts to deal with some of the substantive objections, integrating them into a modified partial ordering of basic colour terms. Kay and McDaniel (1978) is a more sophisticated attempt to take account of counter-examples using the machinery of fuzzy set theory. I am uncomfortable with this accunt as it appears to make a large number of predictions for which there is no evidence. Nevertheless, the attempt to establish a close relationship between set membership functions for linguistic categories and response functions for individual neurons in the visual system is impressive and deserves close scrutiny. Since Heider's work on the development of colour terms refers to the original Berlin and Kay hypothesis, I shall pay no attention to these modifications in what follows.

26. Interestingly, even if it were the case that parents, in teaching colour terms to their children, tended to use objects exhibiting focal colours, this itself would be in need of explanation.

27. Evidence for the child going through a stage where the 'prototype' determines the extension of the colour term is not obviously available. The fact that the children, in Heider's third experiment, responded at all can be seen as providing a measure of support, since, presumably, adults in such a situation would be likely to respond with 'Which X one?'

28. Bowerman contrasts this complexive use of words, based on Vygotsky's (1962) notion of 'associative complex', with the latter's 'chain complex'. According to this last notion, temporally adjacent referents for a word will have some features in common, but this need not be true if one examines non-adjacent referents (cf. Vygotsky's *quah* example). While Bowerman found convincing examples of associative complexes, she does not offer a single instance of chain

complexes. The discussion in Palmer (1977) makes clear the sense in which prototypes are consistent with featural theories of representation.

29. That P should persist as part of the lexical entry for CT is argued for by the existence of cognitive reference points for adults in this domain. Cf. 3.5 above.

30. Nor is it obvious that we would have to stop at this point, for there might be the equivalent of what Fodor (1968) has termed a 'phase two explanation' available by reference to the biological properties of the organism. The well-known work of de Valois and Jacobs (1968) on the visual system of the macaque monkey has demonstrated that, in a system very similar to that of man, there are specialised cells for processing information concerning the wavelengths of light and that these cells have peaks of sensitivity which might be related to the properties of at least the primary focal colours. These findings have been used by Kay and McDaniel in their modification of the original Berlin and Kay position. Note further that Bornstein (1975) has demonstrated the perceptual salience of focal colours in infants and that Bornstein, Kessen and Weiskopf (1976) have produced evidence pointing to the existence of categories of hue similar to the adult categories for the four primary hues in four-month-olds.

31. For more speculation along these lines with some interesting suggestions see Ratcliff (1976).

32. I leave aside any speculation on the nature of X (e.g. should it be a subset of $F_1 \ldots, F_n$ as suggested by Smith, Shoben and Rips 1974). Clearly, any complete model of lexical development will have to address this issue. Bowerman does not.

4 The acquisition of relational terms

1. This is only a sample of the work which could be discussed in this chapter, although, I hope, not an unrepresentative one. Notable omissions are E. Clark's own work on spatial prepositions (Clark 1972a), that in collaboration with Haviland on kinship vocabulary (Haviland and Clark 1974) and Gentner's work on 'transactional' verbs (Gentner 1975).

2. 'Relational terms' is here a convenient label with no theoretical significance. In particular, it is not vital to the discussion of this chapter that such terms be interpreted as denoting intensional entities (cf. Quine 1960), although this might be the natural way to construe the proposals we shall meet.

3. In fact, Donaldson and Balfour studied children's responses under a set of carefully constructed conditions but the finding reported in the text was uniform across these conditions. It is important to emphasise that only *consistency* with the interpretation is claimed here. In the light of Carey's (1978a) work, it seems unlikely that this is the correct interpretation. Nevertheless, it did generate a good deal of theoretical discussion, which is what is of immediate concern.

4. At this point it is convenient to note a fundamental distinction between the data considered relevant in the domain of relational terms and that already discussed in 3.1 from early lexical reference. Clark, in treating both, along

with several other phenomena, as instances of overextension, is pointing to what she considers to be important similarities, but on reflection one notes that there are some quite alarming differences between the two situations. In the case of early reference we have a term X which, as well as being used appropriately, also usurps the domain of another term Y. The result is that what should be called 'Y' gets called 'X' but there is no suggestion that the child *understands* instances of 'Y' as if they had the meaning of 'X'. Correspondingly, for relational terms, there is no evidence with which I am familiar for the child producing instances of 'X' when he is meaning 'Y'. The exact import of these remarks for the foundations of Clark's approach is not clear to me, and I certainly do not wish to suggest that the two sets of observations are theoretically distinct. However, clearly, we should be careful about imposing similarities where they may not exist. See also Huttenlocher (1974) for some relevant discussion.

5. *Wee* is commonly used in Scottish English for *small* and is learned before *small* by many Scottish children.

6. For evidence questioning the generality of this finding, see Eilers, Oller and Ellington (1974), Brewer and Stone (1975), Carey (1978b). The last of these is discussed in more detail in 4.6.

7. The concern with antonymic adjective pairs only constituted half the experiment. The other half examined the semantic field of spatial prepositions and will not be analysed here.

8. Note, again, that there is no evidence, to my knowledge, for children meaning *after* when they say *before*. Cf. n. 4 above. Coker (1978) questions Clark's interpretation of her results, pointing out that they are consistent with children adopting a main-clause-first strategy along the lines suggested by Amidon and Carey (1972).

9. I would refer again to Maratsos (1973) and his conclusion that understanding of *big* actually decreases when the child learns more specific dimensional vocabulary.

10. Obviously this could be extended to take account of the different experimental procedures which have been adopted in other relevant studies. There is little point in complicating the presentation in this manner here.

11. Clark (1972b) is of some help in this respect where, in order to handle such pairs as *thick/thin*, a feature [± Secondary] is introduced following Bierwisch (1967). The idea is that such adjectives are not applicable to the most extensive (and hence primary) dimension of objects.

12. From now on I shall suppress specific reference to Condition I and assume that some version of it can be satisifed. The same will often go for Condition V, although in this case the reason for not discussing it is usually that theorists have simply not been aware of the necessity of producing a theory which will explain how the child's system changes in interaction with the environment. Accordingly, the normal situation is that there is nothing to discuss under this condition, but the reader should bear in mind that this is a serious inadequacy.

13. That there might be some internal linguistic support for the proposal can be

ruled out on the grounds that the relevant analyses of the world's languages do not exist.

14. For extensive discussion of markedness and its several senses, covering the senses which are relevant here, see Lyons (1977b, pp. 305ff).

15. It is far from clear to me that the last step in this passage is cogent. *Why* should having a bias towards choosing greater extents lead to prior acquisition of the semantic feature [+ pol]? This worry also applies to some of the reasoning in Clark and Garnica (1974) discussed in 4.5 and in Clark (1972a).

16. That Bartlett accurately represents Clark's position here can be seen in the following statement from Clark (1973, p. 94): 'both are treated as if they contain the feature + polar; they have not quite reached the stage where the unmarked adjective + polar is in contrast with its opposite, which is eventually specified as − polar'.

17. Again, of course, additional features will be needed to distinguish pairs within one dimension.

18. To be fair to Clark on this I should point out that he does cite a small amount of indirect evidence, which would indicate that he is entitled to refer to this principle as something more than an assumption.

19. Nor is it possible to turn to H. Clark's later work (1973) involving what he calls 'rules of application' to find an explanation as to why the child should understand the *meaning* of the unmarked forms before the meaning of the marked forms (if, indeed, he does), rather than having procedures which enable him to *act as if* this were the case. In particular, the number of 'reference points' involved in their application will not provide the necessary complexity measures, as both the marked and unmarked adjectives require the same number of reference points when used comparatively.

20. This is to disagree with H. Clark (1970, p. 272) when he says that the sentence 'John has more apples than Dick' is ambiguous in that it may or may not carry an implication that both John and Dick have many apples. According to the first interpretation, *more* is being used nominally, says Clark. He goes on to propose that the sentence 'John has less apples than Dick' is unambiguous in this respect and always 'implies that John and Dick have a paucity of apples'. It seems to me that Clark's judgements are simply incorrect here and I (and many others) find nothing odd about a use of the second sentence when both John and Dick are well-appled.

21. All of this, of course, leaves untouched the data from Donaldson and her associates indicating that children were interpreting *more* and *less* as having the meaning of *some* under some conditions. But it also becomes difficult to relate this non-comparative usage in the comprehension of nursery school children to the supposed non-comparative usage put forward by Clark, which is presented as taking place near the beginnings of lexical development.

22. The extent to which this sort of partial understanding of *before* and *after* is justified is not clear to me. Obviously, if the child has an order-of-mention strategy and treats *before* and *after* as 'semantic noise' we would get Stage I behaviour. We would also expect to get Stage I behaviour if the conjunction were missed out, replaced by a nonsense form or by some other conjunction

the child did not understand. This same suggestion is discussed by Carey (1978a) and she cites some anecdotal evidence to support it.

23. There was a tendency for older children to belong to the more 'advanced' groups but Clark does not provide any analysis to show that the correlation between age and stage is significant.

24. To say that the strategy is dispensed with is, perhaps, something of an oversimplification; there is evidence indicating that a similar strategy plays a part in adults' perception of sentences. However, there is a considerable difference between the child relying on a strategy to *produce* an interpretation and an adult finding it easier to remember sentences which accord with a particular strategy. The sense in which the adult is *using* the strategy is somewhat opaque to me. So, while not wishing to discount the psycholinguistic evidence (Clark and Clark 1968), I shall assume in the text discussion that the strategy does disappear.

25. The authors' analysis of *bring* and *take* is similar to that of *come* and *go* in all important respects. The main conclusion that the pair *bring/take* was more difficult than the pair *come/go* has already been mentioned. That *bring* and *take* can be seen as having one additional semantic feature encoding their 'causativeness', when compared to *come* and *go*, makes this conclusion consistent with the predictions of the SFH.

26. It is, perhaps, not insignificant here that, in the lexical entries Carey supplies, she includes a feature [comparative], the exact status of which is not discussed. If it is intended to be a semantic feature, it could be argued that it presupposes a dimension of comparison and that Carey is thereby admitting the acquisition of some general notion of dimensionality (as opposed to information about specific dimensions) early. Without more explicit statements on the nature and role of the features, it is pointless to speculate further.

5 The development of formal grammar

1. For arguments that this view may not, in general, be correct, see R. Clark (1974). It may also be the case that mere production of two-word utterances is not, in itself, sufficient to demonstrate syntactic *knowledge* of the sort supposedly captured by a transformational grammar. This issue will not be pursued further here.

2. It should be pointed out that Chomsky has never seriously presented his theory as a theory of language acquisition in the sense in which I am pursuing an explication of this concept here. This is most obvious from the idealisation to instantaneous learning which his position embraces (see Chomsky and Halle 1968 and, for extensive discussion, Chomsky 1976, pp. 119ff), but whether this idealisation leads to serious problems for linguistic theory is distinct from its inappropriacy as a predictor of the course of syntactic development. For a discussion of some of the issues involved in this idealisation and its relationship to linguistic argumentation, see Churma (1975).

3. It is worth noting here that there are at least two ways of construing theories of

linguistic performance, neither of which has been the concern of those people who have bothered themselves with writing grammars (but see remarks below in connection with aspects of the work of both Bowerman and Bloom). Linguistic performance can be identified with the native-speaker's 'real' abilities and the move from competence to performance of this type would be mediated, principally, by the imposition of short-term memory constraints and plan execution constraints. An alternative is to identify the domain of a theory of linguistic performance with what people actually say under specified conditions, and this will involve reference to contextual and sociological variables which are not necessary in characterising 'real' abilities. Note that the first type of performance theory is no nearer satisfying a traditional version of Condition I than is a competence theory.

4. John Lyons has pointed out to me that there may be some connection between O and P and either 'full' and 'empty' words of the Chinese grammatical tradition or 'content' and 'function' words as understood by such scholars as Fries (1952). It seems to me that, while this connection may be plausible in some respects, there are instances of forms identified as pivots which would be assigned to the class of full words or content words in either of the above usages. See Bowerman (1973) for examples and discussion.

5. This treatment was subsequently extended and deepened by one of the authors (Bellugi 1967, 1968) but these developments will not concern me here. Klima and Bellugi's paper also contains a section devoted to the development of question forms which interacts with their section on negation. However, ignoring this section, as I shall, does not prejudice evaluation in the sense I am concerned with here.

6. The data on which the generalisations are based came from Roger Brown's longitudinal project.

7. Obviously, this grammar could be complicated by indicating the optionality of the negative elements and expanding the Nucleus constituent, but this is hardly necessary for the present discussion.

8. Conceivably, the one grammar for Kathryn could be compared to the grammars from the other children and, in fact, Bloom indulges in informal comparisons of this kind. It requires an assumption of commonality across children to be feasible, and I have taken the view that comparison of within-child grammars provides enough material to begin to see the advantages and weaknesses of the general approach.

9. This is not exactly true, given the left-most N in these structures, as Chomsky's definition of 'subject-of' refers to NP; in the face of the difficulties we are discussing, this seems a trifling objection.

10. Failure to satisfy the condition permits the general linguistic theory to make available grammars which generate all recursively enumerable languages and this was viewed as an intolerable laxity in the general theory by Chomsky (1965) (see Peters and Ritchie 1973 for much more extended discussion and Sampson 1973, 1975 questioning the substance of the debate). Interestingly, in his more recent work, Chomsky has moved away from his 1965 position. Chomsky (1977) suggests that, so long as candidate grammars are sufficiently

'spread' according to an evaluation measure, it may be legitimate to see the child as confronted with the learning of a recursively enumerable language (see Chapter 10 for further discussion). The important point is that, according to certain conceptions that were popular when Bloom was producing her work, she was, by relaxing the constraint on recoverability, presenting the child with an insoluble learning problem. Bowerman (1973) also uses reduction transformations and, so, is no improvement on Bloom as far as this issue is concerned. That she is uneasy about it is exhibited by her statement that (p. 102): 'The optional verb deletion transformations . . . are regarded as specifications of *performance variables which were important enough to warrant representation in the grammars.*' (My emphasis – RMA.) As she has just taken the view that grammars are theories of the child's competence, nothing could be a firmer indicator of her uncertainty as to her domain of enquiry. For more extensive discussion, see Atkinson (1975).

11. It would be possible to ask questions with regard to the intended derived constituent structure (e.g. is the ə intended to be part of the Q when it is present and part of the VP when it is not?) but enough has been said already to cast doubt on the status of the transformational component of the second Gia grammar.

12. For remarks along these lines, see Schaerlaekens (1973).

13. It is worth noting here that the necessity for a VP category has been questioned by, for example, Lakoff and Ross (1967).

14. Bowerman (1973), while being more sophisticated and consistent in many respects, still has problems with lexicon-feature rules and, as already mentioned, includes a reduction transformation. See Atkinson (1978) for a much more detailed treatment.

15. Similar claims for the order of appearance of lexicon-feature rules relative to transformational rules cannot be substantiated, as a theory in which rules introducing features followed the application of transformations would be perfectly intelligible.

16. Brown and Hanlon recognise that their formulation of this rule violates the condition of recoverability of deletions and this is why it is dubbed 'schema'. The implications of this for the status of the set of operations TI – TVII is obvious. For recent views that this sort of truncation process is best handled in a different component of a linguistic theory – a discourse grammar – see Sag (1976), Williams (1977).

17. The formulation of all the rules leaves open questions of derived constituent structure. Perhaps this is understandable for a topic which was so badly neglected by a large number of transformational linguists for a long time, but it is difficult to talk about rules representing 'structural knowledge' unless it is taken seriously.

18. It is a general feature of these rules that perfect aspect is missed out. Presumably, this is because the children in the sample did not employ perfect aspect, but Brown and Hanlon nowhere say this.

19. Strictly speaking SAAD's cannot enter into these predictions as they involve TV, and none of the others, with the exception of NTag's, do. Brown and

Hanlon's discussion of TV and its interaction with TVI is confusing. They say (p. 23): '[TVI] is not applied in the derivation of SAAD sentences, but it is applied in Q, N and Tr. Nevertheless, it does not strictly operate so as to make one sentence more complex, cumulatively, than another, because, whenever it is not applied, TV must be.' There is nothing here to suggest that SAAD's and other sentence types can be cumulatively compared.

20. Actually these figures are somewhat inflated as not all the predictions are independent. If, say, one predicts correctly that SAAD sentences will appear before N and that N will appear before NQ, one can hardly celebrate an independent correct prediction that SAAD will appear before NQ. Taking account of this, there are only 36 independent predictions of which 26 are confirmed. Removing SAAD from the predictions, as the previous note urges, reduces this still further to 27 predictions of which 17 are confirmed.

21. Brown and Hanlon, commenting on similarities in the structural analyses of the transformations involved in the generation of Q, N and Tr sentences, point out, reinforcing the point in the text, that these three sentence-types are learned at about the same time.

22. It is interesting that Maratsos (1978) implicitly assumes a developmental interpretation of the derivational theory of complexity in his critique of standard transformational accounts for understanding the acquisition of a number of structures. He draws attention to (i) prenominal adjectives and possessives, (ii) subjectless complements and (iii) short passives and points out that, on the traditional account, (i) should not be acquired until after the child conjoins and embeds, (ii) should not be acquired until after complements with full subjects and (iii) should not be acquired until after full passives. All of these predictions are incorrect and I find Maratsos' move towards a surface-lexicalist account (Bresnan 1978) of the acquisition of syntactic structure an attractive one. However, as he points out (p. 263): 'in lightening the burdens of those who hope to explain syntactic development, we complicate the work of those who hope to explain lexical development'. A consideration of the plausibility of the lexicalist account of syntactic development must await a more systematic presentation of this view, but for some additional suggestive discussion, see Mayer, Erreich and Valian (1978) and Goodluck and Solan (1979).

23. This reduction immediately indicates that semantic complexity cannot be the *sole* determinant of acquisition order. Kuczaj (1977) contests Brown's claim that the irregular past morpheme is acquired before the regular past. It seems to me that the apparent contradiction in this debate can be resolved by paying close attention to the ages of the children in the two studies and by recognising that children may differ in their skill for inducing generalisations. Thus, it appears that two of Brown's children had had enough linguistic experience of particular cases to reach criterion on the irregular past before they were capable of inducing the generalisation underlying the use of the regular past. Eve, the exception to the ordering in Figure 5.14, was the opposite of this, being precocious enough to formulate the relevant generalisation before she had had enough experience with irregular forms to reach criterion here. This

interpretation is borne out by the fact that Eve was more given to overgeneralisation errors than the other two children in the period under study. It would appear that *all* of Kuczaj's children had already formulated the appropriate generalisation at the time he collected his data, and this is at least plausible, given the relative ages and MLU's of the subjects in the two studies.

24. One only has to consider the transition from T_1 to T_2 to appreciate the problem. This leads us to speculate on the nature of cognitive or perceptual reasons for the child acquiring the semantic dimension of Temporary duration before he acquires those of Containment and Support.

6 Semantic approaches to syntactic development

1. The reasons for this neglect are: (i) For the more standard versions of such proposals, where the rules are transformations operating on case-grammar structures, there has already been extensive relevant discussion in Chapter 5. Much of this would carry over into the present context. (ii) For the realisation rules of Schlesinger (1971), we would immediately confront the question of the availability of a general theory, which, to my knowledge, has never been discussed. Additionally, Brown (1973) raises some difficult formal problems for these rules. (iii) There has been a good deal of notional agreement on the membership of an inventory of semantic relations for two-word utterances, so, on this basis, such an inventory might be seen as constituting the solid core of such speculations.

2. This is not to suggest that the authors of the proposals in question were uninterested in the mapping problem. It is simply that, in some of their work, they choose to focus on a semantic inventory.

3. The semantic relations recognised in Schlesinger's model do not differ significantly from those of Brown. He too does not speculate on acquisition order within this set. For some speculations of this kind, using rather different inventories of semantic relations, see the summary in Bowerman (1976). This paper also admirably emphasises the difficulty of *empirically* justifying a particular set of relational categories, a problem which is distinct from the theoretical respectability of such a set.

4. Brown does discuss the appearance of non-indicative modalities in Stage I (1973, pp. 215–17).

5. A word of warning is appropriate here, as the inventory of cases necessary in a general theory of case-grammar is one of the recurring problems in Fillmore's work in this area (see Fillmore 1971 for worries and discussion). Nor, of course, is Brown using the case-labels as cases in this context.

6. Edwards (1973) does discuss these relations and comments on (p. 418): 'the absence from Piagetian theory and data of the relevant concepts quite so nicely pre-packaged for our use'. To my mind, Edwards' own attempt to identify sensori-motor sources for these relations is less than compelling.

7. Antinucci and Parisi do not comment on the order of appearance of these utterances in the six-month period they studied. Their subsequent discussion only makes sense if we assume that they appear in the order of Figure 6.1.

8. That this might not be their intention is suggested by the existence of the rule of predicate-raising in the generative semantics literature (see McCawley 1971), but at one point they do suggest that *da* substitutes for a configuration involving non-raised predicates. It is not clear what this means for their allegiance to the generative semantics tradition, nor, indeed, what formal problems it might give rise to.

9. There is something quite inappropriate, to my mind, about this sort of claim, as it seems to make explicit the view that, when the child says *mamma da*, she is, in fact, (metalinguistically) predicating something of herself and of language. This is bizarre enough to be wrong. Evidence for these structures is offered by vocatives and the lexicalisation of 'performative' verbs like *see* and *wanna* (cf. Gruber 1975). One might suggest that evidence against them is offered by the non-lexicalisation of *Italian*!

10. It is difficult to take Antinucci and Parisi's claims seriously anyway, if one examines Figure 6.2. There the first argument of *become* is sentential and so, semantically, there is sentential embedding right from the start of development.

11. Ingram (1971) proposes that one-word utterances should be assigned complex semantic-syntactic structures. In fact, he goes further than this and suggests that similar structures are appropriate for pre-linguistic vocalisations and cries. I have a number of difficulties in comprehending the details of his position, not least because of his non-standard use of various sorts of linguistic formalism. Telling criticisms against his analysis are put forward by Greenfield and Smith. Additionally, the notion that one-word utterances, pre-linguistic vocalisations and cries should be seen as abbreviations of *sentences* seems to be highly suspect for reasons advanced by, e.g., Bloom (1973), Dore (1975). I do not believe that a detailed dissection of what Ingram is saying would repay the effort involved. Greenfield and Smith see a number of classical studies as anticipating some of their conclusions, including Guillaume (1927), Werner and Kaplan (1963) and, most notably Leopold (1949).

12. This interpretation is also argued for by Greenfield and Smith's treatment of *informativeness* as the factor which determines the choice of the single word when the child is combining such a word with situational elements (see also Greenfield 1978b, Miller 1978). Whether this notion could also be used for later stages of development is not clear.

13. It is worth noting that this generalised ordering is not the only one which is true of Table 6.1. We could distinguish each of the performative categories or place Object associated with another Object or location in the second category, for example. That Greenfield and Smith do things this way is a reflection of where they want their analysis to take them.

14. If the linguistic development does lag behind the relevant cognitive development, it is not obvious that the linguistic functions have to appear in the same order as their cognitive counterparts. Something could be going on in the time-interval to affect this ordering. For more discussion, see Chapter 8. Additionally, it is not clear, contrary to what Greenfield and Smith suggest, that formal complexity is constant throughout the one-word period. Often,

one-word utterances have marked intonation patterns and are accompanied by gestures and it seems reasonable to suggest that the integration of these with the segmental characteristics of words will lead to differentially complex utterances.

7 The development of speech-acts

1. Cf. similar remarks in Chapter 8 in connection with arguments for a cognitive basis for syntactic structure. Ervin-Tripp (1977) is a recent review of the role of conversation in syntactic development with, to my mind, totally unspectacular conclusions.

2. There is scope for discussion as to whether the system is appropriately called a language at this stage or whether it is better regarded as a primitive communication system. To some extent, Halliday provides this discussion, producing criteria according to which it is a language. It would, however, be possible to consider alternative criteria which the system fails to meet, as Halliday points out. I agree with him that it makes little difference what we call the system at this stage, but feel that there is room for disagreement on whether we emphasise the continuity of functional development, as he does, or the discontinuity of other properties.

3. This rather negative tone should not be misunderstood here. From Dore's starting point, it is not clear that he had any alternatives to the procedure he adopted (but cf. 7.4). I am merely anxious to get clear what that procedure is.

4. Bennett (1976) makes the same point in a critique of Chomsky's view that the 'primary' function of language is not communication. It seems necessary to distinguish between a particular linguistic act and a language in this dispute and, while Chomsky has argued that communicative intention is not a necessary concomitant of every linguistic act, this does not show that such a notion is not central in the definition of a language.

5. Dore's difficulties of imagination are not necessarily insurmountable. It is certainly not incoherent to consider an act of pointing as corresponding to an assertion (but cf. Griffiths' discussion of statements and requests in 7.4). Also relevant is Grice's (1957) discussion of the differences between showing photographs and drawing pictures, where he seems to be saying that the latter can be functionally equivalent to asserting. It is patently non-linguistic and can be imagined as pre-linguistic without too much difficulty.

6. There is some inconsistency between Dore (1974) and (1975) on whether the two components of Figure 7.1 are obligatory or not. The later paper and Figure 7.1 suggest that they are, but the earlier paper allows PSA's to consist of only prosodic patterns, which are seen as encodings of Primitive force.

7. A fuller investigation of the 'functional' tradition, as represented in the work of, e.g., Firth, might reveal a pedigree for Halliday's categories. It would, however, involve lengthy discussion and, as Halliday's explicit strategy in the work under discussion is the one outlined in the text, I feel justified in not pursuing this possibility here.

8. See Sugarman-Bell (1978) for discussion which is very sympathetic to the tone

of this distinction. The idea of using an object to capture an adult's attention is obviously distinct from that described in the next section of using a vocalisation to get an adult to attend to an object.

9. Bates *et al.* also speculate on development *within* the protodeclarative, arguing that Piagetian theory is not helpful here. I shall not discuss this aspect of their work here.

10. This expresses a concern for the *referential* usage of definite descriptions as opposed to the *attributive* usage (see Donnellan 1966 for this distinction). It seems to me that attributive usage is relatively late to develop in children, standardly requiring the use of complex referring expressions, but I am aware of no developmental study of the distinction.

11. Lyons in the works cited in the text argues that quasi-reference is to be distinguished from reference as the latter is a bedfellow of predication, and the reader is referred to these works for a more extensive discussion of the theoretical foundations of the distinction and some programmatic remarks on its significance for the study of child language. It is interesting to note that precursors to the distinction can be found in the categories of judgements embraced in the Port-Royal *Grammar* and *Logic* and in the metaphysics of Brentano (see the distinction between categorical and thetic judgements and its interesting application to Japanese syntax by Kuroda 1972).

12. For more extensive discussion, see Isard (1975) and for a formal framework in which speech-acts are seen as 'changing the context', Apostel (1972).

13. It seems likely that this could be strengthened to a total ordering with Requesting coming later than Attention-directing, particularly if we interpret these labels as referring to communicative (not necessarily linguistic) acts. The primitive request that Griffiths describes requires pointing in order for its content to be conveyed and, of course, pointing is the paradigmatic attention-director.

8 Cognitive reductions

1. Chomsky (1980), working within a framework which no longer uses an extensive set of transformational rules, still postulates principles of grammar for which, in his opinion, 'it would be surprising indeed if we were to find that [they] . . . are operative in other cognitive systems' (p. 4).

2. For the purposes of this section it is not essential that the theories be developmental.

3. Recalling the discussion of Chapter 1, note that each such theory will also have a vocabulary of theoretical terms. To simplify the presentation here I concentrate on formal properties of theories.

4. Both of these latter positions assume that additional conditions, still to be investigated, are satisfied to justify the assertion of total or partial dependence. One further possibility which can be mentioned, but which seems to be sufficiently remote from serious investigation at the moment not to warrant further discussion, is that whereby some properties in P_j are identified in D^* while others are identified in the distinct non-linguistic cognitive domain D^{**}.

Perhaps we are justified, at this stage, in assuming that cognitive development is monolithic once language development is excluded. Bates, Benigni, Bretherton, Camaioni and Volterra (1977), in their very useful survey of possible positions on the language and cognition question, raise the possibility of relating both aspects of development to that of some superordinate capacity. It is evident from their discussion and their employment of Piaget's distinction between figurative and operative structures, that it might not be misleading to regard this superordinate capacity as cognitive *competence* (employing operative structures) to be distinguished from cognitive *performance* (employing figurative structures). But, if this is so, the position they outline is inappropriately biased towards cognition in not recognising a similar distinction for language. Bates *et al.* find the position they describe attractive because it allows a good deal of flexibility in the order of appearance of related cognitive and linguistic behaviour. However, once we see the task of constructing theories of language development as concerned with competence domains (as many workers have), variability in the appearance of *behaviours* will be anticipated anyway, although the question of the temporal priority and explanatory status of the competence level will still be a substantial one.

5. As an example, consider the possibility that syntactic knowledge is, to some extent, independent of cognitive development, whereas the development of speech-acts or 'communicative competence' is totally dependent on cognition. The only thing to be clear about is that there is no conflict in this state of affairs.

6. It is not my task here to investigate what may be involved in this notion, although I would anticipate that something along the lines of the discussion in Chapter 1 would be relevant. It is worth pointing out at this stage that the most popular theories of cognitive development are not presented in the fashion which has become standard in some parts of linguistics and also, to some extent, in non-developmental psychology. They do not provide axiomatisations of sets of representations and procedures for operating on such representations.

7. I shall assume that such a collapsed sequence is a total ordering but nothing hangs on this assumption. If we were to allow cognitive and linguistic theories to appear 'simultaneously' in the ordering, this would complicate some of the subsequent definitions without affecting the arguments. Note that no one–one correspondence between theories in the two sequences is entailed by this procedure and I leave open the possibility that in a collapsed sequence we shall find adjacent linguistic (cognitive) theories. This is merely a reflection of the fact that we are not entitled to prejudge the issue of the number of theories of either type, and the most conservative strategy assumes that the stages on which our theories are based are quite arbitrary, being a function of the methodology of particular studies, time available, etc. As pointed out in Chapter 1, this is not to deny the possibility of there being a number of significant stages of development in any domain.

8. The fact that this developmental sequence would be ruled out anyway on teleological grounds is beside the point here.

9. Quite simply, we are enquiring as to whether the two sets of terms and operations enter the sequences *in the same order*.

10. The distinction between content and structure is clearly recognised in Karmiloff-Smith (1979) where she notes the original emphasis on syntactic structure in Geneva-inspired studies, later giving way to a bias towards the study of content. It is also implicit in Slobin (1973) (see 8.5 below).

11. It is perhaps worth recalling here Brown's argument, discussed in 6.1, for the cognitive basis of the semantics of early two-word utterances. This relied, to a large extent, on the child's abilities to distinguish an object from its attributes, its location and actions performed on it. But, of course, this argument does not establish any ontogenetic primacy for object names over attribute names – *both* rely on the same cognitive development. I have been unable to find any clear argument in Greenfield and Smith (1976) to support McNamara's contention, although the *empirical* claim appears to be substantiated.

12. These speculations can be related to those of Nelson discussed in Chapter 3. Greenfield and Smith (1976) offer some evidence for the cognitive primacy of *change of state* over *process* (see 6.3) citing McNamara, but this evidence does not bear on the varying/unvarying attribute question.

13. Several readings of Cromer (1974) have failed to reveal any succinct statement of the content of the Cognition Hypothesis, but it seems clear that it amounts, at least, to a claim for the truth of the first three conditions in 8.2.

14. It might be objected that the L's could be regarded as grammars as L_2 will not be identical to L_1, containing a generalisation of Affix-hopping to apply to *-en* of *have-en*. There are two points to consider in this connection. First, according to Cromer's own emphasis, nothing has changed between L_1 and L_2 as far as the grammatical system is concerned. Second, and more importantly, if we treat the L's as grammars in this way, the collapsed sequence will not satisfy the relevant conditions. To see this we have only to note that the vital cognitive notion in C is 'relevance' and we would expect this to be a translation of some new theoretical term in L_2. However, no such theoretical term exists; all we have in L_2 is the generalisation of Affix-hopping and, by no stretch of the imagination, is it possible to see this as translatable into 'relevance'.

15. Similar reservations must be expressed concerning Cromer's analysis of Bloom's (1968) treatment of the development of negation. Interpreted syntactically, it falls foul of dealing with notions which are not standardly accommodated in syntax; interpreted semantically, it fails to make contact with any substantial cognitive theory.

16. Note that this is not necessary as witnessed by the non-contradictoriness of *John broke the doll but now it's fixed*; what is being exploited here is not a linguistic fact concerning the semantics of *break* but probabilistic knowledge about the world. See Chomsky (1976), Pulman (1977) for extensive discussion.

17. One thing which seems clear here is that there is antagonism between this claim and Cromer's discussion of Perfects, which could be seen as implying that the endurance of a state of affairs resulting from a past event into the present encounters the notion of 'relevance'.

18. Note that such a translation is obviously too simple as it stands, because the past forms occurring with CHANGE OF STATE verbs are not taken account of and they do not involve only NON-REAL. Also the prohibition of present tense forms being used in imaginative verbal play appears unjustified. I shall ignore such complications for the sake of the argument.

19. I have assumed that this is a more appropriate sequence than (C_1, L_1, C_2, L_2) as the cognitive distinction between REAL and NON-REAL is seen as a property of mature sensori-motor intelligence; as such, it would precede *any* linguistic reference to past events.

20. Given the success of the non-conservers on the comprehension tasks, it is tempting to say that their poor showing on the production tasks represents a rather superficial linguistic disability, i.e. one would hardly be justified in concluding that these children did not know the significance of the expressions in question.

21. There are two further criticisms which could be developed. The first is that we have only been concerned with a small subset of both substantive and formal aspects of the linguistic theory assumed by the investigation, and, even if the reduction were successful with regard to the categories and properties considered here, this would still leave a large residue of linguistic constructs untouched. The exact constitution of this residue would, of course, depend upon the linguistic theory being manipulated but it is safe to say that *no* linguistic theory is exhausted by the terms and properties in Figure 8.1. The second point is that there is no question of the cognitive and linguistic theories being order-isomorphic or intermeshed because of the unstructured nature of the collapsed sequence. The stronger of these two conditions would not be satisfied by virtue of the relevant cognitive development being complete before the linguistic development gets started, but it is an interesting question (not investigated, to my knowledge) as to whether any parallels can be drawn between orderings in C and G, as these theories are understood by Sinclair.

22. Without more detailed information it is impossible to say that the sequence is to any degree intermeshed giving us, say, a collapsed sequence of the form $(C_1, L_1, C_2, L_2, C_3, L_3)$, but there is nothing in the age norms presented by Greenfield *et al.* to rule out this possibility.

23. In later studies (Greenfield and Schneider 1977, Goodson and Greenfield 1975, Greenfield 1978c), Greenfield has abandoned the strict parallelism between action sequences and sentences which is implied by the study under consideration. She says (1978c, p. 444): 'This theoretical formulation has been in terms of common structural features in more than one domain rather than specific parallels between sentences and action patterns. A major reason for this is that, while any two domains may have similar principles of operation, the actual combinatorial possibilities may be quite different due to design features of the two media.' Bates *et al.* (1977), discussing this possibility, refer to it as an *analogue* position on the relationship between language and cognition.

24. Hierarchisation is specifically attended to in Goodson and Greenfield (1975) and Greenfield (1978c). However, what these discussions fail to take account

of is that hierarchisation *per se* is not what is seen as vital in the structures defining grammatical relations. Particular hierarchical configurations are necessary for the definition of, e.g. 'subject-of', 'main verb-of', 'direct object-of', and nothing in Greenfield's work on action sequences has the required degree of specificity in this respect. For relevant discussion of hierarchisation in non-linguistic cognitive systems, see, e.g., Sampson (1975, p. 127).

25. It is remarkable that Tzotzil, a VOS language, should be cited in this respect, since one would expect at least some Tzotzil children to use this dominant word-order.

26. In this role they were opposed to grammatical transformations. For summary and development of Bever's position, see Bever (1974, 1975), Fodor, Bever and Garrett (1974), and for effective criticism of some of Bever's suggestions, Grosu (1975).

27. Interestingly, at this point, Slobin makes remarks which would seem to indicate that he is not a definitionalist when he says (p. 181) that: 'although one can talk about order of acquisition in terms of semantic or cognitive complexity, there is clearly a point at which formal linguistic complexity also plays a role'. The observations which lead to this remark concern Bowerman's work on yes/no questions in Finnish and Omar's work on the acquisition of Arabic plurals. The most interesting way to look at these findings from my point of view is discussed below (8.6).

28. Serbo-Croatian uses a combination of suffixes and prepositions, and the suffixes are the part of the locative system which is learned first.

29. That Slobin wishes the principle to be extended within the linguistic domain is apparent from some of the examples he uses which require attention not to the ends of *words* but to the ends of *sentences*. Of course, this may raise a difficulty for the principle as, within any linguistic utterance, there are a number of levels of temporally ordered sequences of events, e.g. syllables, morphemes, words, phrases and sentences. To see these levels being manipulated in an experimental context with adults, see Savin and Bever (1970), Foss and Swinney (1973), McNeill and Lindig (1973). Note also the recent research of Newport, Gleitman and Gleitman (1977) suggesting that sentence-*initial* position is privileged for small children processing input.

30. We could infer on the basis of such a (hypothetical) result that the set of properties in question are characteristic of cognitive systems which are unique to man, but, of course, this is a distinct issue from the autonomy of any aspect of language development. For the former we need to make cross-species comparisons; for the latter, we can restrict our attention to humans.

31. It is worth noting here that the sort of property Chomsky has in mind when discussing this sort of argument has become more abstract throughout his writings (cf. structure-dependence of rules with the constraints on rules discussed in e.g. Chomsky 1973, 1977). Certainly, it is difficult to imagine such constraints as subjacency or the specified subject constraint having any role outside the linguistic system. Further to this point we should note that it is not clear that Chomsky is concerned with systems of expression in the sense

in which this phrase is being used here. It would be quite possible that the system of grammar, as envisaged by Chomsky and his associates, should have properties which make it independent of any non-linguistic cognitive system, while the system of expression should share all its properties with such systems. Whether child language theorists have been concerned with studying Chomskyan grammars or expression systems is, of course, a difficult question, briefly mentioned in Chapter 5.

9 Social reductions

1. One of Bruner's aims is to attempt to produce functional/interactional explanations for phenomena which have given rise to innateness claims. It is worth pointing out that the domain of turn-taking in conversation is not one which has led to such claims.
2. Given Bruner's later speculations, it could well be that he would turn to play, where clearly, it is possible to suggest that actions must be interpreted non-literally, for non-linguistic interactional correlates to non-literal inter-pretations. To my knowledge, this possibility has not been pursued in the literature.
3. I must emphasise that this is not to say that the Chomskyan position on innateness is correct, but merely to point out the magnitude of the task of showing that it is not *in all respects*.
4. Although a reference to Chomsky (1965) follows, it is unclear in this context what the reference of 'subject-predicate rules' in the cited passage is supposed to be, since such functionally defined notions are not explicitly mentioned in the rules appearing in the grammars which Bruner appears to be trying to make contact with.
5. For identical observations, see Menn (1973).
6. To examine this question meaningfully would require a specification of what aspects of the addressee's cognitions must be available to the speaker in connection with each deictic form and *this* information must then be seen as important in the behaviours to which Bruner draws our attention. For some programmatic discussion of the sort of information in question, see Atkinson and Griffiths (1973).
7. Clark's argument and others of a similar kind seem to be crying out for the distinction Lyons (1972b) draws between *communicative* and *informative* (cf. also Chapter 7). According to this distinction, the child's reaching could be viewed as informative but not communicative in the primitive phase.
8. Clark says (p. 252); 'the gestural form, though necessarily bearing a resem-blance to the previous form of the social act, reflects an entirely different mental organisation on the part of the child'.
9. I use 'symbolic' here as a deliberately vague cover term for all categories of signs. If there is a lesson to be learned from Peirce (1932) it is that we are not usually in a position to assign signs to categories in a completely unequivocal way.

10. For the most extensive discussion of these three 'stages' of linguistic development, see Bloom (1973).

10 Learnability and mechanisms of learning

1. This is not to suggest that workers in this area are not interested in taking account of, and ultimately explaining, the course of development. The strategy which has been adopted has been one of first attempting to establish that certain systems can be learned. A second stage in the enquiry is to see whether the systems remain learnable as we make more and more realistic assumptions about, e.g. the nature of the input data, the processing capacities of children, the actual course of development, etc. It is probably fair to say that, with notable exceptions (see below), this stage of the activity is still in a fairly rudimentary state.

2. The work of Wexler and his associates has been almost exclusively concerned with the learning of (components of) grammars. There are at least two obvious reasons for this: within transformational theory, syntax has been seen as generative, thereby producing the most obvious learnability problems, and, more importantly, syntactic theories have been articulated in a sufficiently precise way for the formal manipulations necessary in learnability proofs to be possible. For further discussion, see 10.2.

3. Wexler and Culicover raise the possibility that there might not be a single fixed learning procedure which the child resorts to throughout syntactic development. This could be because there are individual differences across children or, more interestingly, because learning procedures themselves are subject to development. In this latter case learning procedures might themselves constitute an appropriate domain of study within language development. For now, Wexler and Culicover are surely correct in assuming that we should see how much progress we can make on the assumption that the learning procedure is fixed.

4. A few words of amplification are in order here to prevent misunderstanding. For Gold, data are presented in a sequence and a permissible sequence of data is one which includes all sentences in the target language. The criterion of learnability is referred to as 'identification in the limit' and insists that for every language in the class in question and for every permissible sequence of data from that language, there must be some finite time at which the learner chooses the 'correct' grammar for the language and continues to choose this grammar from then on. This cashes in on the intuition that a child modifies his grammatical system in the light of incoming data until he develops the correct grammar; from this point on, his grammar is stable. Whether this is a correct assumption about the adult linguistic state is not something I am concerned with here. For Gold 'correct' can be identified with 'observationally adequate', i.e. once the learner has acquired a grammar which generates the strings of the target language and no non-strings, he has identified the language in the limit. Questions of descriptive adequacy are not raised.

5. Note that, in general, it is not the infinite cardinality of the class of languages

being investigated which leads to unlearnability. Thus, there are infinite classes of infinite languages which are learnable under text-presentation according to Gold's criterion (for an example, see Wexler and Culicover 1980, p. 44). In particular, classes of recursively enumerable languages may be learnable in this way, as what is crucial is the relationships of the sets of sentences in the languages, not the cardinality of the languages. This leaves open the possibility that, by severely restricting the class of possible grammars, learnability from text could be achieved. For discussion along these lines, although with important reservations about the nature of the data relevant to grammar induction, see Koster (1979). Wexler and Culicover do not adopt this strategy in their text, as they believe that radical restrictions of the required sort are not consistent with the general function of transformational rules. Koster is writing in a climate where transformational rules play a much less significant part in the overall theory than is the case in the standard theory on which Wexler and Culicover largely base themselves. For Koster there is, in core grammar, only one transformational schema – move α – which is universal and which is trivially learnable. I shall not pursue the analyses of the learnability properties of more recent versions of transformational grammar in the text. For some discussion, see Wexler and Culicover (1980, pp. 486ff).

6. For an interesting discussion and negative evaluation of heuristic learning procedures, see Pinker (1979, pp. 234ff).

7. For extensive discussion, see Wexler and Culicover (1980, pp. 63ff). The suggestion that the input to the child is specially tailored to the child's linguistic needs and, therefore, makes language acquisition possible is also effectively demolished by Wexler and Culicover. The empirical correctness of the view that Motherese is causally efficient in language development is already in considerable danger from the work of Newport, Gleitman and Gleitman (1977) and Feldman, Goldin-Meadow and Gleitman (1978). The additional slant that Wexler and Culicover supply to the debate is that there is also a serious *logical* problem with the argument. There is no *a priori* reason to believe that simplified input is going to make language acquisition easier without having to assume innate linguistic properties.

8. In connection with this view of a transformational component, various complexities arise to do with deletion. These are not relevant to the level of discussion in the text and the interested reader can consult Wexler and Culicover (1980, pp. 523ff).

9. What is interesting in this connection is whether the child is also presented with ungrammatical strings which are not labelled as such (cf. the earlier discussion of informant-presentation), and what the implications of such presentations would be for syntax learning. For some discussion, see Wexler and Culicover (1980, pp. 481ff) and 10.3. It is perhaps worth pointing out here the two senses in which 'degenerate' has been used in connection with input to the child in the recent literature. Chomsky's (1965) original usage was interpreted by most commentators as implying a high proportion of false starts, hesitations, etc. in adults' speech to children and it is this interpretation

which is relevant to this note. The demonstration that there were not many such 'errors' was then taken by some to argue against Chomsky's views on linguistic innateness (see papers in Snow and Ferguson 1977 for summary). There is, however, another interpretation which claims that the input data are 'structurally degenerate' in the sense that they do not contain enough information in themselves to enable the child to induce the grammar of his language. It is this sense which is exploited by Wexler and Culicover in their argument against the view that simplified input makes language acquisition easier. Simplified input is going to be *more* degenerate in this latter sense than non-simplified input.

10. There are two remarks worth making here with regard to my conditions from Chapter 1. The first is that an enumerative procedure would make little sense from the point of view of Condition III, i.e. if the procedure were simply guessing grammars on the basis of an enumeration, there would be no reason to expect the guesses to become increasingly complex in any interesting way (unless, of course, the enumeration was itself constructed in terms of increasing complexity). Second, the formulation of Condition V I offered in Chapter 1 is consistent with a mechanism of gradual modification rather than an enumerative procedure. Wexler and Culicover (1980, p. 92) contains an interesting, though programmatic, discussion of one way in which an enumeration procedure might be consistent with gradual modification. What their discussion shows, however, is that it might be possible to look at a sequence of grammars and not always be in a position to decide whether they had arisen as a result of enumeration or as a result of gradual modification. This conclusion does not make the view that the child uses enumeration procedures any more plausible because of the requirement of access to all previous data.

11. Wexler and Culicover are aware that there are other possibilities for the operation of learning mechanisms. They say (p. 100): 'This property of LP [the learning procedure] has been assumed for conceptual clarity and mathematical and conceptual simplicity, not because it is necessarily correct. In fact, it is probably wrong, because it means that there is no direct concept in LP of correction or modification of a transformation. If a transformation T is to be modified to T', it must be by rejection of T on datum d and hypothesization of T' on some later datum d'. Certainly the assumption of the possibility of direct modification is consistent with our intuitions about intelligent learning procedures.' Pinker (1979) sees further difficulties in the assumption that rejection or hypothesisation of any of the transformations in the candidate set is equiprobable. Where intelligence can be built into this sort of procedure is undoubtedly going to be the subject of much future research.

12. Note that this is a totally different point from that which says that short simple sentences make for easy learning. Here we are taking as given the fact that adults do use short sentences when talking to children and asking what the consequences of that are for learning. The major consequence is that more constraints have to be put on the child's initial hypotheses if he is to learn from simple data and from errors on simple data. Of course, this is the complete converse of the conclusion which is standardly drawn from the observation.

13. There are major aspects of Wexler and Culicover's approach which have not been mentioned in the text. Perhaps the major omission is that, along with assuming a probabilistic mode of data presentation, they also assume a probabilistic criterion of learning. This has no effect on any of the issues I am concerned with here.

14. It would seem likely that these constraints would also contribute to the solution of the problem of *strong learnability* (cf. strong generative capacity), whereby the learner must not only induce a grammar which generates the correct language (or maps base structures onto the correct surface strings) but induce a grammar which assigns the correct structures to strings in the language (maps base structures onto correct surface structures). This problem has not, to my knowledge, been solved, hence my usage of single quotation marks for 'correct' in the text.

15. I do not wish to suggest here that such a set of assumptions is itself plausible, although much of the work discussed in Chapter 3 operates with it. I am merely concerned to raise a possibility. Alternatives to enumeration are not difficult to speculate about. For example, a learning procedure might accept a lexicon plus a new datum consisting of a word and a representation of what the child takes to be the referent of the word (for the sort of concrete nominal learning in which E. Clark 1973 and Nelson 1974 are particularly interested). A match between this (word, representation) pair and the existing entry in the child's lexicon for this word would lead to no modification in the lexicon, a mismatch would lead to modification which could be more or less conservative, etc. Given that explicitly negative information is presented to the child in this domain and assuming that the child has some way of representing this, it might be that such information is particularly efficacious as far as modifying lexical entries is concerned, perhaps prompting the child to adopt a less conservative strategy of modification. All of this is speculation but I submit that it is intelligible speculation and worthy of serious investigation. Similar considerations are, of course, applicable to the sort of learning mechanism envisaged by Wexler and Culicover. Certainly, if one wished to pursue an analogy between the child's grammatical hypotheses and general scientific hypotheses, it seems unlikely that the child would abandon a hypothesis which is faced with only one conflicting datum: scientific hypotheses are usually robust and can accommodate a good deal of negative evidence before being abandoned.

16. For clarification it should be pointed out that Wexler and Culicover are assuming a 'grammar' for semantic representations which itself consists of rewriting rules defining constituency. This grammar, however, does not order constituents.

17. For a systematic evaluation of Anderson's system, see Pinker (1979, pp. 251ff).

18. One exception to the claim that linguistic theories are insufficiently formalised to allow for serious discussion of learnability problems is, perhaps, provided by phonology. In a very brief discussion Wexler and Culicover suggest that there might be interesting learnability problems in this domain. This is because they cannot see a way in which the child can be presented with

information about underlying form and superficial form at the same time (cf. presentation of base structure and surface string in syntax learning). It seems to me that the move away from abstractness which has characterised much recent work in phonology could facilitate solution of these problems. Of course, when there are morphological alternations, it could be argued that the child is supplied with information on the underlying form via his understanding of the situation and his lexicon. I shall not speculate further in this direction here.

19. Wexler and Culicover are certainly guilty of a misplaced emphasis when they contrast two pictures of the presentation of information to the learning device as in Figure 10.1. (b), of course, simply ignores the left-hand end of (a) and

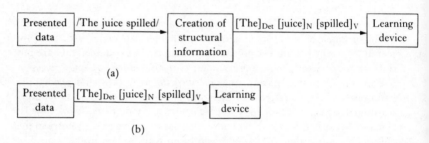

Figure 10.1 (from Wexler and Culicover 1980, p. 63)

makes clear the authors' decision to ignore questions of pre-analysis. However, their statement that (*ibid.*): 'Since the middle box in (a), *creation of structural information*, is not analyzed in the theory, (b) is a picture that will do as much work as (a)', is misleading. This may simply be an unfortunate phrasing, but, as it stands, the statement is false: (a) makes the relevant assumption explicit and is committed to an overall theory including a middle box which does some work; (b) buries the assumption.

20. Again, there are numerous possibilities one could contemplate in these circumstances. To mention just one, on the assumption that the downgraded part of the input leaves some trace, the child will 'know' that such an instance is not to be treated as an instance for learning transformational rules. As an alternative he may focus on 'local' (e.g. morphological) properties of the part of the utterance to which he has attended. This might be consistent with Newport *et al.*'s (1977) observations on the learning of nominal inflections, but I would not wish to push the point too hard at this stage of enquiry.

Bibliography

Adams, K. L. & Conklin, N. F. (1973). 'Towards a theory of natural classification.' In *Papers from the Ninth Regional Meeting Chicago Linguistic Society*. Chicago: Chicago Linguistic Society.

Amidon, A. & Carey, P. (1972). 'Why five-year-olds cannot understand *before* and *after*.' *Journal of Verbal Learning and Verbal Behavior* 11: 417–23.

Anderson, J. (1976). *Language, Memory and Thought*. Hillsdale, N.J.: Erlbaum.

Antinucci, F. & Miller, R. (1976). 'How children talk about what happened.' *Journal of Child Language* 3: 167–89.

– & Parisi, D. (1973). 'Early language acquisition: a model and some data.' In Ferguson, C. A. & Slobin, D. I. (eds).

– & Parisi, D. (1975). 'Early semantic development in child language.' In Lenneberg, E. & Lenneberg, E. E. (eds).

Apostel, L. (1972). 'Illocutionary forces and the logic of change.' *Mind* 81: 208–24.

Atkinson, R. M. (1975). Review of Bowerman (1973). *Journal of Linguistics* 11: 87–101.

– (1978). 'Explanations in the study of child language development.' Unpublished doctoral dissertation. University of Edinburgh.

– (1979). 'Prerequisites for reference.' In Ochs, E. & Schieffelin, B. B. (eds).

– (1980). Review of Lock (1978). *Journal of Child Language* 7: 579–90.

– & Griffiths, P. D. (1973). 'Here's *here's*, *there's*, *here* and *there*.' *Edinburgh Working Papers in Linguistics* 3: 29–73.

Austin, J. L. (1962). *How To Do Things With Words*. Oxford: Clarendon Press.

Baron, N. S. (1977). *Language Acquisition and Historical Change*. Amsterdam: North Holland.

Barrett, M. D. (1978). 'Lexical development and overextension in child language.' *Journal of Child Language* 5: 205–19.

Bartlett, E. J. (1976). 'Sizing things up: the acquisition of the meaning of dimensional adjectives.' *Journal of Child Language* 3: 208–19.

– (1978). 'The acquisition of the meaning of colour terms.' In Campbell, R. T. & Smith, P. T. (eds).

Bates, E. (1976). *Language and Context: the Acquisition of Pragmatics*. New York: Academic Press.

–, Benigni, L., Bretherton, I., Camaioni, L. & Volterra, V. (1977). 'From gesture to the first word: on cognitive and social prerequisites.' In Lewis, M. & Rosenblum, L (eds).

–, Camaioni, L. & Volterra, V. (1975). 'The acquisition of performatives prior to speech.' *Merrill-Palmer Quarterly* 21: 205–26.

Bellugi, U. (1967). 'The development of negation.' Unpublished doctoral dissertation. Harvard University.

– (1968). 'Linguistic mechanisms underlying child speech.' In Zale, H. (ed.). *Proceedings of the Conference on Language and Language Behavior.* New York: Appleton-Century-Crofts.

Bellugi-Klima, U. (1969). 'Language acquisition.' Unpublished paper.

Bellugi, U. (1971). 'Simplification in children's language.' In Huxley, R. & Ingram, E. (eds). *Language Acquisition: Models and Methods.* New York: Academic Press.

Bennett, J. (1976). *Linguistic Behaviour.* Cambridge: Cambridge University Press.

Berlin, B. (1977). 'Ethnobiological classification.' In Rosch, E. & Lloyd, B. (eds).

–, Breedlove, D. E. & Raven, P. H. (1973). 'General principles of classification and nomenclature in folk biology.' *American Anthropologist* 75: 214–42.

– & Kay, P. (1969). *Basic Color Terms.* Berkeley: University of California Press.

Bernstein, B. (1971). *Class, Codes and Control I: Theoretical Studies towards a Sociology of Language.* London: Routledge & Kegan Paul.

Bever, T. G. (1970). 'The cognitive basis of linguistic structures.' In Hayes, J. R. (ed.).

– (1974). 'The ascent of the specious or there's a lot we don't know about mirrors.' In Cohen, D. (ed.).

– (1975). 'Functional explanations require independently motivated functional theories.' *Papers from the Parasession on Functionalism.* Chicago: Chicago Linguistic Society.

Bierwisch, M. (1967). 'Some semantic universals of German adjectivals.' *Foundations of Language* 3: 1–36.

– (1970). 'Semantics.' In Lyons, J. (ed.). *New Horizons in Linguistics.* Harmondsworth: Penguin.

Bloom, L. (1968). 'Language development: form and function in emerging grammars.' Columbia University doctoral dissertation. University Microfilms.

– (1970). *Language Development: Form and Function in Emerging Grammars.* Cambridge, Mass.: MIT Press.

– (1973). *One Word at a Time.* The Hague: Mouton.

–, Lightbown, P. & Hood, L. (1975). 'Structure and variation in child language.' *Monographs of the Society for Research in Child Development* 40 (2) (Serial No. 160).

Boden, M. A. (1977). *Artificial Intelligence and Natural Man.* Hassocks: Harvester Press.

Bornstein, M. H. (1975). 'Qualities of color vision in infancy.' *Journal of Experimental Child Psychology* 19: 401–19.

–, Kessen, W. & Weiskopf, S. (1976). 'Color vision and hue categorization in young human infants.' *Journal of Experimental Psychology: Human Perception and Performance* 2: 115–29.

Botha, R. (1973). *The Justification of Linguistic Hypotheses.* The Hague: Mouton.

Bower, T. G. R. (1966). 'The visual world of infants.' *Scientific American* 215: 80–92.

– (1974). *Development in Infancy*. San Francisco: Freeman.

Bowerman, M. (1973). *Early Syntactic Development: A Cross-linguistic Study with Special Reference to Finnish*. Cambridge: Cambridge University Press.

– (1974). 'Learning the structure of causative verbs: a study in the relationship of cognitive, semantic and syntactic development.' *Papers and Reports on Child Language Development (Stanford University)* 8: 142–78.

– (1976). 'Semantic factors in the acquisition of rules for word use and sentence construction.' In Morehead, D. M. & Morehead, A. E. (eds).

– (1978). 'The acquisition of word-meanings: an investigation into some current conflicts.' In Waterson, N. & Snow, C. (eds).

Braine, M. D. S. (1963). 'The ontogeny of English phrase structure: the first phase.' *Language* 39: 1–13.

– (1971). 'The acquisition of language in infant and child.' In Reed, C. (ed.). *The Learning of Language*. New York: Appleton-Century-Crofts.

Brainerd, C. J. *et al*. (1978). 'The stage question in cognitive-developmental theory.' *The Behavioral and Brain Sciences* 1: 173–213.

– *et al*. (1979). 'Continuing commentary on Brainerd *et al*. (1978).' *The Behavioral and Brain Sciences* 2: 137–54.

Braunwald, S. R. (1978). 'Context, word and meaning: towards a communicational analysis of lexical acquisition.' In Lock, A. (ed.).

Bresnan, J. W. (1978). 'A realistic transformational grammar.' In Halle, M., Bresnan, J. W. & Miller, G. (eds).

Brewer, W. F. & Stone, J. B. (1975). 'Acquisition of spatial antonym pairs.' *Journal of Experimental Child Psychology* 19: 299–307.

Brown, R. (1973). *A First Language: The Early Stages*. London: Allen & Unwin.

– & Fraser, C. (1963). 'The acquisition of syntax.' In Cofer, C. N. & Musgrave, B. S. (eds). *Verbal Behavior and Learning*. New York: McGraw Hill.

– & Hanlon, C. (1970). 'Derivational complexity and order of acquisition in child speech.' In Hayes, J. R. (ed.).

Bruner, J. (1975a). 'The ontogenesis of speech-acts.' *Journal of Child Language* 2: 1–19.

– (1975b). 'From communication to language: a psychological perspective.' *Cognition* 3: 255–287.

– & Scaife, M. (1975). 'The capacity for joint visual attention in the infant.' *Nature* 253: 265–66.

Brush, L. R. (1976). 'Children's meaning of *more*.' *Journal of Child Language* 3: 287–89.

Bühler, K. (1934). *Sprachtheorie*. Jena: Fischer.

Campbell, R. T. & Smith, P. T. (eds) (1978). *Recent Advances in the Psychology of Language*. New York: Plenum.

Carey, S. (1978a). '*Less* may never mean "more".' In Campbell, R. T. & Smith, P. T. (eds).

– (1978b). 'The child as word learner.' In Halle, M., Bresnan, J. W. & Miller, G. (eds).

Carter, A. L. (1975). 'The transformation of sensori-motor morphemes into words: a case study of the development of *more* and *mine.' Journal of Child Language* 2: 233–250.
– (1978a). 'The development of systematic vocalizations prior to words: a case study.' In Waterson, N. & Snow, C. (eds).
– (1978b). 'From sensori-motor vocalizations to words: a case study of the evolution of attention-directing communication in the second year.' In Lock, A. (ed.).
Chafe, W. L. (1970). *Meaning and the Structure of Language.* Chicago: University of Chicago Press.
– (1977). 'The recall and verbalization of past experience.' In Cole, R. (ed.).
Chomsky, A. N. (1957). *Syntactic Structures.* The Hague: Mouton.
– (1964). *Current Issues in Linguistic Theory.* The Hague: Mouton.
– (1965). *Aspects of the Theory of Syntax.* Cambridge, Mass.: MIT Press.
– (1968). *Language and Mind.* New York: Harcourt, Brace & World.
– (1970). 'Remarks on nominalizations.' In Jacobs, R. & Rosenbaum, P. (eds). *Readings in English Transformational Grammar.* Waltham, Mass.: Blaisdell.
– (1973). 'Conditions on transformations.' In Anderson, S. & Kiparsky, P. (eds). *Festschrift for Morris Halle.* New York: Holt, Rinehart & Winston.
– (1974). 'Questions of form and interpretation.' *Montreal Working Papers in Linguistics* 3: 1–42.
– (1976). *Reflections on Language.* London: Temple Smith.
– (1977). 'On *Wh*-movement.' In Culicover, P. W., Wasow, T. & Akmajian, A. (eds).
– (1980). 'Rules and representations.' *The Behavioral and Brain Sciences* 3: 1–15.
– & Halle, M. (1968). *The Sound Pattern of English.* New York: Harper & Row.
Churma, D. G. (1975). 'Child language acquisition and the justification of linguistic hypotheses.' *Papers from the Eleventh Regional Meeting Chicago Linguistic Society.* Chicago: Chicago Linguistic Society.
Clark, E. V. (1970). 'How young children describe events in time.' In Flores d'Arcais, G. B. & Levelt, W. J. M. (eds).
– (1971). 'On the acquisition of the meaning of *before* and *after.' Journal of Verbal Learning and Verbal Behavior* 10: 266–75.
– (1972a). 'Some perceptual factors in the acquisition of locative terms by young children.' In *Papers from the Eighth Regional Meeting Chicago Linguistic Society.* Chicago: Chicago Linguistic Society.
– (1972b). 'On the child's acquisition of antonyms in two semantic fields.' *Journal of Verbal Learning and Verbal Behavior* 11: 750–58.
– (1973). 'What's in a word?' In Moore, T. E. (ed.).
– (1974). 'Some aspects of the conceptual basis for first language acquisition.' *Papers and Reports on Child Language Development (Stanford University)* 7: 23–51.
– (1975). 'Knowledge, context, and strategy in the acquisition of meaning.' In Dato, D. (ed.). *Proceedings of the 26th Annual Georgetown University Round Table: Developmental Psycholinguistics: Theory and Applications.* Washington D.C.: Georgetown University Press.

– & Garnica, O. (1974). 'Is he coming or going? On the acquisition of deictic verbs.' *Journal of Verbal Learning and Verbal Behavior* 13: 559–72.

Clark, H. H. (1970). 'The primitive nature of children's relational concepts.' In Hayes, J. R. (ed.).

– (1973). 'Space, time, semantics and the child.' In Moore, T. E. (ed.).

– & Clark, E. V. (1968). 'Semantic distinctions and memory for complex sentences.' *Quarterly Journal of Experimental Psychology* 20: 129–38.

Clark, Roger (1978). 'The transition from action to gesture.' In Lock, A. (ed.).

Clark, Ruth (1974). 'Performing without competence.' *Journal of Child Language* 1: 1–10.

Clowes, M. (1969). 'Pictorial relationships – a syntactic approach.' In Meltzer, B. & Michie, D. (eds). *Machine Intelligence 4*. Edinburgh: Edinburgh University Press.

Cohen, D. (ed.) (1974). *Explaining Linguistic Phenomena*. Washington, D.C.: Hemisphere Publishing Corp.

Coker, P. L. (1978). 'Syntactic and semantic factors in the acquisition of *before* and *after*.' *Journal of Child Language* 5: 261–77.

Cole, P. & Morgan, J. L. (eds) (1975). *Syntax and Semantics 3: Speech Acts*. London & New York: Academic Press.

Cole, R. (ed.) (1977). *Current Issues in Linguistic Theory*. Bloomington, Indiana: Indiana University Press.

Collier, G. A. (1973). Review of Berlin and Kay (1969). *Language* 49: 245–8.

– *et al.* (1976). 'Further evidence for universal color categories.' *Language* 52: 884–90.

Cooper, D. (1975). *Knowledge of Language*. Dorchester: Prism Press.

Cromer, R. (1968). 'The development of temporal reference during the acquisition of language.' Unpublished doctoral dissertation. Harvard University.

– (1974). 'The development of language and cognition: the cognition hypothesis.' In Foss, B. (ed.). *New Perspectives in Child Development*. Harmondsworth: Penguin.

– (1976a). 'Developmental strategies for language.' In Hamilton, V. & Vernon, M. D. (eds). *The Development of Cognitive Processes*. London & New York: Academic Press.

– (1976b). 'The cognitive hypothesis of language acquisition and its implications for child language deficiency.' In Morehead, D. M. & Morehead, A. E. (eds).

Culicover, P. W., Wasow, T. & Akmajian, A. (eds) (1977). *Formal Syntax*. New York & London: Academic Press.

– & Wexler, K. (1977). 'Some syntactic implications of a theory of language learnability.' In Culicover, P. W., Wasow, T. & Akmajian, A. (eds).

Davidson, D. (1974). 'Belief and the basis of meaning.' *Synthese* 27: 309–23.

de Valois, R. & Jacobs, G. H. (1968). 'Primate colour vision.' *Science* 162: 533–40.

Derwing, B. L. (1973). *Transformational Grammar as a Theory of Language Acquisition*. Cambridge: Cambridge University Press.

Donaldson, M. & Balfour, G. (1968). 'Less is more: a study of language comprehension in children.' *British Journal of Psychology* 59: 461–72.

- & Wales, R. (1970). 'On the acquisition of some relational terms.' In Hayes, J. R. (ed.).
Donnellan, K. (1966). 'Reference and definite descriptions.' *Philosophical Review* 75: 281–304.
Dore, J. (1974). 'A pragmatic description of early language development.' *Journal of Psycholinguistic Research* 3: 343–50.
- (1975). 'Holophrases, speech acts and language universals.' *Journal of Child Language* 2: 21–40.
- (1978). 'Conditions for the acquisition of speech acts.' In Marková, I. (ed.).
-, Miller, R. T., Franklin, M. B. & Ramer, A. (1976). 'Transitional phenomena in early language acquisition.' *Journal of Child Language* 3: 13–28.
Dougherty, J. W. D. (1978). 'On the significance of a sequence in the acquisition of basic colour terms.' In Campbell, R. T. & Smith, P. T. (eds).
Durbin, M. (1972). 'Basic terms off-colour.' Review of Berlin & Kay (1969). *Semiotica* 6: 257–77.
Edwards, D. (1973). 'Sensory-motor intelligence and semantic relations in early child grammar.' *Cognition* 2: 395–424.
Eilers, R. E., Oller, D. K. & Ellington, J. (1974). 'The acquisition of word meanings for dimensional adjectives: the long and the short of it.' *Journal of Child Language* 1: 195–204.
Eimas, P. D., Siqueland, E. R., Jusczyk, P. & Vigorito, J. (1971). 'Speech perception in infants.' *Science* 171: 303–6.
Ervin-Tripp, S. (1977). 'From conversation to syntax.' *Papers and Reports on Language Development (Stanford University)* 13: K1–K21.
Feldman, H., Goldin-Meadow, S. & Gleitman, L. (1978). 'Beyond Herodotus: the creation of language by linguistically deprived deaf children.' In Lock, A. (ed.).
Ferguson, C. A. (1977). 'New directions in phonological theory: language acquisition and universals research.' In Cole, R. (ed.).
- & Garnica, O. (1975). 'Theories of phonological development.' In Lenneberg, E. & Lenneberg, E. E. (eds).
- & Slobin, D. I. (eds) (1973). *Studies of Child Language Development.* New York: Holt, Rinehart & Winston.
Ferreiro, E. & Sinclair, H. (1971). 'Temporal relationships in language.' *International Journal of Psycholinguistics* 6: 39–47.
Ferrier, L. (1978). 'Word, context and imitation.' In Lock, A. (ed.).
Fillmore, C. J. (1968). 'The case for case.' In Bach, E. & Harms, R. T. (eds). *Universals in Linguistic Theory.* New York: Holt, Rinehart & Winston.
- (1971). 'Some problems for case grammar.' *Monograph Series on Languages and Linguistics* 24: 35–56. Washington, D.C.: Georgetown University Press.
- (1977). 'Topics in lexical semantics.' In Cole, R. (ed.).
Flavell, J. (1963). *The Developmental Psychology of Jean Piaget.* Princeton, N.J.: Van Nostrand Co. Inc.
- (1971). 'Stage-related properties of cognitive development.' *Cognitive Psychology* 2: 421–53.
- (1972). 'An analysis of cognitive-developmental sequences.' *Genetic Psychology Monographs* 86: 279–350.

Flores d'Arcais, G. & Levelt, W. J. M. (eds) (1970). *Advances in Psycholinguistics*. Amsterdam: North Holland.

Fodor, J. A. (1968). *Psychological Explanation*. New York: Random House.

– (1976). *The Language of Thought*. New York: T. Y. Crowell & Co.

– (1978). 'Computation and reduction.' In Savage, C. W. (ed.). *Perception and Cognition: Issues in the Foundations of Psychology. Minnesota Studies in the Philosophy of Science: IX*. Minneapolis: University of Minnesota Press.

–, Bever, T. G. & Garrett, M. F. (1974). *The Psychology of Language*. New York: McGraw Hill.

Foss, D. J. & Swinney, D. A. (1973). 'On the psychological reality of the phoneme: perception, identification and consciousness.' *Journal of Verbal Learning and Verbal Behavior* 12: 246–57.

Fries, C. C. (1952). *The Structure of English: An Introduction to the Construction of English Sentences*. New York: Harcourt, Brace & Co.

Gardner, R. A. & Gardner, B. T. (1969). 'Teaching sign language to a chimpanzee.' *Science* 165: 664–72.

– & Gardner, B. T. (1975). 'Evidence for sentence constituents in the early utterances of child and chimpanzee.' *Journal of Experimental Psychology: General* 104: 244–67.

Garnica, O. (1971). 'The development of the perception of phonemic differences in initial consonants in English speaking children.' *Papers and Reports on Child Language Development (Stanford University)* 3: 1–29.

– (1973). 'The development of phonemic speech perception.' In Moore, T. E. (ed.).

Gentner, D. (1975). 'Evidence for the psychological reality of semantic components.' In Norman, D. A., Rumelhart, D. E. & the LNR Research Group. *Explorations in Cognition*. San Francisco: Freeman.

Gibson, E. J. (1969). *Principles of Perceptual Learning*. New York: Appleton-Century-Crofts.

Gold, E. M. (1967). 'Language identification in the limit.' *Information and Control* 10: 447–74.

Goodluck, H. & Solan, L. (1979). 'A reevaluation of the basic operations hypothesis.' *Cognition* 7: 85–91.

Goodson, B. D. & Greenfield, P. M. (1975). 'The search for structural principles in children's manipulative play: a parallel with linguistic development.' *Child Development* 46: 734–46.

Gopnik, A. (1978). 'The analysis of proto-demonstratives in the one-word period.' Unpublished paper.

Greenberg, J. (1966). 'Some universals of grammar with particular reference to the order of meaningful elements.' In Greenberg, J. (ed.). *Universals of Language*. Cambridge, Mass.: MIT Press.

Greenfield, P. M. (1978a). 'How much is one word?' *Journal of Child Language* 5: 347–52.

– (1978b). 'Informativeness, presupposition and semantic choice in single-word utterances.' In Waterson, N. & Snow, C. (eds).

– (1978c). 'Structural parallels between language and action in development.' In Lock, A. (ed.).

–, Nelson, K. E. & Saltzman, E. (1972). 'The development of rule bound strategies for manipulating seriated cups: a parallel between action and grammar.' *Cognitive Psychology* 3: 291–311.

– & Schneider, L. (1977). 'Building a tree structure: the development of hierarchical complexity and interrupted strategies in children's construction activity.' *Developmental Psychology* 13: 299–313.

– & Smith, J. (1976). *The Structure of Communication in Early Language Development*. New York: Academic Press.

Grégoire, A. (1937). *L'apprentisage du Langage*. Paris: Libraire Droz.

Grene, M. (1976). 'Aristotle and modern biology.' In Grene, M. & Mendelsohn, E. (eds). *Topics in the Philosophy of Biology*. Dordrecht: Reidel.

Grice, H. P. (1957). 'Meaning.' *Philosophical Review* 66: 377–88.

– (1968). 'Utterer's meaning, sentence-meaning and word-meaning.' *Foundations of Language* 4: 225–42.

– (1975). 'Logic and conversation.' In Cole, P. & Morgan, J. L. (eds).

Grieve, R. & Hoogenraad, R. (1977). 'Using language if you don't have much.' In Wales, R. J. & Walker, E. C. T. (eds). *New Approaches to Mechanisms in Language*. Amsterdam: North Holland.

Griffiths, P. D. (1974). 'That there deixis I: *that*.' Unpublished paper.

– (1976). 'The ontogenetic development of lexical reference.' Unpublished doctoral dissertation. University of Edinburgh.

– (1978). 'Asking and answering.' Unpublished paper.

– (1979). 'Speech acts and early sentences.' In Fletcher, P. & Garman, M. (eds). *Studies in Language Acquisition*. Cambridge: Cambridge University Press.

–, Atkinson, R. M. & Huxley R. (1974). 'Project report.' *Journal of Child Language* 1: 157–8.

Grosu, A. (1975). 'A plea for greater caution in proposing functional explanations in linguistics.' *Papers from the Parasession on Functionalism*. Chicago: Chicago Linguistic Society.

Gruber, J. S. (1975). 'Performative-constative transition in child language.' *Foundations of Language* 12: 513–27.

Guillaume, R. (1927). 'Les débuts de la phrase dans le langage de l'enfant.' *Journal de Psychologie* 24: 1–25.

Halle, M. (1961). 'On the role of simplicity in linguistic description.' In Jakobson, R. (ed.). *Structure of Language and its Mathematical Aspects. Proceedings of the Twelfth Symposium in Applied Mathematics*. Providence, R.I.: American Mathematical Society.

–, Bresnan, J. W. & Miller, G. (eds) (1978). *Linguistic Theory and Psychological Reality*. Cambridge, Mass.: MIT Press.

Halliday, M. A. K. (1967). 'Notes on transitivity and theme in English: Part II.' *Journal of Linguistics* 2: 199–244.

– (1970). 'Functional diversity in language as seen from a consideration of modality and mood in English.' *Foundations of Language* 6: 322–61.

– (1973). *Explorations in the Functions of Language*. London: Arnold.

– (1975). *Learning How to Mean*. London: Arnold.

Hamburger, H. & Wexler, K. (1975). 'A mathematical theory of learning transformational grammar.' *Journal of Mathematical Psychology* 12: 137–77.

Hamburger, V. (1957). 'The concept of development in biology.' In Harris, D. B. (ed.).

Harris, D. B. (ed.) (1957a). *The Concept of Development*. Minneapolis: University of Minnesota Press.

– (1957b). 'Introduction.' In Harris, D. B. (ed.).

Harris, Z. (1951). *Methods in Structural Linguistics*. Chicago: University of Chicago Press.

Haviland, S. E. & Clark, E. V. (1974). '"This man's father is my father's son": a study of the acquisition of English kin terms.' *Journal of Child Language* 1: 23–47.

Hayes, J. R. (ed.) (1970). *Cognition and the Development of Language*. New York: Wiley.

Heider, E. R. (1971). '"Focal" color areas and the development of color names.' *Developmental Psychology* 4: 447–55.

Hempel, C. & Oppenheim, P. (1948). 'Studies in the logic of explanation.' *Philosophy of Science* 15: 135–75.

Hewes, G. W. (1973). 'Primate communication and the gestural origin of language.' *Current Anthropology* 14: 5–32.

Hickerson, N. (1971). Review of Berlin & Kay (1969). *International Journal of American Linguistics* 37: 257–70.

Holland, V. M. & Palermo, D. S. (1975). 'On learning *less:* language and cognitive development'. *Child Development* 46: 437–43.

Hubel, D. H. & Wiesel, T. N. (1962). 'Receptive fields, binocular interaction and functional architecture in the cat's visual cortex.' *Journal of Physiology* 160: 106–54.

Huttenlocher, J. (1974). 'The origins of language comprehension.' In Solso, R. L. (ed.). *Theories in Cognitive Psychology: The Loyola Symposium*. Potomac, Md.: Erlbaum.

Ingram, D. (1971). 'Transitivity in child language.' *Language* 47: 888–910.

Isard, S. (1975). 'Changing the context,' In Keenan, E. (ed.). *Formal Semantics of Natural Languages*. Cambridge: Cambridge University Press.

Jacobs, R. & Rosenbaum, P. T. (1968). *English Transformational Grammar*. Waltham, Mass.: Blaisdell.

Jackendoff, R. S. (1977). 'Constraints on phrase structure rules.' In Culicover, P. W., Wasow, T. & Akmajian, A. (eds).

Jakobson, R. (1968). *Child Language, Aphasia and Phonological Universals*. The Hague: Mouton.

–, Fant, G. & Halle, M. (1952). *Preliminaries to Speech Analysis*. Cambridge, Mass.: MIT Press.

– & Halle, M. (1956). *Fundamentals of Language*. The Hague: Mouton.

Kaplan, E. L. (1969). 'The role of intonation in the acquisition of language.' Unpublished doctoral dissertation. Cornell University.

Karmiloff-Smith, A. (1979). *A Functional Approach to Child Language*. Cambridge: Cambridge University Press.

Karttunen, L. (1968). 'What do referential indices refer to?' Unpublished paper.

Katz, J. J. (1972). *Semantic Theory*. New York: Harper & Row.

– & Postal, P. M. (1964). *An Integrated Theory of Linguistic Description*. Cambridge, Mass.: MIT Press.

Kay, P. (1975). 'Synchronic variability and diachronic change in basic color terms.' *Language in Society* 4: 257–70.

– & McDaniel, C. K. (1978). 'The linguistic significance of the meanings of basic color terms.' *Language* 54: 610–46.

Keenan, E. O. (1974). 'Conversational competence in children.' *Journal of Child Language* 1: 163–83.

– (1975). 'Evolving discourse – the next step.' *Papers and Reports on Child Language Development (Stanford University)* 10.

– & Schieffelin, B. B. (1976). 'Topic as discourse notion.' In Li, C. (ed.). *Subject and Topic*. New York: Academic Press.

Kempson, R. M. (1977). *Semantic Theory*. Cambridge: Cambridge University Press.

Kiparsky, P. & Menn, L. (1977). 'On the acquisition of phonology.' In McNamara, J. (ed.).

Klima, E. (1964). 'Negation in English.' In Fodor, J. A. & Katz, J. J. (eds). *The Structure of Language: Readings in the Philosophy of Language*. Englewood Cliffs, N.J.: Prentice Hall.

– & Bellugi, U. (1966). 'Syntactic regularities in the speech of children.' In Lyons, J. & Wales, R. J. (eds).

Kornfeld, J. (1971). 'Theoretical issues in child phonology.' In *Papers from the Seventh Regional Meeting Chicago Linguistic Society*. Chicago: Chicago Linguistic Society.

– & Goehl, H. (1974). 'A new twist to an old observation: kids know more than they say.' *Papers from the Parasession on Natural Phonology*. Chicago: Chicago Linguistic Society.

Koster, J. (1979). 'Some remarks on language learnability.' Paper presented to Paris Conference on Learnability, September 10–11.

Kuczaj, S. A. (1977). 'The acquisition of regular and irregular past tense forms.' *Journal of Verbal Learning and Verbal Behavior* 16: 589–600.

Kuroda, S.-Y. (1972). 'The categorical and the thetic judgement: evidence from Japanese syntax.' *Foundations of Language* 9: 153–85.

Lakoff, G. (1971). 'On generative semantics.' In Steinberg, D. D. & Jakobovits, L. A. (eds). *Semantics: An Interdisciplinary Reader in Philosophy, Linguistics and Psychology*. Cambridge: Cambridge University Press.

– (1972). 'Linguistics and natural logic.' In Davidson, D. & Harman, G. (eds). *Semantics of Natural Language*. Dordrecht: Reidel.

– & Ross, J. (1967). 'Is deep structure necessary?' Indiana University Linguistics Club.

Lass, R. (1980). *On Explaining Language Change*. Cambridge: Cambridge University Press.

Lenneberg, E. & Lenneberg, E. E. (eds) (1975). *Foundations of Language Development*. New York: UNESCO.

Leopold, W. (1939). *Speech Development of a Bilingual Child: I.* Evanston, Ill.: Northwestern University Press.

– (1949). *Speech Development of a Bilingual Child: III.* Evanston, Ill.: Northwestern University Press.

Lewis, M. M. (1936). *Infant Speech: A Study of the Beginnings of Language.* London: Routledge & Kegan Paul.

Lewis, M. & Rosenblum, L. (eds) (1977). *Interaction, Conversation and the Development of Language.* New York: Wiley.

Lock, A. (ed.) (1978). *Action, Gesture and Symbol.* London & New York: Academic Press.

Lounsbury, F. G. (1956). 'A semantic analysis of the Pawnee kinship system.' *Language* 32: 158–94.

Lyons, J. (1966). Discussion of McNeill contribution. In Lyons, J. & Wales, R. J. (eds).

– (1975). 'Deixis as the source of reference'. In Keenan, E. (ed.). *Formal Semantics of Natural Language.* Cambridge: Cambridge University Press.

– (1977a). 'Deixis and anaphora.' In Myers, T. (ed.). *The Development of Conversation and Discourse.* Edinburgh: Edinburgh University Press.

– (1977b). *Semantics*, vol. 1. Cambridge: Cambridge University Press.

– & Wales, R. J. (eds) (1966). *Psycholinguistics Papers.* Edinburgh: Edinburgh University Press.

McCawley, J. D. (1968). 'The role of semantics in a grammar.' In Bach, E. & Harms, R. T. (eds). *Universals in Linguistic Theory.* New York: Holt, Rinehart & Winston.

– (1971). 'Prelexical syntax.' In *Monograph Series on Languages and Linguistics* 24: Washington, D.C.: Georgetown University Press.

McNamara, J. (1972). 'The cognitive basis of language learning in infants.' *Psychological Review* 79: 1–13.

– (ed.) (1977). *Language, Learning and Thought.* New York: Academic Press.

McNeill, D. (1966). 'Developmental psycholinguistics.' In Smith, F. & Miller, G. (eds). *The Genesis of Language.* Cambridge, Mass.: MIT Press.

– & Lindig, K. (1973). 'The perceptual reality of phonemes, syllables, words and sentences.' *Journal of Verbal Learning and Verbal Behavior* 12: 419–30.

Macrae, A. (1976). 'Movement and location in the acquisition of deictic verbs.' *Journal of Child Language* 3: 191–204.

Maratsos, M. (1973). 'Decrease in the understanding of the word *big* in preschool children.' *Child Development* 44: 747–52.

– (1976). *The Use of Definite and Indefinite Reference in Young Children: An Experimental Study in Semantic Acquisition.* Cambridge: Cambridge University Press.

– (1978). 'New models in linguistics and language acquisition.' In Halle, M., Bresnan, J. W. & Miller, G. (eds).

Marková, I. (ed.) (1978). *The Social Context of Language.* New York: Wiley.

Marshall, J. (1979). 'Getting off the ground: or The Höffding First-step.' Paper presented to Paris Conference on Learnability. 10–11 September.

Matthei, E. (1978). 'Children's interpretation of sentences containing reciprocals.'

In Goodluck, H. & Solan, L. (eds). *Papers in the Structure and Development of Child Language*. University of Massachusetts Occasional Papers in Linguistics 4.

Mayer, J., Erreich, A. & Valian, V. (1978). 'Transformations, basic operations and language acquisition.' *Cognition* 6: 1–13.

Menn, L. (1973). 'On the origin and growth of phonological and syntactic rules.' In *Papers from the Ninth Regional Meeting Chicago Linguistic Society*. Chicago: Chicago Linguistic Society.

Mikeš, M. (1967). 'Acquisition des catégories grammaticales dans le langage de l'enfant.' *Enfance* 20: 289–98.

Miller, M. (1978). 'Pragmatic constraints on the linguistic realizations of "semantic intentions" in early child language.' In Waterson, N. & Snow, C. (eds).

Miller, W. & Ervin, S. (1964). 'The development of grammar in child language.' In Bellugi, U. & Brown, R. (eds). *The Acquisition of Language (Monographs of the Society for Research in Child Development* 29 (1)). 9–34.

Mischel, T. (ed.) (1971). *Cognitive Development and Epistemology*. New York: Academic Press.

Moore, T. E. (ed.) (1973). *Cognitive Development and the Acquisition of Language*. New York: Wiley.

Morehead, D. M. & Morehead, A. E. (eds) (1976). *Normal and Deficient Child Language*. Baltimore: University Park Press.

Mowrer, O. H. (1960). *Learning Theory and Symbolic Processes*. New York: Wiley.

Nagel, E. (1957). 'Determinism and development.' In Harris, D. B. (ed.).

Nelson, K. (1973a). 'Structure and strategy in learning to talk.' *Monographs of the Society for Research in Child Development* 38 (1–2) (Serial No. 149).

– (1973b). 'Some evidence for the cognitive primacy of categorization and its functional basis.' *Merrill-Palmer Quarterly* 19: 21–39.

– (1974). 'Concept, word and sentence.' *Psychological Review* 81: 267–85.

– (1979). 'Features, contrasts and the FCH: some comments on Barrett's lexical development hypothesis.' *Journal of Child Language* 6: 139–46.

Newport, E., Gleitman, L. & Gleitman, H. (1977). 'Mother, I'd rather do it myself: some effects and non-effects of motherese.' In Snow, C. & Ferguson, C. A. (eds).

Ochs, E. & Schieffelin, B. B. (eds) (1979). *Developmental Pragmatics*. New York: Academic Press.

–, Schieffelin, B. B. & Platt, M. L. (1979). 'Propositions across utterances and speakers.' In Ochs, E. & Schieffelin, B. B. (eds).

Omar, M. (1973). *The Aquisition of Egyptian Arabic by Native Speakers*. The Hague: Mouton.

Paivio, A. (1975). 'Neo-mentalism.' *Canadian Journal of Psychology* 29: 263–91.

Palermo, D. S. (1973). 'More about *less*: a study of language comprehension.' *Journal of Verbal Learning and Verbal Behavior* 12: 211–21.

– (1974). 'Still more about the comprehension of *less*.' *Developmental Psychology* 10: 827–29.

– (1976). 'Sémantique et acquisition du langage: quelques considérations théoriques.' *Bulletin de Psychologie* (special issue). 251–8.

Palmer, F. (1965). *A Linguistic Study of the English Verb*. London: Longmans.

Palmer, S. E. (1977). 'Fundamental aspects of cognitive representation.' In Rosch, E. & Lloyd, B. (eds).

Park, T.-Z. (1970). 'The acquisition of German syntax.' Unpublished paper.

Peirce, C. S. (1932). *Collected Papers*. Cambridge, Mass.: Harvard University Press.

Peters, P. S. & Ritchie, R. W. (1973). 'On the generative power of transformational grammars.' *Information Sciences* 6: 49–83.

Pinker, S. (1979). 'Formal models of language learning.' *Cognition* 7: 217–83.

Postal, P. M. (1964). *Constituent Structure: A Study of Contemporary Models of Syntactic Description*. The Hague: Mouton.

– (1966). Review of A. Martinet *Elements of General Linguistics*. *Foundations of Language* 2: 151–86.

– (1970). 'On the surface verb *remind*'. *Linguistic Inquiry* 1: 37–120.

Power, R. J. D. & Longuet-Higgins, H. C. (1978). 'Learning to count: a computational model of language acquisition.' *Proceedings of the Royal Society London. B* 200: 391–417.

Pulman, S. G. (1977). 'Formal grammar and language use – their interaction in the analysis of modals.' Unpublished doctoral dissertation. University of Essex.

Putnam, H. (1970). 'Is semantics possible?' In Kiefer, H. & Munitz, M. (eds). *Language, Belief and Metaphysics*. New York: State University of New York Press.

– (1975). 'The meaning of *meaning*.' In Putnam, H. *Mind, Language and Reality*. Cambridge: Cambridge University Press.

Pylyshyn, Z. (1973). 'The role of competence theories in cognitive psychology.' *Journal of Psycholinguistic Research* 2: 21–50.

Quine, W. V. O. (1960). *Word and Object*. Cambridge, Mass.: MIT Press.

Ratcliff, F. (1976). On the psychophysiological basis of universal color terms.' *Proceedings of the American Philosophical Society* 120: 311–30.

Reich, P. A. (1976). 'The early acquisition of word meanings.' *Journal of Child Language* 3: 117–23.

Ricciuti, H. N. (1963). 'Geometric form and detail as determinants of similarity judgements in young children.' In *A Basic Research Program on Reading*. Final report: Cooperative Research Project No. 639. US Office of Education. 1–48.

Richards, M. M. (1976). '*Come* and *go* reconsidered: children's use of deictic verbs in contrived situations.' *Journal of Verbal Learning and Verbal Behavior* 15: 655–65.

Rips, L. J. (1975). 'Inductive judgements about natural categories.' *Journal of Verbal Learning and Verbal Behavior* 14: 665–78.

Rips, L. J., Shoben, E. J. & Smith, E. E. (1973). 'Semantic distance and the verification of semantic relations.' *Journal of Verbal Learning and Verbal Behavior* 12: 1–20.

Romney, A. K. & d'Andrade, R. G. (1964). 'Cognitive aspects of English kin terms.' In Romney, A. K. & d'Andrade, R. G. (eds). *Transcultural Studies in Cognition. American Anthropologist* 66: 146–70.

Rosch, E. H. (1973). 'On the internal structure of perceptual and semantic categories.' In Moore, T. E. (ed.).

- (1975a). 'Cognitive representations of semantic categories.' *Journal of Experimental Psychology: General* 104: 192–233.
- (1975b). 'Cognitive reference points.' *Cognitive Psychology* 7: 532–47.
- (1977). 'Principles of categorization.' In Rosch, E. & Lloyd, B. (eds).
- & Lloyd, B. (eds) (1977). *Cognition and Categorization*. Hillsdale, N.J.: Erlbaum.
- & Mervis, C. B. (1975). 'Family resemblances: studies in the internal structure of categories.' *Cognitive Psychology* 7: 573–605.
-, Mervis, C. B., Gray, W. D., Johnson, D. M. & Boyes-Braem, P. (1976). 'Basic objects in natural categories.' *Cognitive Psychology* 8: 382–439.
Sag, I. (1976). 'A logical theory of verb phrase deletion.' In *Papers from the Twelfth Regional Meeting Chicago Linguistic Society*. Chicago: Chicago Linguistic Society.
Sampson, G. (1973). 'The irrelevance of transformational omnipotence.' *Journal of Linguistics* 9: 299–302.
- (1975). *The Form of Language*. London: Weidenfeld & Nicolson.
Saunders, J. W. (1970). *Patterns and Principles of Animal Development*. London: MacMillan.
Sauvageot, A. (1948). *Esquisse de la Langue Finnoise*. Paris: Klincksieck.
Savin, H. B. & Bever, T. G. (1970). 'The non-perceptual reality of the phoneme.' *Journal of Verbal Learning and Verbal Behavior* 9: 295–302.
Schaerlaekens, A. (1973). Review of Bloom (1970). *Cognition* 2: 371–76.
Schiffer, S. (1972). *Meaning*. Oxford: Oxford University Press.
Schlesinger, I. M. (1971). 'Production of utterances and language acquisition.' In Slobin, D. I. (ed.). *The Ontogenesis of Grammar*. New York: Academic Press.
- (1974). 'Relational concepts underlying language.' In Schiefelbusch, R. & Lloyd, L. (eds). *Language Perspectives: Acquisition, Retardation and Intervention*. University Park Press: Baltimore.
- (1975). 'Grammatical development – the first steps.' In Lenneberg, E. & Lenneberg, E. E. (eds).
- (1977). 'The role of cognitive development and linguistic input in language acquisition.' *Journal of Child Language* 4: 153–69.
Schwartz, R. G. & Folger, M. K. (1977). 'Sensori-motor development and descriptions of child phonology: a preliminary view of phonological analysis for Stage I speech.' *Papers and Reports on Child Language Development (Stanford University)* 13: 8–15.
Searle, J. (1969). *Speech Acts*. Cambridge: Cambridge University Press.
- (1975a). 'A taxonomy of illocutionary acts.' In Gunderson, K. (ed.) *Minnesota Studies in the Philosophy of Language*. Minneapolis: University of Minnesota Press.
- (1975b). 'Linguistics and the philosophy of language.' In Bartsch, R. & Vennemann, T. (eds). *Linguistics and Neighbouring Disciplines*. Amsterdam: North Holland.
- (1975c). 'Indirect speech acts.' In Cole, P. & Morgan, J. L. (eds).
Seidenberg, M. S. & Petitto, L. A. (1979). 'Signing behavior in apes: a critical review.' *Cognition* 7: 177–215.

Shatz, M. (1977). 'The relationship between cognitive processes and the development of communication skills.' Unpublished MS.

Shields, M. (1978). 'The child as psychologist: construing the social world.' In Lock, A. (ed.).

Shipley, E. F., Smith, C. S. & Gleitman, L. R. (1969). 'A study of the acquisition of language: free responses to commands.' *Language* 45: 322–42.

Shotter, J. (1978). 'The cultural context of communication studies: theoretical and methodological issues.' In Lock, A. (ed.).

Shvachkin, N. Kh. (1948). 'The development of phonemic speech perception in early childhood.' English translation in Ferguson, C. A. & Slobin, D. I. (eds).

Simon, H. A. (1962). 'An information processing theory of intellectual development.' In Kessen, W. & Kuhlman, C. (eds). *Thought in the Young Child (Monographs of the Society for Research in Child Development* 27 (2) (Serial No. 83)).

Sinclair, H. (1971). 'Sensori-motor action patterns as a condition for the acquisition of syntax.' In Huxley, R. & Ingram, E. (eds).

– (1975). 'The role of cognitive structures in language acquisition.' In Lenneberg, E. & Lenneberg, E. E. (eds).

Sinclair-de-Zwart, H. (1969). 'Developmental psycholinguistics.' In Elkind, D. & Flavell, J. (eds). *Studies in Cognitive Development: Essays in Honor of Jean Piaget*. New York: Oxford University Press.

Slobin, D. I. (1970). 'Universals of grammatical development in children.' In Flores d'Arcais, G. B. & Levelt, W. J. M. (eds).

– (1971). 'Developmental psycholinguistics.' In Dingwall, W. O. (ed.). *A Survey of Linguistic Science*. Maryland: University of Maryland.

– (1973). 'Cognitive prerequisites for the development of grammar.' In Ferguson, C. A. & Slobin, D. I. (eds).

– (1977). 'Language change in childhood and history.' In McNamara, J. (ed.).

Sloman, A. (1978). *The Computer Revolution in Philosophy*. Hassocks: Harvester Press.

Smith, E. E., Shoben, E. J. & Rips, L. J. (1974). 'Structure and process in semantic memory: a featural model for semantic decisions.' *Psychological Review* 81: 214–41.

Smith, N. (1973). *The Acquisition of Phonology*. Cambridge: Cambridge University Press.

Snow, C. & Ferguson, C. A. (eds) (1977). *Talking to Children*. Cambridge: Cambridge University Press.

Sober, E. (1975). *Simplicity*. Oxford: Oxford University Press.

Stampe, D. (1969). 'On the acquisition of phonetic representation.' In *Papers from the Fifth Regional Meeting Chicago Linguistic Society*. Chicago Linguistic Society.

Stich, S. P. (1971). 'What every speaker knows.' *Philosophical Review* 80: 480–96.

Strawson, P. F. (1964). 'Intention and convention in speech acts.' *Philosophical Review* 73: 439–60.

Sugarman-Bell, S. (1978). 'Some organizational aspects of pre-verbal communication.' In Marková, I. (ed.).

Taylor, C. (1971). 'What is involved in a genetic psychology?' In Mischel, T. (ed.).

Trevarthen, C. (1974). 'Conversations with a two-month old.' *New Scientist* 62(896): 230–35.

– & Hubley, P. (1978). 'Secondary intersubjectivity: confidence, confiding and acts of meaning in the first year.' In Lock, A. (ed.).

Velten, H. V. (1943). 'The growth of phonemic and lexical patterns in infant language.' *Language* 19: 281–92.

Vygotsky, L. S. (1962). *Thought and Language*. Cambridge, Mass.: MIT Press.

Waterson, N. (1970). 'Some speech forms of an English child: a phonological study.' *Transactions of the Philological Society*. 1–24.

– (1971). 'Child phonology: a prosodic view.' *Journal of Linguistics* 7: 179–211.

– & Snow, C. (eds) (1978). *The Development of Communication*. Chichester: Wiley.

Watson, J. B. (1928). *Behaviorism*. New York: Norton.

Weiss, P. A. (1939). *Principles of Development*. New York: Holt.

Werner, H. & Kaplan, B. (1963). *Symbol Formation*. New York: Wiley.

Wexler, K. & Culicover, P. W. (1980). *Formal Principles of Language Acquisition*. Cambridge, Mass.: MIT Press.

–, Culicover, P. W. & Hamburger, H. (1975). 'Learning-theoretic foundations of linguistic universals.' *Theoretical Linguistics* 2: 213–53.

White, L. (1979). 'The responsibility of grammatical theory to acquisitional data.' *Montreal Working Papers in Linguistics* 14: 241–75.

Williams, E. S. (1977). 'Discourse and logical form.' *Linguistic Inquiry* 8: 101–39.

Wittgenstein, L. (1953). *Philosophical Investigations*. Oxford: Blackwell.

Woodfield, A. (1976). *Teleology*. Cambridge: Cambridge University Press.

Index